Dear Britt —

Hope you like my
translation — let me
know what you think —
Call me when you're
back. Have a good
trip.

Ann

Dec 17, 1993

WORLD LITERATURE
IN TRANSLATION

LARS AHLIN

CINNAMONCANDY

Translated with an Afterword by
HANNA KALTER WEISS

GARLAND PUBLISHING, INC.
NEW YORK & LONDON 1990

Library of Congress Cataloging-in-Publication Data

Ahlin, Lars Gustav, 1915–
    [Kanelbiten. English]
    Cinnamoncandy / by Lars Ahlin; translated with an afterword by Hanna
Kalter Weiss.
        p. cm.—(The Garland library of world literature in translation; 1)
    Translation of: Kanelbiten.
    Includes bibliographical references.
    ISBN 0-8240-3183-0
    I. Title. II. Series: Garland library of world literature in translation; v. 1.
    PT9875.A33K313   1990
    839.7'372—dc20   90-3043

Printed on acid-free, 250-year-life paper
Manufactured in the United States of America

To
MICHELLE, DONALD,
and
RACHEL

CINNAMONCANDY
Kanelbiten

1

Sylvia Månsson was almost ready. Standing with her back against the light, she held an oval mirror in one hand. In her other hand was a translucent, crimson comb.

In ten minutes she would ride her bike, pedal slowly through the streets among droves of other cyclists. After yet another ten minutes she would enter the large gate, no longer feeling weary and depressed. Her life had taken a sudden turn. Only a few weeks ago she had been unhappy with her washed-up, dreary existence, had often felt like screaming, just to feel that she was still alive. But that had changed. Now she felt an infusion of spicily honed tension flowing through her, at times increasing to a wonderful sensation of being reborn.

Gratefully she glanced at the golden morning light outside her attic window. She raised her hands. Finally a blue sky, finally a breath of summer. An exquisite sense of kinship between herself and the light, the fragrance in the warm air, overcame her, underscored by the soft cooing of a lonesome dove, probably perching near her dovecote somewhere underneath the black tin roof.

It did not take her more than a minute to finish combing her hair. During the week her hair was the least important item. No one at work had a chance to see it. Whenever she did not wear a plain turban during her working hours, she at least covered her head with a colorful piece of cloth. Her black hair was her source of pride. Friends had often commented on its silken luster. Smiling to herself she thought of Stellan, her lips ripening with longing. He had told her that he could mirror himself in its dark, mysterious brilliance.

3

Humming, Sylvia surveyed her looks without a trace of concern. There had been a time when she believed that everything depended on lusciously painted lips and correctly plucked eyebrows. Such ideas had often guided her actions in the past, but she knew better now; had known it for quite some time. No, if luck depended on anything more than chance, then it was a good disposition. A good disposition is contagious—it creates warmth and excitement.

A sudden frown appeared between her eyebrows. Though still holding the mirror, she was not conscious of doing so. For a split second a brooding thought created a vacuum between her and the world. What about her heart? Was she really that forgetful? Could a general and superficial notion influence her so easily? Her spirits dropped. She was often given to fits of melancholy. Was not despair her true nature? A sense of hopelessness at the implacable bottom of it all? No one suspected it. Everyone considered her cheerful, spirited, quick-witted and actually someone who did not take life very seriously. No one would ever believe that pain could tear her apart as she desperately cried and wailed for rescuers who would not materialize.

There was one who knew it.

The second passed. Again, she looked at a face that lived and wanted to live, because underneath it all there was a will that controlled her features, a desire that willingly assumed the playing of a role.

Sylvia put away mirror and comb and resumed her humming. It was a proud woman that now lifted her face to look down her sides, experiencing the arrogance her heart revealed: she was magnificent, complicated, complex. Unlike others, she was familiar with both darkest distress and purest happiness. Actually, she was simply enviable. Ordinary wretches don't know how to live. They are dead. If things don't go well for them, they don't get anything out of life. Whereas she . . . her innate intensity reassured her that love and happiness would come her way shortly.

The dove cooed and a soft breeze made the curtains billow against the wall. Sylvia Månsson had a flashing recollection that something in her expectations was not as it should be. The melody stopped abruptly on her joyous lips. Turning around, she looked at her daughter, standing only a few steps away from her and, strangely enough, hardly aware of what the mother was doing.

Britt-Mari was holding her mother's watch against her ear, listening with closed eyes, her head slightly tilted. The girl's smile was a mixture of grief and enchantment. As her gaze changed, the mother was unable to express the thought that had suddenly struck her. But her quick glance soon abated as a new sentiment took hold of her. Fascinated, she looked at her daughter as if she were a beautiful picture.

There was the newly scrubbed skin and the white forehead, gleaming like mother-of-pearl. There was the fragile abandon of the finely drawn lips with their strange expression of some persistent pain. There were the clear lines of chin and cheeks, and the rosy labyrinth of her exposed ear. There was the soft curve of her hairline, and the cascade of reddish-blond hair, tied with a white string into a ponytail, cascading halfway down the lightblue dress through the loop her arm described. The total submission in the bearing of her head and arms in connection with the commonplace object under scrutiny aroused a contradiction of sentiments. The combination of both scruples and happiness expressed in the girl's face somehow made the brown hint of freckles even more appealing.

What are you up to? the mother asked, chuckling to set her mind free.

I'm just listening.

Britt-Mari looked up, trying to say something. But she suddenly realized that she could not. It was impossible. She simply couldn't. The mother sensed the seriousness of the girl.

May I have my watch? she asked.

Britt-Mari stretched her arm forward, holding out the watch. But instead of taking it, the mother turned away and switched the radio on. Then, not waiting for the latest hit to end, the mother turned back to the girl. Stroking the girl's shoulders lightly, she bent down and pulled a funny face,

Did you think it was the heart of a canary?

Giggling, she finally took the watch and fastened it around her wrist. Solemnly Britt-Mari shook her head. No, not the heart of a canary. She had thought of something entirely different, something her mother never must know.

Britt-Mari had seen herself as an adult, standing in a watchmaker's shop and listening to the ticking of a hundred clocks.

The idea was to buy the watch for herself, that's at least what she imagined. Only first she wanted to listen for a while to the strange music that echoed from walls and shelves. She closed her eyes to listen to the fragile, silvery sounds organizing into a solid, steadfast rhythm. A sudden feeling of being grown up and mature took hold of her. What did it mean to be grown up and mature? To have entered a final form. No more internal changes. If there were any after that, they would be external changes only. All the wily surprises of growing up would no longer wreak havoc with one's life and miserable shortcomings would be a thing of the past.

How could she talk to her mother about anything like that? She needed only to look at her to understand that she had conjured up something most offensive and perhaps just plain inexcusable.

The music of the hundred clocks was timeless. This music would never change. It knew neither beginning nor end. Only constant repetition. It was solidly permanent. Always beautiful. Always the best. That's how grown-ups lived. That's how they felt. Time to them was but a dim rumor. Growing up a tale far removed. And death but distantly valid. Real music did not disturb them. Not its beginnings, not its endings, not its artfully contrived luxuriance, not even the experience of abandonment the listener feels after it stops. Grown-ups never feel abandoned. Music enriches them. It teaches them clever tricks of defense and methods of building up their strength so they can conquer the world. But for the young, the old and the weak this modern, timebound music creates an impractical world and false precepts. This music's subtle, at times even brutal force demands strength from those who listen to it.

Have you wound it up?

Yes.

You've been taking care of it now?

Ever since I got it from the watchmaker.

Why do you look so sad? I'm not accusing you at all. I just think that it's funny the way you stand there watching me and remembering everything.

I have plenty of time. It's you who must go to work.

Stop now. By the way . . .

A wave of uneasiness took hold of Sylvia Månsson, but she controlled her feelings.

Gosh, turn the radio off, she said. I don't know why I ever turned it on.

She felt no regrets. But her feeling of uneasiness persisted. It was not that she was unnecessarily sympathetic toward the unhappy woman she had been this past winter. And before, long before that. The girl has seen too much, she thought suddenly, has witnessed everything. Taking her engagement rings from the table, Sylvia Månsson slipped them nervously over her fingers, convinced that the girl would never understand the new thing that had come her way. No, she would not even trust her mother's words. Sylvia sensed the girl's searching looks on her back. The girl's beauty was not lovable, not in the eyes of those who knew her well, certainly not those who could see through her charming appearance. The girl's beauty was a mask, hiding an ugly maturity. The wisdom of the uncanny stared through her eyes. Of course, the child was unable to catch the drift. She distrusted all happiness and remained on guard against every change for the better. Besides, at her age, how could she know anything about life?

I'm an egoist. Do you hear me, Britt-Mari? Your mother is a terrible egoist.

Not that she really felt guilty. This was just a formal declaration. Her tone of voice belied the contents of the words she uttered, and her facial expression revealed something totally different. She merely felt sorry for herself under the scrutiny of Britt-Mari's quiet gaze.

You understand what I'm saying. Your mother thinks only of herself. I want to have my own way. Things will be fine for me. Not for you.

Why do you say that, Mommy?

What else is there to say? Look outside the window, and perhaps then you'll realize how terribly egoistical I am.

Stadsberg mountain is so beautiful today.

What pleasure is it to you if you . . .

Britt-Mari spoke softly, hoping to calm her mother down and lead her thoughts in a different direction. As a rule it was easy to make her mother forget annoying troubles. Sometimes just a smile would do. She tried it.

Don't you understand what I'm saying? the mother said heat-edly. Britt-Mari's hope disintegrated.

It had been so good lately. Not at all like last winter.

Looking at this beautiful weather makes me feel like a criminal, the mother resumed, exaggeration in both body and voice. You shouldn't be here, and you wouldn't be if I hadn't. . . . No, don't interrupt me. I'm a disgusting egoist who said No when, as usual, you were invited again to summer camp. I did it out of selfishness, without thinking of you. Instead of swimming in the water and lying on the cliffs by the seashore in the sun, getting a tan . . .

She stopped because she had forgotten the point she wanted to make. The girl's face remained unchanged. She realized that the girl would never understand, but continue to consider her mother the same irresponsible being she was last winter. The child's maturity was cold and stunted. Having seen only the adverse side of life, she believed that this was it, or at least the important, crucial, lasting part. As if life were not constant flux. As if there existed no lofty heights to counteract the deepest depths.

Well, I've told you the way it is, she said mechanically. The silence in the girl's gaze bothered her. Now you know how I feel.

It's unnecessary, Mom. Why should you think of camp when you know that it was impossible.

Why was it impossible?

You know that.

Do I? You don't dare tell me.

You know that we need one another. That's why.

You little hypocrite. You're faking. I've said it before. You too. Tell the truth. It was I who needed you to stay with me. My needs, mine. But what about yours?

To be with you, Britt-Mari said simply, hoping that it would be over for this time around.

You need sunshine and swimming and peace and quiet more than I, the mother said sullenly.

Britt-Mari looked away, overcome with a sense of care. She heard her mother step across the floor and knew intuitively that she would never forget her experience that time in the watchmaker's shop. She would forever long to get back there. Shouldn't she? Would she be really grown up, feel as calm, dignified and secure some day?

Perhaps it's not too late yet, the mother said. What was the date set for your group's departure?

Britt-Mari stood still, listening.

When was it you went last year?

I don't remember.

It must've been around this time. I'll inquire. Perhaps there's still one free space. If so, you'll go and get what you need. People tend to listen to me, even though there may be some obstacles. If I really make the effort . . .

Mommy.

I'm thinking of what's best for you.

Mommy.

Sooner or later there must be an end to this pampering and mollycoddling. We can't go on forever to . . .

Britt-Mari suspected nothing. Certainly not that she had become superfluous, a block in the way. But she felt the hurt coming from her mother and cried out. Then she got frightened of her own voice and pressed her hand against her mouth. It was her turn to be stunned, incapable of moving an eyelid, or a finger. She could utter no sound, shed no liberating tear.

The mother perceived the girl's frozen numbness and was touched. Despite their differences, they were alike in their reaction to great distress. Sylvia Månsson went over to her daughter. Her sympathy masked the reason for the girl's hurt. Forgetting instantly what she had just said and thought, she pulled Britt-Mari's hand with mild determination away from her mouth to press a kiss on it. Putting her arms around the girl's slender waist, she rocked her gently.

Mommy's girl. Mommy's only support in the whole wide world.

With a hushed, heartfelt voice she mumbled these words a few times, then bent down again and kissed the girl on her freckled nose.

Cinnamoncandy. My sweet, lovely Cinnamoncandy.

Britt-Mari responded instantly and regained her mobility. Opening her eyes, she cast a devoted look at her mother as she lifted her hands to stroke her across her hips and upward, toward her breasts.

I can't live without you, she whispered, her teeth bared in a miserable smile.

And I can't without you, the mother whispered.

Happy and refreshed, the mother gave a sudden laugh.

I forgot to show you something yesterday. Come and see. How could I ever forget?

Her hands playfully spread out, she walked with mincing steps over to the table and put her hands over the zipper of her shopping bag. With a sudden flip she separated the rest of the zipper and pulled out a dark-red scarf made of a sheer, translucent material. Gingerly Britt-Mari stretched her hand out, but the mother threw the scarf into the air before she could reach it.

Look, the mother cried as the delicate, strawberry-red fabric descended on her fingertips.

She wound it around her hand and covered her entire forearm. Then she moved her fingers back and forth to bring out the sheerness of the material. Mockingly pretending to be the Black Witch, she threatened Britt-Mari.

You'll look stunning with it, Britt-Mari said, conjuring away her cares.

Britt-Mari watched her mother wind the scarf around her head without even looking in the mirror. She reveled in her mother's tricks, her happiness and vitality, as she dived down to reach the great storehouse of love she held for her. Her mother had just time enough left to repeat her instructions: the food to be bought, the closet to be cleaned, the dispatch note to be signed with her mother's name and witnessed by Mrs. Hagberg—if it arrived today. Then the mother threw her a kiss from the door and was gone. Britt-Mari stood still and listened. She heard her mother hum a tune on her way downstairs: the first kiss was tender . . . it had not poisoned her adoration. Turning her face toward the open window, Britt-Mari caught sight of the Stadsberg, the mountain that formed part of the old city.

The mountain looked bright and smiling today. Both its woods and the very rock. Even the steep cliffs and ravines looked friendly in the golden morning light. The dove on the roof began to coo just as Britt-Mari folded her hands together. She managed to complete three of her most secret signs. First the triangle, then the bird, last the chalice. She did not go any further. Gripping her skirt impetuously, she whispered with a tiny chirp: No.

Then she ran out of the room, through the kitchen, in her hurry forgetting to lock the kitchen door. As she slammed it shut, the noise came like a blow in her back. She did not notice. All she knew was the feeling that she would choke if she were not to see her beautiful mother one more time. I've got to see her, she panted. See her, see her. She watched her mother disappear in the traffic, her mother with the glowing red turban that made her head look as proud and cool as a tulip.

2

Britt-Mari's wild hopes crumbled when she reached the slow curve on the other side of the high church walls. There was no one to stop her mother, no one to detain her. The outer limits of her viewing range quivered in the blue haze of the rising sun. No red turban glided past, no proudly radiating head drifted through the obscured horizon. She saw only sparse clusters dashing past on bicycles. They had no time to lose. The plant's sirens were about to howl. After that the churchbells would ring, their sounds coming from the depths of another era.

Out of breath like an old woman, Britt-Mari pressed her arms against her breast to stop her panting. She was unaware that she was crying, did not understand that a certain feeling of happiness chained her to the spot. I'm going to tidy up so neatly, she whispered to herself, her viewing range dissolving in her eyes. She was hardly talking to any living soul when she promised: I'll pick some flowers to put in your room, and I'll rinse your stockings.

The day stretched long before her. Turning, she walked on with dreamfilled steps, smiling at some secret inner happiness. When she came to the high walls, she stepped aside with a sense of discomfort, away from their proximity. Up on the hill, where the tile-red walls of the church might burn in the fiery sunshine and its belfry often pierced the clouds, she had no trouble taking endless, lonely walks, stirred by some forbidding or lighthearted dream. But the walls always frightened her, except perhaps on evenings when the setting sun made their granite sparkle and the velvety moss look radiant.

She hurried across the street where a park with mighty trees sloped down to the river. The city's tallest bird-cherry grew in that park and it stood in full bloom just now. She went over and sat down on a bench close to the tree. Thousands of tiny cherryblossoms covered the grass around its trunk. Even though the crown was not overly full, the clusters were fresh and blindingly white. Snowlike—no blue shimmered in this whiteness. There was nothing compared to its purity.

The river was a running water, though that was not easy to see from where she sat on the bench. There was nothing floating on its surface. No rowboat was out there. She remembered the creek that came splashing down Stadsberg by the water works. It rippled and gushed in small torrents, and the higher one followed its path the clearer became its waters. One could drink it. The higher up and the deeper in the woods, the better the water. But, she thought, one must not be too hot and perspiring when drinking. Why? One might die. Why? She had no answer to that question. Perhaps it was not even true. Just something she had heard, maybe from a child who knew nothing. Something about a big fellow who had drunk some water and fallen dead on the spot. And yet, he had been drinking from a well, not the creek. That warning did not concern the water from the creek at all. That she hadn't voiced her opinion when . . .

The sirens went off, one after another. Columns of boxes, hard as steel, stretched higher and higher up into space. As if a voracious hunger had awakened invisible wild animals who now tore through their hunting grounds where they knew their prey was easy game.

Britt-Mari pushed her hands under her thighs. Surely, her mother had made it to work, punched in on time. Now the people were streaming into the great hall where her mother's new turban made a great impression.

Her mother's tales often frightened Britt-Mari. There were long stretches of time when she did not hear her talk about anything special, only about her drudgery and weariness. Other times there were many events, narrow escapes and catastrophes. Was she sure that her mother told her everything? Britt-Mari would have felt better if she at least for once could have seen her mother's workplace. Well, if only she could have a peek at the machine her mother ran. This machine above all took on a most frightening aspect. In her fantasy it had the form of a strange animal, created and developed by remarkable men. It was full of capricious and bloodthirsty nerves, its functions were highly incomprehensible and its actions beyond her understanding.

This terror had struck her abruptly and without the slightest warning one recess this past winter. Talking to a friend, she had stretched her hand out and suddenly seen the skin break and there was blood all over the hand. She never reached her friend's shoulder. A raw force had settled in her neck that made her bend down and vomit in the snow. She felt at a loss, unable to answer her girlfriends' anxious questions. She ran away from school and classes. Not home. No, she kept running in the direction of her mother's workplace. She saw the smoke coming out of the plant's chimney, drawing words in the grey of the winter sky, reverberating on her eyes as: accident, accident.

By the time she reached the plant she was so convinced of her vision's strange meaning that she dared to walk straight into the building. Only under the cool gaze of the gatekeeper did the acuteness of her terror finally subside. She noticed the skeptical wrinkle around his mouth, the frown on his forehead, the expression of a mean, introverted sensuality, and knew instinctively that she needed to be on guard. That was why she never even told him her name and did not ask for her mother. But she did not turn and walk away. Keeping her voice low, she asked the face in the cubbyhole a question,

Has there been an accident recently?

The face did not move, but its lips parted, baring a row of decayed teeth,

Speak up so that I can hear you.

Has there been an accident?

Has there been an accident? Who says so?

Its neck stretching forward, the face slid through the milky-white glasspanes that framed the cubbyhole. She felt a whiff of death coming from its mouth,

Who says there's been an accident here?

I was just wondering.

Who has sent you here?

I came by myself.

There's been no accident here.

Are you sure?

Wouldn't I know if there'd been an accident around here? You're very stupid.

With a bored gesture he pushed the window shut, only to open it again. There was Britt-Mari, standing in front of him, laughing out loud. She would always blush when she remembered the way she had behaved at the time. She was still giggling when she ran out of reach of his rage.

Troublemaker, he screamed behind her. Troublemaker, I'll teach you to make fun of me . . .

Afterwards she cruised through the city with quick, easy steps. Not with a sense of luck, or gratitude, or humble happiness. No, it was exhilaration. Then, later at home, she felt sick and went to bed, suffering imaginary pains. But she got up again and again, acting on one brainstorm after another: took her temperature, tried to find her pulse, investigated her tongue and eyes in the mirror, gulped down water with honey, even fixed enormous sandwiches and cleared out all leftovers, took a laxative. When her mother came home she told her about her attack, though without telling her its cause, whose origin was beyond her comprehension anyway. Mother was wonderful all evening, sitting with her and comforting her. Her girlfriend Elsa also dropped in, corroborating both truth and untruth. She brought along Britt-Mari's forgotten mittens, explaining that she had washed them. That's why they were still wet.

Look out for your hands, Mommy. Be careful about your fingers. And make sure that your clothes don't get caught. Always check that your buttons are buttoned, especially around your wrists. Don't forget to sew them on real tight-tight. That's necessary. It doesn't take much. The least bit. . . . Why do you wear shoes with laces? They can come loose and it's easy to step on them and fall. Is it true that you never take off your haircover, or the turban? You have such beautiful hair, Mommy. You remember what you told me. What happened to that flirty doll who wanted to show off her new hairstyle? She got scalped. It took no more than a second. The new boss never got to see her great hairdo. The damage was permanent, you remember that. That must never happen to you, Mommy. I pray to God that it will never happen to you.

The churchbells announced earthly time with dark, heavy sounds, eternally unchanging, stroke by stroke. It is the time of superficiality, whose thin, unreal film envelops our lives. Britt-Mari sat on the darkgreen bench, hunchbacked, her head hanging down and her thin shoulderblades showing through her dress. Her reddish-blond hair fell in a curve around her neck and shoulders. She dropped into herself. Not like a stone that is helpless when it falls. No, with winged strength and outstretched heart, trying to reach to the bottom of her love and lock her heart in there. She tightened her lips so as not to burst out in shouts of joy and triumph.

Her love was boundless. Her affection inexhaustible. There were no demands she was not willing to carry out. She would offer herself. Her entire life. She would give everything. As soon as she would hear her name, she would answer the call: Cinnamoncandy, Cinnamoncandy. She would tear herself apart to allow the mouth that called to feel the sweetness of life.

Britt-Mari shivered and pulled her hands out. A dog had started nosing against her legs and was busily licking her sandals. It was Felix, the poor, neglected dog of the janitor. Britt-Mari scratched one of his bent ears with her hand. An unintelligible radiance gleamed in her eyes.

Felix whimpered a ringing stanza before he sat down, draping his tail around one of her legs and looking at the girl as if he understood her.

Pappa loved her, she told the dog. That explains it all, doesn't it? Of course, I don't remember anything. But Mommy has been telling me as long as I can remember, He carried me on his hands, I was like a queen in his eyes, there was nothing I wanted that. . . . At that time she never dreamed of having to work in a plant year after year.

Britt-Mari lifted her left hand and pointed upward,

Now you understand Pappa's worry where he is. He can see me here. He can hear what I'm telling you.

Something strange frightened her and she let go of the dog's ear. Feeling a sudden chill, she looked around, ready to run, wondering with an absolutely normal little girl's voice,

Gosh, why am I sitting here?

She stretched her legs forward, their skin shimmering coral red and violet and alkali green. Jumping up, she started rubbing them.

So far it's the sunshine that is warm, she told Felix, who sat watching her.

She remembered suddenly that just a while ago she had shouted at the dog not to bother her. Hadn't she even kicked him? Now she wanted his forgiveness. She had been excited. Not seeing her mother on the street, she had run down in the hope of finding her mother still in the backyard with her bike, perhaps the tires needing air, or the hub some oil. It was then that Felix had appeared and bothered her with his jumping up against her legs.

I was so unhappy, she explained. If you understood what I told you, you'd forgive me.

After that she took the path that cut through the park out to Storgatan, talking and thinking words to the dog. She had renamed him for her personal use. Really, the name Felix was disparaging. She remembered another dog by that name, a ridiculous and creepy dog that belonged to a chimney-sweep who abused it. No, she called him Grepp, and now she promised him sugar bits for the next time and assured him that she meant to ask the janitor's wife to give her permission to wash him—because your mistress neglects you something awful, Grepp, Grepp! Right now there was plenty of room for that in the backyard. Oh, she would lather Grepp until he looked as white as a polar bear and scrub him properly until his fur was as shiny as it could possibly be.

Your mistress doesn't realize how beautiful you are.

3

At this early hour Storgatan was almost deserted. All the stores and offices were still closed and many people still in bed. Those having definite, fixed working hours usually tend to sleep as late as possible in the morning. Getting up right before going to work makes them feel keenly their lack of time for themselves. But not my Mommy, Britt-Mari thought as she looked out over the river and became aware of the empty streets and tightly drawn curtains behind the windows in the Norrmalm section of the city. Sylvia

Månsson offered gladly half an hour's sleep every morning for some time to relax in bed with the daily paper and coffee.

Look, Britt-Mari said, and pointed with her finger.

The sanitation department had rinsed Storgatan. The asphalt looked as shiny as if it had been raining during the night. In contrast the pale-yellow stone slabs of the sidewalks were dry. Perhaps it was their color that made it so obvious where an early cleaning woman had thrown out her mop- and rinse-water.

Britt-Mari hesitated when she reached the streetcrossing at Allégatan. While she kept on talking to Grepp, she asked herself, Why? But she had no answer to her question. Not about her hesitation. That had happened before. But why her patience so often fell short. Why would her impatience so often take over despite all her good intentions?

She was prone to a feeling of being hemmed in in her attic. All it took was to sit down on a chair or to stretch out on her bed in the kitchen. Unable to do anything. Her dreams and feelings would knock, senselessly baiting, like flies against a window pane. It is difficult to be alone, she thought, when I want to live in a world that is totally different from the one I am living in. It is difficult to accept myself when it's clear how I'm going to be. Why did her patience always fall short so unexpectedly? Just now, this very moment. Nothing had worried her before. She knew what she had to do and she was willing to do it.

An old man passed her, an empty newspaperbag hanging over his shoulder. When his steps died away, the idea that he had stopped to stare at her hit her with sudden force. There was no traffic to speak of now. Without turning her head, she cut across the street. Grepp followed on her heels.

You think, of course, that I'm a real slovenly lazybones, she said, bending down to tighten his collar. Bark at me. Go upstairs and make up the beds, bark. Go upstairs and run the vacuum cleaner, bark. Go upstairs and rinse Mommy's stockings, bark.

But Grepp only licked her hands. Turning a corner, she saw something that looked like a good excuse for a detour. There was another park on this side, a mere wedge of a green island consisting of some young trees, a flowerbed in bloom surrounding it. These were maple trees, planted three years ago. One of them with its darkly burning red leaves differed from the others.

My tree, Britt-Mari said, pointing. Come, let's say hello to it. As she stood by the young tree, she could hear the heralding sounds of a hundred bells. She abandoned herself to a strange spell, which cleansed and stained her conscience at the same time. She tried to invoke the tree's growth by holding her hands down, all the while lifting her head and stretching her neck. All her muscles tightened, became rigid. She did not give in. Her breathing stopped. Her fists pressed against her thighs. The tendons of her neck protruded like stiff roots. Her chin was distorted as she sucked her lips in between her teeth. Her straining made her blood gush and both forehead and neck turned a bloody red. It seemed as if her upper torso had disengaged itself from her hips, and a sensation of something unreal and airless spread around her middle. She felt as close to defeat as to victory.

She succeeded. The physical surge toward perfection lasted for only a short second when her entire body expanded and enlarged. Round breasts extended from her ribcage. Her hips and thighs took on their final shape. The gates were wide open, but she stood still, waiting. Her hair changed to a new hairdo. A dress of classical cut draped around her body. Rings settled on her fingers. Darkgreen earrings adorned her earlobes. Her shoes rose up on high heels. She was ready to walk forth, but hesitated a moment before continuing to step into the world of adults. For a split second a young woman in her newly acquired maturity encompassed the memory of a miserable young thing.

One second only, after minutes of extreme effort and concentration. One mere second. But it was enough for her to experience both blessing and terror.

Britt-Mari relaxed. Small pearls of perspiration were glistening on her forehead. She was still trying to remember the details of her experience. Through her fatigue she tried to fill in plausible incidents and possible impressions. Hadn't she been on her way to a very definite encounter? Or was she merely cool and chic? Hadn't she experienced the rich perfume of a grown woman? Or was it simply an instant in a little girl's misled heart looking for sympathy? No, it was her love, with boundless understanding, with encouraging advice, with strict command: hold out, hold out!

The bitterness on Britt-Mari's lips turned to disgust.

The most important aspect was missing. What was in her gaze? It was not her clothes, not her hairstyle, not her jewelry that mattered. It was the look of the young woman's eyes she needed to meet. What was her face like? It should radiate purity and daring and strength. There should be no cowardice, no soiled simplicity, no indifference to malice and laxity, no depraved adult pleasures. It should show a willingness to fight. It mustn't forgive the girl who used to . . .

Britt-Mari stared at a telephone booth into which she often used to duck. Unable to look away, she could feel the censure she so well deserved emanating from the booth.

In her daydreams she called the telephone booth The Lady. She had several reasons for associating the booth with the woman her mother called Aunt and whose snapshot she saved in an album. There she wore a red-checkered, wide skirt—one could easily figure that. The short jacket of her suit was green. That wasn't too bad. The crown of the maple tree might fit over her hair, like a hat. This telephone booth seemed like a lady from the past. Britt-Mari could enter her and give her voice, stand inside her and make high and mighty faces and well-mannered gestures. She could even lift the receiver and pretend to talk with the fellow she was in love with, with her best girlfriends, with an old woman who was her worn-out mother, with her personnel in her big department store, with her maid, with her children's nanny, with her own children: be good and do what you're asked; I want it, my dear, I'm used to being listened to; in my opinion, I shall do what I can, I'm invited out tonight, no that must certainly never happen, I'll never rest until I've straightened out that misunderstanding; girls must be protected, get moving, I'm in a hurry . . .

Britt-Mari walked down Storgatan with defiant steps, her lips pursed with scorn. Having lost all self-esteem, she was highly indifferent to the judgment of the world. Grepp followed faithfully, off and on jumping forward and yapping to remind her of his presence.

The door to a café stood open. She looked in. The chairs were stacked, seats upside down, on the tables. A woman was mopping the floor. To show herself how inconsiderate she could be, Britt-Mari asked,

I'd like to buy a lump of sugar.

A lump of sugar?

Yes, the dog is terribly starved, she declared with a cold, sober voice.

Get moving, and don't bother me, the woman said. She bent down to take the washrag off the mop.

Turning to Grepp, Britt-Mari declared a profound truth,

There you can see, Grepp. The world is mean and the people nasty. Just what I've always said.

Are you crazy? the woman asked, surprised.

Crazy? Just look at the facts, my dear. What happened? All I wanted was to buy a lump of sugar for my dog. But you not only refused, you didn't even take me seriously.

Britt-Mari took off, steeped in dignity. The woman, busily rinsing her rag in the bucket, gave a jerk and ran to the door. Standing a short distance away, Britt-Mari stood nonchalantly wiggling her foot over the gutter.

I'll show you how to buy sugar lumps, the woman screamed.

Britt-Mari shrugged her shoulders and walked on to the marketplace. There was more life and bustle. Although there was no market today, quite a few stands had set up shop at the Storgatan intersection. More traders were arriving constantly with their carts and trucks. For a while Britt-Mari ambled through, watching as they unpacked and listening intently to their conversations, until people noticed her curiosity. She moved on without talking to anyone. Being the observer, she sensed a slow numbing of her feelings as to what she saw.

At a distance a blue streetcar rattled around the corner to its stop at Esplanade. She crossed the street. A bus came to a halt a few steps away from her. She turned around. A row of cabs stood in line at the taxistand, waiting. City Hall looked like an abandoned castle. The light over the police station was broken on one side. She turned around again, stopping at the bus stop, pretending to wait for a bus ride. But she lost her patience before any bus arrived whose driver she could have pestered. Eventually she settled down on a bench on Esplanade. Life around her drifted into the distance. The air she breathed thinned out, became light and poisonous, like gas. Suddenly she gave a flutter with her arms, jumped up and ran off.

This went on for hours. The streets changed her and she changed the streets. She lived ten lives, died through nine of them. She pleaded and begged. Deliver my soul. Save my heart. Infuse my body with patience. She hated and damned. Kill them. Hurt them. Skin them alive. She scoffed and played the fool. Heedlessly dropping on her feet, she frightened an old lady. She confused an old man, telling him about the big red spot on the back of his jacket. He turned both head and jacket to reach and see.

And so it continued. Walking into the fishmarket, she asked to buy meat. Are you blind? the man asked. In a meatmarket she asked for herring. Where do you have your eyes? she was asked. Then she wanted to buy two meters of lace in a paintstore, which made the salespeople scoff with derision. But through it all she retained her violet gaze, declaring with clear-tolling voice, I love lace, surely you have lace, the most wonderful thing there is.—She spread confusion, elicited dawns of blushes and shame. There is nothing easier than playing nuts, she thought, disappearing with a silly giggle, her arms somewhat stiff and sprawling. People gasp when they see signs of abnormality in a face that seems fully normal. Just baring one of her pointed eyeteeth was often enough.

Release came on Bergsgatan. Without knowing it, she had come to a construction site. She posted herself in front of it, enveloped in tranquility.

There was once a workman who fell from the scaffold here. A young man still, just twenty-four years old. It happened early one morning. The man was standing up there in the air on a board. Bareheaded. His hair was red and he had a funny, almost black mark on the back of his neck. He wore a new pair of workjeans. For the first time there were nails in its pockets and a hammer in the tiny pocket down by his calf. That was strange, because usually a ruler goes in there. The pocket proved too small for the hammer's handle. Holding his jeans with one hand and the head of the hammer with the other, he needed to pull in two directions to get the hammer out. He tugged hard at the handle once more and finally got his hammer out, still standing up there.

He fell from the high scaffold. It happened early one morning. His blueclothed living body fell. Still young, only twenty-four years old. He had been married for three. His bluejeans were shiny. The incident blinded the five witnesses. They turned their heads, or lifted a protective arm against their foreheads, or simply closed their eyes.

With closed eyes she could see him fall. Had seen it a thousand times. She loved the one who fell. She knew him well. Not just on the outside, not just a row of incidents. She knew his inside, had listened to him talk, lived with him her entire life. In reality she had not seen him long enough to remember the changes in his features. But she knew that he had seen her, talked to her, carried her in his arms, dreamed of her future. She had inherited his haircolor and features and body and temperament. Although a girl, she is his spitting image.

It was in her love that he fell with outstretched arms. Love cannot be blinded. It does not shy away from scrutiny. Her love sees the fall turn. He who fell did not stop helplessly on the ground. No, his fall continued upward. There is a curve just at this point. Her love can see that. She who loves can see with closed eyes what really happened. It is not death that grieves. Often a longing overcomes her to fly through this invisible curve herself.

He did not fall early one morning many years ago. He fell just now. Fell in her love upward.

Britt-Mari remained in front of the construction site until her awareness of the present receded and the experience became a memory. She had witnessed a falling raindrop return to its glitteringly blue cloud, shimmering in all the colors of a rainbow. In heaven's eternal soil, she thought. Courageously she returned to the surface of the life she lived. The constant change of interests, the incessant variations of feelings could not always show in her features. Given to contradictory moods, she baffled people. Some considered her puzzling, others difficult to understand. And there were those who found her frightening.

Let's stop playing around, she told Grepp. We both need something to eat.

4

The money order finally arrived a few days later. Holding the paper in her hand, Britt-Mari felt her self-esteem rising to heights of nobility. It was great to receive a money order. Absolutely enviable. The mailman now had the impression that those living on the other side of this door weren't just anybody, but people of means, with all kinds of social connections. Really, the very service in the post office was a marvel. A simple forward push of a piece of paper could separate lots of bills from those otherwise inaccessible bundles. She could never stop being amazed at their great number and their different exchange values. Their very existence was a miracle. She wondered about the world's treasures and their mystical distribution, the mere fact that there was a need for all this. What did a person do to get all these sums? There were always people standing in line before these windows and the heaps of wealth needed constant replacement. Strange that people saw nothing special in this solemn ceremony, were completely nonchalant about it. She knew that there were many banks in the city, though she had never been in one of them.

Death sent the money order Britt-Mari held in her hand. She did not want to let go of it. It came from her father.

Rearranging the table in her mother's room for her needs, she moved the vase, folded the tablecloth back and spread out a newspaper. She got out pen and ink and pulled the chair in place, all the while holding on to the check. Then she sat down to read every single word and number printed on it.

Storgatan 33, apt. 5 A.

That was their address. She always savored the answer she could provide when people asked her where she lived. It was pretty posh to live in this part of the city, especially on Storgatan. The A in her address marked it for the best part of the apartment building, indicating that their entrance hallway led directly out to the street. Those living in B, C and D needed to go through the inner courtyard. The house itself was very distinguished—the oldest apartment complex of stone. The great fire had burned down even the church, but had not ruined the house in whose attic she was now sitting. Called the Stockholm Building, it was completed the very year that terrible fire broke out. In every respect, hers was an address to brag about. Britt-Mari had never been above doing just that.

She dipped the pen into the inkwell and started writing. Sylvia Månsson, she lettered without changing her handwriting. As always, this was easy for her. With thin, fragile contours, her letters were open and wide. The ring over the å was big and airy. Then she penned a period after the name.

All she needed now was a blotting paper. But even though she remembered leaving it in one of her workbooks, she decided to wait for the ink to dry. She looked out the window and was surprised about the sudden change in the weather. Dark clouds were scudding high over the Stadsberg. A windgust burst through the open window and made the curtains flutter. Before she could get to the window, the curtains were sucked outside, whipping and whirring about like two flags. She had a hard time getting them inside again and the window shut. When finally done, she sensed a sudden silence spreading around her. Life seemed to exist just on the other side of the window pane.

Some strange power took possession of her. She felt weak and passively drawn toward the window. She became oblivious to her very existence and her forehead kept sliding back and forth across the pane.

A feeling of happiness took hold of her. With a cry of delight she watched, her mouth wide open, the panorama before her. Something was happening to the Stadsberg. Just a moment ago it had looked so insignificant under the high cirrus clouds. But suddenly it was taking on powerful dimensions. Heavy rainclouds came gushing down as if wanting to put the mountain in its rightful place. The sun, still illuminating it from the southern end of the sky, made the vertical precipice glow like a light-yellow pansy above the green of the hardwood forest and between the climbing pines. Or look like the mask of a mighty face. A hard, chiseled, indestructible face. The mask of a god.

When the sunlight disappeared, the face turned dark. A black-blue velvet curtain fell across the sky and instantly the face came alive. It came closer, its features softening in a show of melancholy, longing and visions. Slowly it took on the characteristics of a dying man and Britt-Mari felt a sudden urge to lift her hands. She panted. A feeling of closeness to the mountain enabled her to justify its majesty. She sensed its mild essence.

The rain was pouring down in driving veils that quickly grew wider and heavier as they lost their white glitter and fine, powdery quality. Woven into a mighty tapestry, the rain drenched the earth, conquering district after district under its power. Eventually it overtook the black tin roof where its clatter slowly turned to grey monotony.

The girl's hands dropped down to her shoulders, her slender fingers still vibrating with her divination of happiness, care, ecstasy, and zest for life.

Then she witnessed another spectacle. The dove appeared and, despite the pelting rain, stood its ground on the roof. Far from sinking down against the tin roof in dovish delight, it struggled hard to stretch its neck in order to pick and ruffle its feathers to expose them to the rain, lifting and spreading one wing at a time to do so. Its entire body began to slant. With a final, powerful flap it folded its wings again. Then it began slowly to stretch each foot, letting the raindrops smash against the red toes.

Britt-Mari stood and watched for a long time. She had always idolized the bird's shape, felt in her hands how well it might fit in them, sensed in her palms the wonders of caressing it, the dove's head and neck gliding forth between thumb and forefinger. The form of the small head was clear perfection. She could think of only one instance where this perfection was absent: at feeding time with all the other doves. Its impetuous picking made it look depressingly insane.

The girl wondered just how long the dove would enjoy standing in the rain. In the end the dove's delight surpassed the patience of the girl.

5

Magda Hagberg sat at her kitchen table, busily ripping apart the lining of a suit. Hagberg himself sat in the next room. The door in between was closed. Judging from the sounds coming through, Britt-Mari understood that he was pressing some garment he had altered or turned. Hagberg was a tailor, though not a very good one. Disdainfully, her mother called him a patch-tailor. No good at making new suits, he made his living doing alterations. Rumor had it that he had learned his craft in an institution. His wife helped him. She was also excellent at mending and repairing. Britt-Mari's mother had known her for a long time.

It must be a wonderful feeling to have money coming in on a regular basis, Mrs. Hagberg sighed.

Britt-Mari took a sip from the glass of juice in front of her and looked across its edge.

That depends.

In order to diminish the difference in their finances, Britt-Mari quoted her mother,

Pension sounds so great, but it's rather small when you get it.

Yes, but it does come and arrive on time, Mrs. Hagberg insisted.

When I turn sixteen it'll stop coming for me.

That's still a few years away, Mrs. Hagberg said, with a hard pull separating the sleeve from the rest of the lining.

Holding it against the window, she eyed it carefully. Her lips were dry and cracked, looking more like yellow apple peelings than human skin. Britt-Mari regretted having accepted the juice. She hardly liked Aunt Magda. It was always an effort, but she tried very hard to like her. Still, sometimes this seemed impossible. Aunt Magda's fat, pale-yellow cheeks resembled pressed marzipan, and she sighed often, looking kind of joyful even when she talked about dreadful things. And there was always something sad for her to tell, often even worse.

Filthier than the bag of a vacuum cleaner, Mrs. Hagberg said and shook the sleeve with energetic disgust. This comes from a lush.

She glanced at the door behind which her husband was work-ing, his banging reverberating through the entire house. Sliding her elbows forward over the oil cloth until her face seemed to hang just above the center of the table, she turned to Britt-Mari,

He doesn't get any customers nowadays, she whispered. Only trash—pigs, drunks, bums or cheats. He can't make it. Never could. He's no real man. If not for me, he'd be in . . .

Her finger pointed down to the floor. Britt-Mari was silent, gaz-ing into the red juice in front of her.

He hits me, Mrs. Hagberg whispered as if it were a secret. As if the entire building didn't know; at least all the tenants in the C and D sections had more than once heard them scream and cuss. Once they even found it necessary to call the police.

Hit back, Britt-Mari advised vehemently, startled at hearing her voice uttering her most secret thoughts. Surely you're stronger than he, she added quietly.

I'm a woman.

So what?

Don't talk so loud. Hagberg may hear you and come in here, wondering who it is.—You know very well that a woman can't come to blows if she wants to be ladylike.

Then leave him.

Leave him?

Yes, run away from him. He can blame himself, I should think. No other woman would take it from him.

Good. Then there won't be anyone for him to hit any more. He'd be alone and have to take care of himself.

It's obvious that you're but a child, Britt-Mari. Of course, no one expects you to know about these things. But life is a lot more difficult than you think. You can't simply draw a line through things you don't like and go on from there.

Mrs. Hagberg brooded, lost to the world, her body slowly lapsing into a slight wobble. Her wide-open eyes stared blindly ahead. In a sudden flash of recognition, Britt-Mari perceived it all. Her hands trembled against the oil cloth.

They may be dead, but some people simply live on. Even though all their dreams are torn to shreds and literally obliterated, all crav-ings for style and truth crossed and broken to pieces, their strong

bodies and stubborn willpower will not let them give up. A disgraceful acceptance replaces all reverence and piety for their own hu-
manness. Defeated, they have reached a point where their pain is
twisted into a strange feeling of pleasure. Britt-Mari knew it instinctively. Mrs. Hagberg did not want improvement, not even a cleansing reconciliation. Hers was not a call for help as she realized that
she was not strong enough to fight all that was wrong in her life.
She simply lived on. She complained, but she had accepted her fate.

Look here, Mrs. Hagberg said, coming alive again. The smile on
her lips spread slowly to her eyes and forehead.

Her face took on a soft-yellow tint as she pulled the sleeve of
her dress up to her shoulder. Her arm was covered with bruises of all
shapes and discolorations.

That's where he pinches me, she said, her hands stroking and
demonstrating on her body. Most of the time his fists land here, and
his kicks here, almost always. I could show you other places.

She paused. Obviously Britt-Mari was not the object of her attention. Her thoughts were concentrating on something abstract in
front of her, people in general, their opinions, the entire world. She
sat as if she were in a showcase window where shame and suffering
and pleasure co-mingled and established a special framework. Britt-
Mari hid her hands under the table, trying hard to disengage their
present form in order to construct a new configuration with her fingers
and palms. She intertwined her fingers, then loosened them again,
twisted them backward, let them circle around without touching each
other. Then she twisted her fingers to form a violent, ugly union,
but disengaged them again immediately without sympathy. Finally
she brought them together in a new, pure form she could not remember ever having tried before. Her thumbs linked up with her
forefingers in two rings while the knuckles of her other fingers were
set sharply against each other. Since she could only sense the effect,
but not see it, she decided to reshape her hands again as soon as she
got outside and look at them then.

I could show you some other places, Mrs. Hagberg repeated. But
I don't dare to now. He might come in.

The dull thud of his iron sounded through the closed door and
the bangs of his wooden beater rang like pistol shots.

I would leave him, Aunt Magda.

You reach a point when you no longer expect anything from life, Mrs. Hagberg said. Carefully, she pulled her sleeve down.

I would hit back until the very end.

Whatever else I've put up with, there's still one thing no one has ever been able to take away from me. I've never forgotten to behave like a lady. I've always been mindful of that, and I'll always be, no matter what happens. I'm a lady.

She returned to her dirty coatlining. Sipping her juice, Britt-Mari looked around in the neat, clean kitchen. There were two shelves filled with shining copper pots and other oldfashioned copper utensils. Above the couch hung an embroidered wallhanging, showing a bay and a couple resting on a warm beach, a bridge and a red cottage. Home Sweet Home it said with sun-yellow letters across the sky.

It's because you and Mr. Hagberg both have dark hair, Britt-Mari burst forth with sudden heat.

What's that you're saying?

You know very well. Dark and dark never match.

What kind of nonsense is that you're saying?

Do you mean that you never knew that?

Never knew what?

No, you really didn't know then. You couldn't have known, because everything *did* go wrong here.

What went wrong?

Your marriage.

My marriage?

Uncomprehending, Mrs. Hagberg continued to pull at her black lining. Had she forgotten her battered arm? How serious had she been about what she had just said about him in that room over there? Britt-Mari felt a sudden sympathy for Aunt Magda. Looking around in the kitchen, she was impressed by certain things, like the shiny, well-kept copper utensils, no longer in use except as wall decorations.

Darkhaired must marry blondes, and blondes darkhaired, she declared. Only those marriages are happy. It's because people don't know this that there are so many unhappy marriages. Think of Mom and Dad. My Mom is dark. Dad was reddish-blond, like me. And there has hardly been a marriage as happy as theirs.

In that case you're looking for a darkhaired fellow when the time comes.

Absolutely. Because I know.

Her enthusiasm left her. In a sadder mood, Britt-Mari pressed her fingertips against her cheeks in contemplation. She needed to be honest about the truth.

Well, I just might fall in love with a blond guy anyway. Even those who know about it could fall in love with the wrong person. Wasn't that what happened to you, Aunt Magda?

Mrs. Hagberg wheezed forth a muffled laugh.

It's not good for you to think so much, she said and pulled away another piece of the lining.

Surely you were in love with Uncle Hagberg?

It's better not to answer some questions. I know that I'm a woman. Shouldn't I have the same feelings other women have?

Her malicious sigh made Britt-Mari lose all sympathy for her again. If there weren't so much to discuss, she would have gulped down the juice and left right then. But just when she wanted to continue to insist on the importance of hair color for the success of love between man and woman in general, and for marriage in particular, a slight move of Mrs. Hagberg's hand and her whispered "quiet" stopped her.

There comes Hagberg.

Mrs. Hagberg's façade resumed its expression of suffering when the door opened and the man called,

Well, my job is done. Time for a suds.

Britt-Mari's dislike for Aunt Magda dissolved when she saw the man. The tailor was skinny and short. One of his legs was about two decimeters shorter than the other, and he wore a black-painted steel-construction under that foot. When walking without his cane, he tended to wobble and his arms kept jerking. She watched him trample over to the refrigerator and take out a bottle of beer. He leaned against the cold stove and gulped the beer down right out of the bottle. His Adam's apple moved up and down his long throat like a little animal that had settled under his skin.

I need to go to the post office, Britt-Mari declared and finished the rest of her juice. Hagberg took the bottle away from his mouth.

The post office? he asked.

She's got to get her loot, Mrs. Hagberg said. She sighed.

Well, there are those who're sitting pretty soft, Hagberg said. He started stroking his thigh with his left hand. Britt-Mari could not help but notice that his pants encased his thighs as tightly as gloves cover hands. Now he was scratching himself on that spot.

How is your beautiful Mom doing nowadays? he wanted to know.

Thanks. All right. Britt-Mari's answer was as short as she could possibly make it.

Hagberg snickered and pushed his hand further up his thigh.

Does she have male company these days? Or can I apply? He continued snickering as his hand kept on stroking his thigh. Britt-Mari pulled her black, shiny raincoat off the rack and rushed toward the door. But there she stopped suddenly and turned around. She stepped quickly over to the man who was still leaning against the cold stove. First she pulled his hand away from his thigh. Then she hit him across his chest. For a moment he stood very still, doing nothing either against her or with himself. He made no sound. Her face was extremely white as she with long steps walked over to Mrs. Hagberg and kissed her yellowish, marzipan-looking cheeks, whispering a silent prayer against the forehead of the woman, who was struck dumb. Then, without looking at anyone, she disappeared with deliberate, elongated steps from the kitchen. She did not know that she was leaving. She was unaware that she was already halfway down the iron stairs of Entrance D, but when she heard the vile howls from upstairs, she whispered,

You helped me, Pappa. You helped me.

6

Two hours later a violent rainshower forced Britt-Mari into a doorway. Water was dripping down her hair, face and clothes. She loved it. Remembering the dove, she wanted to stand in the rain with arms stretched so high that the pounding rain could hit her armpits. She was excited about everything that was happening around her. The quiet rapture that had taken possession of her ever since she decided to go downtown had not left her for a minute. It was a pleasure to stand in the doorway and beat her sandals against the cobblestones and watch the raindrops leaping off her raincoat. It was a delight to think of an experience like going to the post office, or to remember some of those fabrics she had seen in the stores, to think of Mother's promise, to know how good Mother was with sewing . . .

She pulled her raincoat slightly apart to get her purse. She needed to find her handkerchief.

To stand here, inhaling the damp air, to dry her cheeks, her neck and especially her ears, to check her money in her purse once, twice, even three times, then pull out yet another handkerchief and place it over her hair like a lace mantilla, to stand here jumping up and down, watching the heavy raindrops splash down with such force . . .

It's great! It's simply marvelous! she cried out, loudly, right into the rain. There was nothing in sight, no people, no streetcar, no automobiles. On the other side of the street, where an iron fence graced the sidewalk, was the railroad park with its immense poplars and chestnut trees.

Not until she leaned backward against the wall in the doorway did she realize that she was not alone. It began when she detected a pair of brown shoes and the tip of a small walking stick; further up a chocolate-brown suit became visible, then a dark-red tie against a light-green shirt, all topped by an extremely white student cap. Having skipped over the face at first, she now took time to study it carefully. He was dark and had brown eyes. There was an air of strained aloofness about him as if he were feigning total indifference. His complexion was unusually dark. Though quite clear, it looked rather dull, like the underside of a leaf. Almost like nougat, she thought.

You think, of course, that I'm making a fool of myself? she asked, trying to look serious.

Not at all, he answered with a quick glance in her direction. He seemed bent on surrounding himself with indifference, and it annoyed her.

You just graduated? she asked.

It occurred to her that if she were but a few years younger she would address him in a more informal way. And she would do the same if she were a few years older. But as it was, she had to be formal. It sounded stilted to her ears and it made it more difficult for her. But she soon realized that it was to her advantage to be formal with him. She felt an urge to put on airs. She wanted to impress him.

A week ago, he said.

Here in the city?

No.

Then you don't live here?

Yes.

Well then, you must have graduated here.

No, in Stockholm.

Then you know Stockholm!

No.

But you just said that you went to school there.

It doesn't follow that when you go to school somewhere that you know the place. As long as you go to school you don't learn a thing.

That's the most stupid thing I've ever heard.

That's the way it is.

Are you going to go on with your studies?

I'm about to start.

What?

Life.

In what way?

I'm going to study the highest thing of all: man.

Now you're stupid again. The highest is God.

The highest is man.

The highest is God. But you can't study Him, of course. Have you already picked the man you're going to study?

He shrugged his shoulders, indicating that her question was hardly worth an answer. Thinking that he was joking with her—as she was doing with him—Britt-Mari clapped her hands and pointed her finger at him. She liked his deep, quiet voice and the calm way his brown eyes looked at her.

I can guess your choice, she said. You're going to study yourself.

She saw him blush and moisten his lips. She felt a sudden threat coming from him, something she could not explain. She saw him change as he stood before her, his shoulders slightly leaning against the wall, the tip of his walking stick between his legs. If he had looked handsome before, he now looked handsomely alive. A complete stranger to her just a moment ago, he aroused in her a strange feeling of knowing him well. His eyes seemed to beg for something. His lips were pleading. And his hands reflected a longing to touch her.

Britt-Mari burst into tears. Her shoulders shaking, she buried her face in her hands. Her handkerchief dropped from her head like a lost wing. The young man watched her, startled, unable to utter a word. His right hand stirred, but he stopped his momentary impulse to rescue the girl's soiled handkerchief from the black pool of rainwater at their feet.

Eventually Britt-Mari's curiosity got the better of her. She stopped crying and peeked through her fingers to see whether it was really true.

No, it was not true. He was merely handsome. Her hands came down. The young student frowned, his blood pulsing in his neck. It was obvious that he was upset, but Britt-Mari no longer cared. The inexplicable had not happened. She bent down to pick up her kerchief, too wet now for wiping herself dry. For lack of something better, Britt-Mari wiped away her tears with her hands.

What's the matter with you? he asked.

Nothing. Nothing at all.

Then why did you start crying all of a sudden?

Because I'm very unhappy, Britt-Mari said simply and matter-of-factly.

But you weren't before. I even heard you shout: It's marvelous.

One may try, but there's no way to ignore terrible grief.

But you looked so beautiful. Really. If you can bear to hear me say that.

It's no great help in my present predicament.

How old are you?

What does that matter? You're informal with me. But I'm going to continue to address you in a formal way because there's an immense distance between us.

Really, the way you express yourself!

The way I suffer, how can I express anything but suffering?

A tender look that was a mixture of pain and hope flickered across the student's face. His eyes expressed fascination and fear at the same time. Without being conscious of it, he began playing with his stick.—Clenched into a tight fist, Britt-Mari's hand hit the air around her several times.

Why am I suffering? I've lost my money. A large sum. But that's hardly anything you'd understand. Britt-Mari's look of dismay singed past the student's eyelashes, forehead and tip of his cap before dissolving somewhere beyond the roof.

How much? His question sounded strained.

Twenty-five crowns. Two tens and a five.

Terrible grief! Great predicament! Extreme suffering! And all that about something as trivial as money.

Trivial! Well, I knew that you'd never understand. I'm a poor girl. My father is dead. My mother slaves in a factory. Twenty-five crowns means food for an entire week. She's going to hit me. You share in my mother's hourly wages and see what happens. She'll ground me for a whole month. And that in the summer, during vacation. I'll have to sit up on the roof all day long and feed her canaries.

Why on the roof?

I told you that it's summer. Can't you understand? It's because we live up in an attic, an apartment no more than a hole.

Well, what are you going to do now?

Don't know yet, but it's going to be something drastic.

You're not considering suicide?

That's entirely possible.

I'm going to prevent that.

How?

By giving you that piddling amount of money.

Now really! What do you take me for?

I'm wealthy.

You mean your dad is.

All right, then.

Honestly, where's your upbringing? When I ask you what you think of me, you tell me that you're wealthy.

I should have said that I want to help you. I really do want to
help someone in need, especially if it concerns you. And it's money
you need, right?

Britt-Mari turned her head quickly. Again she did not dare to
look at him. Again she watched his appearance changing. His eyes
were begging, his lips pleading, his hands longing to touch her. Her
heart throbbed while she waited for something to happen. It's my
eyes playing tricks on me, she thought. Her imagination could transform rain into a violet-blue episode as well as the darkest calamity.
She turned her eyes toward the wall and lowered her eyelids when
she felt him come closer. He stood close, right next to her, his new
wallet open in his hands. She could not help but ogle it as he pulled
out two tens and a fivecrown bill.

This is for you. He said it hesitantly in his low, deep voice.

Her eyes went from his hands up to his face and she realized
that it was not as she had imagined. A strange sense of loss overcame her suddenly, impelling her to probe as deeply as possible for
the utter truth. Instead of pushing away his hand, she took the money
he offered her. Holding the notes between the fingers of one hand,
she touched his shoulder lightly with the other. Her probing eyes
scanned his face with an inquisitive, sensitive urgency.

Why are you so kind to me?

I, too, was a problem child, he said with a sudden rigidity (because he didn't think that I would take his money, she mused afterward). I know how it feels. That's why I'm two years late graduating.

No, that wasn't true. She withdrew her hand from his shoulder,
no longer feeling any loss. She did not even hear what he said, but
pushed the money down into her mother's purse with a sense of self-
righteousness. Smiling distractedly under the sudden torrent of his
words, she could no longer understand what she could ever have
seen in his conceited visage.

As far as I'm concerned, there's a hellish abyss in my heart, she
interrupted him. Turning away from him, she waited a while. Then
she spun her head around and looked at him,

But there's also a sundrenched mountain top.

Having said that, she walked squarely out into the rain. Soon,
under her cape, she knitted her hands together as she pulled them
ever closer to her heart while she walked on with long, deliberate

strides. She pressed her thumbs backward until eventually she could feel her heart throb in her fingertips. With a sense of dread she wondered what would have happened if she really had fallen in love with this student there in the doorway. If she had, what would she be now? A mistress? No, someone hopelessly in love—a wet kitten, as miserable as a mangy rat, as helpless as a fly without wings, drenched far down to her inmost being.

7

That afternoon Britt-Mari finally got around to doing what she had put off for too long already. Their gas range looked terrible. Looking down its opening, she knew that it needed a good scrubbing. There's no better word than filthy mess to describe this, she thought as she draped her mother's oldest apron around her. It reached far below her knees. Then she pulled her mother's gloves over her hands, even though they were much too large and their fingers were torn besides. She smiled about her outfit. Just right for scouring this dirty range, she mused.

There was a knock at the door and it opened before she could answer. Gertrud stepped inside, her eyes red from crying, her face sullen. Gertrud the Stupid, the Klutz who was repeating their grade.

May I visit for a while? she asked, seemingly miserable from loneliness and boredom, like an old woman, or a childless housewife.

Of course; only I can't be very entertaining just now, as you see, Britt-Mari said.

Despite her sullen looks and red-rimmed eyes, Gertrud's large mouth widened to a grin. Britt-Mari turned to her range to attack the dirt, whistling at first, though later with angry grunts. Coffee grounds, grease and caked-on oatmeal were easy to explain. But what about potato peels and things that looked like eggshells, and presumably were. How could that get in there? Even a wishbone of a chicken, like a tiny slingshot for a doll. It was an eternity since they had last feasted on chicken. Britt-Mari could not remember when.

Had her mother gnawed on it while standing over the stove, then thrown it aside just like Britt-Mari would do whenever she grabbed a tidbit and ate it on the sly?

D'you remember last winter, when we were best friends? Gertrud asked.

Britt-Mari shrugged her shoulders and decided not to answer. It took her a little while before she realized that Gertrud was sitting on her bed, instead of on the chair next to it. Well now, this was going too far. Britt-Mari spun around and told her off with a violence that even shocked and baffled Stupid. And Britt-Mari was relentless. Under no circumstances could she permit Miss Klutz to sit on her bed and the thin blanket that covered it.

Gertrud got up and seated herself on the chair, more sullen than before. Finally she said,

You surely don't act like we were best friends last winter.

Britt-Mari swallowed the answer she had ready on her tongue. Stupid wouldn't understand anyway, she told herself and shrugged her shoulders. Scrubbing deeper into her mess, she pulled out the knife she had been looking for lately. Unbelievable. She threw the knife into the sink and continued her scrubbing, mindful of a nagging discomfort lurking in her back, which worsened as time went on. Gertrud continued her staring. Britt-Mari sensed that her classmate had come for a special reason.

The last time they had met was ten days ago, the last day of the schoolyear. Britt-Mari purposely avoided her. She had planned never to notice her again, but turn the other way whenever she was around. She wanted desperately to forget whatever transpired between them last winter, put it completely out of her mind. There must never be a repeat of what had happened. However difficult things might get, here at home, or with her mother, she would never again confide in others. Whatever had possessed her? A girl like Gertrud at that! Why her, of all people?

Britt-Mari did not want to remember that Gertrud's stupidity had reassured her that she would simply listen without comprehending anything, as to a terrible tale that frightens for a short while, or for as long as it is told. But Gertrud proved craftier than that. She was not frightened. Not only had she comforted Britt-Mari at the time, but Britt-Mari's weakness had given her a certain power over her that bound her to Stupid for a long, troubling month.

Aren't you going to offer me anything?

Britt-Mari did not answer. Instead, she started humming the latest popular hit. It sounded like moaning or yelping. Only after repeating the tune several times did Britt-Mari's voice finally stabilize. By the time she finished her job and closed the oven door, her words rang out clearly: My heart is an abyss, but also a sparkling mountain top. The words fitted exactly to the tune of the refrain. Without bothering to give Gertrud a second look, she walked over to the sink to clean her brush and rag. She repeated her words, more defiantly this time. What was she afraid of, really? Gertrud was and remained the sum of her experience: never again.

Never again, she thought, finally turning to face Gertrud. But her face blushed to a bloody red when she saw that Gertrud was opening up the buttons on her bodice. Her breasts were heavy and well-developed and her altered, hand-me-down dress stretched tautly over them.

What on earth are you doing? Britt-Mari shouted.

My bra is too snug. I always get Mother's discards. And this morning I thought I'd finally buy some with my own money.

Britt-Mari did not believe her. With cold scorn she declared,

If you try that trick once more I'm going to throw this rag right into your puss.

Without blinking Gertrud buttoned her bodice up again.

I got fired today, she said, watching Britt-Mari's diligence at the sink. But perhaps you didn't even know that I had a job?

Britt-Mari did not answer.

Well, I started when school let out. At Sonja's Diners. I washed the dishes every morning and evening. Actually, it wasn't morning exactly. I started at noon and got out at 7.00 P.M. every day. Sundays too. Although, as it turned out, it was one Sunday only. I made three crowns per day and two meals. Mother thought that was pretty good pay for the job. Now I'll get my rap at home when I tell her that I've been kicked out. They couldn't keep me any longer, and they didn't want to either. I begged to stay, but they only yelled at me and showed me the door.

She stopped to collect the whole range of her feelings.

Sonja's Diners, she said, contempt in her voice. The owner's name isn't Sonja at all, but Gunvor. Why wouldn't Gunvor's Diner do? Gunvor's Diners can't possibly sound cheaper. And how can you call a joint with just one room Diners? It should've been Gunvor's Diner, really.

Britt-Mari was not listening. She had the water faucet running full force. Two small Chinese coffee cups, that's what you're going to have for breasts, her mother had told her many a time. One nice day they'll be there. Translucent like fine china. It may take a while yet. You have that kind of body. Don't be impatient. You'll always be slim. You should be happy about that. If it doesn't make sense to you now, it will once you hit thirty-five and see what others your age look like.

I broke too many dishes, Gertrud said.

Who had this bright idea that you should wash dishes? Britt-Mari asked, wiping her hands dry on her oversized apron.

Why, d'you think that I can't wash dishes?

I don't think anything. Sorry.

It wasn't my fault that I broke so much. You should've seen the place. Old-fashioned. Cramped. And dark.

Why did you come here?

I just got the idea.

In that case I think that you should get the idea to leave now.

D'you mean that you won't let me sit here?

I've got some shopping to do before Mom gets home, Britt-Mari lied. She regretted it immediately.

Pulling off the apron and tossing it down, she was about to hurl an insult at the girl. But suddenly she changed and uttered with an affected smile,

Even though it isn't polite, I must tell you that I can't stand to see you here for another minute. Make yourself scarce, or I'll throw you out.

Britt-Mari stopped making faces. She cast a studied, sidelong glance full of loathing the way she had seen someone do it in some movie she had watched with her mother. Britt-Mari could feel Gertrud's shudder. Stupid was not angry, did not pretend that it was raining outside. The Klutz was not dumb. It dawned suddenly on Britt-Mari that Gertrud had an advantage over her. Gertrud's eyes showed a ghastly, admirable cunning, becoming ever stronger as it slowly spread over her entire face. Its resources seemed without limits. Not spontaneous, but studied, it was the continuation of that dreadful cunning she had shown last winter.

Okay. Then I don't mind telling the things I know.

Gertrud got up. She let her sweaty hands run along the buttons between her breasts, which looked like heavy, fat cheeses and were too large for her hand-me-down dress, probably from some lady for whom the mother did the cleaning. Her fingers clasped the edge of her neckline, ruffling the material with an absent-minded purposefulness.

You don't know a thing about me, Britt-Mari said quietly, beseeching. The eyes that met hers were the gates of evil.

I know what I know; this came from the mouth with the wide-spaced, milkwhite teeth, which should have been and remained stupidity's gate.

What do you think? That I'm interested? Or possibly frightened?

That's the way it looks!

Beat it before I stick our carving knife in you!

Gertrud gave a throaty laugh,

You little red louse. I could squeeze you between my thumbs and spill all your juices.

She started walking toward the door, her movements indicating her certainty that she would be stopped. Britt-Mari looked at the window with a prayer to the heavens and their light to hurry up and save her. The rain had stopped, but the clouds hung low and heavy still. The naked crags of Stadsberg hovered suspended between the roots of its pines like a grey load of washed workclothes on the clothesline. Britt-Mari reverberated with self-accusations: I am worse than she, I'm much worse than she. It gave her the strength to stop Gertrud.

What's that you heard?

Not only heard. I've seen too.

My Mom?

Yes, with her latest. It was just dandy to see how lovey-dovey they were together. Not just your Mom. Him too.

You're lying.

Am I? I even followed them, almost all the way. I know who he is and where he lives.

You were dreaming.

They stood in the entrance for a long time. D'you think I couldn't see what they did? It was like watching necking in the movies.

You spy.

I was just walking home from Sonja's Diners. It was past ten o'clock, and I was pretty tired, the way one gets when working as hard as I did. Can I help it that your Mom and her latest beau took the same street I did?

Gertrud knew how to appreciate the silence that followed. Once again she had managed to cross and humiliate so that it wounded and hurt. One of those who always let her know that she was inferior, always, either the way she looked, or in her tone of voice, or with stabs and blows, or nasty words, always, in school, on the street, at home, and now at work too. Panting with excitement, Gertrud watched Britt-Mari through half-closed eyes. A quick leer broke her lips apart, like a white dagger. She swallowed the leer as she again panted with excitement. Yet another leer followed, as cutting, as milky-white as before. Finally her words summed up what she had accomplished,

Well, at least you got enough to shut you up.

As soon as she was alone Britt-Mari threw herself on her bed. She could not remain too long in the hole she had dug for herself. She rushed against the door, pelted and kicked it with fists and feet as if a fire had broken loose and she were locked inside. But not even that gave her any peace. She needed to condemn herself to death.

She received her sentence with iron self-control.

The carving knife lay in its usual place. The largest mirror in the house hung inside the closet door. All she needed to do was to swing the door open. She stood in front of her mirror image, lifted the knife's edge against her neck and slid it slightly across her skin. She thought: I have to do it in earnest. That made her consider the pain involved: how it would feel. With a keen edge it wouldn't hurt for quite a while. If dull, the pain would break forth, warm and deep.

She scrutinized her neck all the way up to her mouth.

She saw the unspeakably pure smile of forgiveness on her face and she started to cry. The carving knife dropped out of her hand as she jumped up. Then she ran around, hiccuping with joy over having seen a thing so beautiful. It could not have been herself she had seen, certainly not the person she had acted today. Life's most secret finger had touched her face and so called forth God's pure image to comfort her and give her courage by letting her perceive, for a silver-split second, the glory awaiting her. There are no millstone cares in any human life, all made of precious metals because something great is in store for us. Waiting is the perfect form.

Britt-Mari held her hands, like blinders, in front of her eyes when she passed the mirror. Trembling, she walked behind it and pushed the door shut. That done, she overcame the temptation to look at herself a second time. Leaning her forehead against the door she prayed for patience—stubborn and enduring patience.

She left the carving knife lying on the floor as a symbol of something not to be afraid of. Not until she heard the mother's footsteps outside the door did she rise and pick it up.

8

Britt-Mari hardly needed her mother's oral confirmation to be convinced. A hundred telling, small details during the evening all pointed to the same fact. Her mother was in love. Deeply in love.

The last time that happened Britt-Mari was not at home. That was last summer when she was at summer camp. She hated camp because she could not get along well with youngsters her own age or younger. They were too childish for her, too immature, not serious enough. She found them sullen, sulky, naggy. At camp she had to steal that which was to her more essential than water. For one week she could well get along without water. But she could not survive without meeting herself at least once every day. She turned into a dusty, stinging nettle by the wayside. And pity the young, resolute counselor who came near her then.

I learned it last winter, she mused.

She was lying in her bed in the kitchen, waiting for her mother to turn off the light in her room. She realized that she had been too ignorant at the time and consequently unable to help when her mother needed her. It was her mother's habit to get rid of fellows who tried to hang on. Some she had liked, but they fell out of favor. When I say it's over, I do mean it, her mother used to say. After that she was inaccessible and elusive, feigned insurmountable obstacles. No one was ever able to bother her seriously, though there were many unbelievable incidents.

She was ingenious at finding excuses. It gives me the shivers to think of that fellow as your stepfather, she might say. He would never understand you, my Cinnamoncandy. He would be your death and mine. Or: I couldn't stand to have that character around me night and day for the rest of my life; I don't have the strength to fuss and shoot the breeze for more than one week per year. Or: Right now we know what we have, and have it our own way, but he's the kind who's generous today and stingy tomorrow. Or: Who'd believe that he's religious and wants me to come along to prayer meetings as soon as we get married; I'd rather die. Or: That guy has no future, I can't throw away my pension for anyone like that. Or: A person may lose her common sense for a spell and feel careless and easy, but then she's got to clear her head and choose someone who'll not prevent her from using God the Father's greatest gift to a single woman.

In all these cases there was never any real love involved. But love came with Q, Britt-Mari reflected, picking a seldom used letter of the alphabet to designate him.

Something went wrong with Q in early September, and the horrible aftermath lasted through the winter. Britt-Mari could do nothing except keep close to her mother. But that established merely physical closeness. It took quite a while before the mother found it worthwhile to look at her daughter. Their close relationship did not return until the hours they could spend together became precious. That developed during the winter like this: Their time of togetherness rolled before them like a red ball, for each one of them in her own way, in her own time—a ball neither one could reach on her own. They had to stretch for it in unison, or else it would not stay; only hand in hand could they catch it. That miracle happened every day. The instant they met, the red ball expanded to a fairy-tale balloon and took them along on sublime journeys of togetherness.

The door to her mother's room stood slightly ajar, leaving a narrow strip of light streaking across the floor, like a drawn sword. When darkness finally swallowed it, Britt-Mari started counting to twelve, then to nine, then to seven, and finally to three. Then she got up and tripped over to her mother in the darkness. She heard her mother reach for the light switch,

Don't turn it on, she said.

Her mother gave a deep chuckle in the dark and Britt-Mari could sense her getting comfortable between the pillows, edging further upward and streaking her fingers through her black hair as if to organize her thoughts. Britt-Mari sat down on a footstool. Not even the faintest glimmer of light hovered in front of the curtains.

Mommy.

Aren't you coming here? I thought you'd come in to cuddle up. Her mother's voice sounded somewhat disappointed.

Mommy . . . Britt-Mari started.

Something in the girl's voice made her mother suspect that she was about to say something she had actually wanted to postpone for a while. The mother's voice took on a coy, cooing timbre,

I can guess what you want to ask me. You may calm down; I know already. Of course, you want to talk to me about the dress material I promised you.

Mommy.

Don't worry, I know exactly what you need. Question is only whether I can get the material I want you to have. If I find it, I promise you that I won't count the pennies. You know how difficult it is to buy for you. Most colors clash with yours. If I could just find something in black. Yeah, clear black, a silky black background with cinnamon-brown. Exactly. A cinnamon-brown design against a black background. That's what I want you to have. Can't you see it? I can picture the material made up into a dress already, and the dress on you.

Mommy. I know that it's late and I don't want to hurt you. I'll leave right away if you tell me that you're not altogether sure of yourself yet.

Britt, I am certain.

Britt-Mari saw a fiery red flame light up in the darkness. It had not singed her mother's lips yet. A beautifully colored piece of glass still surrounded the flame.

He too?

Yes.

Are you happy?

Yes.

Do you think it will last?

I haven't even thought of that.

How long has it been?

Perhaps two weeks now.

Is he blond?

No, he's dark.

But Mommy! Then you know already how it'll end. He is dark!
Oh, that's why I felt there's something . . .

You're marvelous, the mother whispered. You don't know how
wonderful you really are. I can't understand it myself. Really. Only
some short moments. Like now. In the dark. I could scream with
horror if you'd as much as touch me now. Can you hear me, Britt-
Mari? But it would be something entirely different. Not horror. It's
pain. Pain makes me cry out, pain that I cannot always feel who you
are. And it's because I'm happy that sometimes I do still feel that
way.

Britt-Mari stood in the darkness, her head hanging. It was not
she who was swirling around in this heavy, immovable dizziness. It
was the darkness. This frightening, wonderful something was happening outside herself.

I'm afraid, her voice trembled.

Me too, me too, the mother quivered.

You too?

Yes, me too.

You, the happy one?

Just because of it, Britt.

Mommy.

Don't blame yourself. What do we determine? Who makes our
decisions? It's been preordained long before we know it.

Do you think that he's going to jilt you?

I don't think anything.

But aren't you afraid that he'll leave you?

I'm afraid for myself. I've become afraid on my behalf. Yes, again.

Me too. Why do we become afraid for ourselves?

I don't know.

Neither do I, Mommy.

A happy person has no conscience.

I know it, Mommy.

Just like an unhappy person. Besides, a happy person is stronger than an unhappy one. That's why he's able to hurt so much more.

I know. It's true.

Nothing may stand in our way. If you've seen happiness you go straight for it and don't worry about anything you trample on your way.

Those who love see happiness. Those who see happiness are happy already.

Not until today did he tell me that he's married. But it didn't bother me at all.

Did he talk about getting a divorce in order to marry you?

We haven't gotten that far yet. Today I had the impression that he's a coward. Cowardly to the core. And I didn't care. That's when I realized that I couldn't live without him.

Do you mean to say that his daring is not equal to his love?

Yes.

I recognize that. No one really dares as strongly as one loves. Even the worst are capable of love. We seem to be created for it. But to be daring about our love . . .

I do, Britt. I dare. And that's why I'm afraid.

I do too, Mommy. I dare. For just once.

Just once and always thereafter, or else it's the end.

Britt-Mari groped about with her arms in the darkness.

No, not you, she cried out, her body stiffening.

Again she had the feeling of standing on the outside. It was the darkness, and something in the darkness was whirling around, heavily, implacably. Darkness had come alive.

Haven't I always dared? the mother complained. Didn't I start a long time ago? Indifference is life's rarest drink. I've never been able to find it, either awake or sleeping, either in the morning or at night. Have I ever stopped daring? You don't realize how accusing your eyes sometimes look at me.

Have you noticed that?

She must have seen that I fold my hands and grow up suddenly to get away from her and the way I am Britt-Mari thought. A sudden cold gripped her.

I've seen that you were never allowed to live like other children. When I needed grown-ups, I made you an adult, and when I had friends, I pushed you back into childhood. Shouldn't it be my fault?

I don't understand a thing of what you're saying.

I ruined your childhood. You'll understand that some day.

Being a child pure and simple is disgusting, just as disgusting as loving pure and simple. Children never dare. It's important to dare. Children are simply unable to dare. It's impossible to do until you've taken on final form. And what child has taken on final form?

You don't hear your own words, but I do.

A small child looks cute when it's playing with its toes. That's about all.

A carefree child, playing. Tossing its ball against the wall. Jumping rope in the park. It's jumping, for the simple joy of jumping, its hair flying in the breeze. Two girls walking arm in arm, giggling. Two boys comparing the blades of their pocketknives.

The sun is shining. The sun is not shining.

Children never need to make indifference their excuse.

Children can't even comprehend how indifferent they are.

You don't understand that a person may be driven to a point of begging for indifference, pleading: make me indifferent, for God's sake make me indifferent so that I don't have to face myself the way I am, and others the way they are; come my way with your grey looks, your silent world, your narrow lips, come with the small, anemic people, save me from having to hear the gasps.

I'm afraid of becoming indifferent.

Me too.

Indifference makes me angry.

Me too, the mother cried out. She pulled herself up on her elbows.

Silence hovered around their heads like a bird who is silently flying around and around a treetop in the darkness. Together mother and daughter began to cry, both of them unconscious of what they were doing. They fumbled for each other's hands and cheeks, and there was pain in their bodies when they stretched out. Something like a dry wind kept flushing through them for a long time. They forgot each other. Their bodies were lying in the same bed, but they forgot each other and their bodies. Later, returned to space, time and body, they both wondered how far away from all this a human can remove himself and still find life, and life, and life always.

9

She is dancing by herself, an ocarina in her hand, along the fence that surrounds the railroad's garden of pleasure. Between the red slats she sees two coiled silver snakes. The clock behind her has stopped ringing. The old fairy-tale, candy-cane-striped crossing bars at the railroad tracks are pointing upward again. Her hand has struggled hard with the round safety arm! Now her heart eagerly drinks release and deliverance from the mighty wheels of the locomotive.

They roll on, roll, swallow.

Her eyes drink it all in, experience it all. There is no enjoyment without giddiness. Longing must overcome dangers. Roving eyes, powerful circles full of temptation. Enter your gaze. Enter your strength. Through your gate into the heart of life. There is no perfection without death. Death is a beautiful eyelid that closes upon the vision of life's eternal majesty. The king's eyes did not bid farewell. They are waiting, full of knowledge. Every day. See you again.

She beheld the small, light-yellow petals the linden dropped on her hair. The vanishing train became a mountain on the chase, its cars became cliffs on the run toward a ten-mile-long sundown.

She is dancing by herself with an ocarina in her hand, passing close by the fence that surrounds the railroad's garden of pleasure. She is dancing, leaping high into the burning sundown in the West. At home the two lovers are burning. She has not met him yet. They have found each other. They cannot endure others to see them.

He's rather shy about meeting you, the mother said.

Don't mind me, Britt-Mari answered. I'm not going to exist until he wants me to.

Are you sure that you don't mind? the mother repeated.

Her foodshopping done, she was busy preparing a festive dinner. In the pantry pilsner and vodka stood ready. There has been nothing like this since last fall. This is the first time she is preparing dinner for him. The first time in her home. But he preferred not to meet her daughter. Not yet. Or was it her idea? It would have been utterly strange to make the girl leave after dinner.

Of course I don't. You know how much I love to cruise through town. Sneak about like a young fox and forget the time. Usually you don't like the idea that I'm not afraid of people, or that I meet some weird characters. But so far nothing has happened to me.

What's that you're taking along? the mother asked, her eyes full of tears—a reaction to the onions she was slicing.

The ocarina he gave me.

That you had to ask for something as cheap as an ocarina.

I like it.

He wanted to buy you a present; you should have asked for something more valuable.

The ocarina is valuable.

Well, there'll be other times, the mother said, daringly facing the onions again. Men love beef with onions. Real men need lots of onions. Onions make them more manly and they become more self-confident with onions in their stomach. The mother laughed when she said that.

Standing by the door, Britt-Mari tried to play a ditty before leaving. She could see that her mother had already put her out of her mind. She loved the outline of her dull-finished terracotta ocarina and felt a thrill of delight coursing through her body every time she touched it. Its surface felt to her skin the way birdcherries tasted in her mouth. Rugged. Bitter. Pungent.

See you later then . . . good-bye . . . bye, Mommy.

Gee, haven't you left yet? the mother said, staring after her.

It was clear that she disappeared from her mother's mind quicker than out the door.—What had she told him? That her girl would be in good company with her schoolfriends?

She leaps into the sunset, dancing close by the fence that surrounds the railroad's garden of pleasure. People solidify into lampposts, watch her burst past them. Some foolish calls curl back to their owners and, like dogs, lift their legs. Run, run on, quickly, westward. An eternal sunset might keep burning for you if you are quick enough. At home the two lovers are burning. There is no darkness in the middle of June. Later on tonight they will dance in the communal park where they have a choice of three dance pavilions. Rowdypavilion, Snobpavilion and Decency. Dusk will set in a strange way. A heavenly dove, ruffling its fine down, will soar high in the midnight sky. Downy-light colors will sail in dreamy softness and liberty. A nightly rainbow will span, faintly burning, over the mountain and dawn's blush will tint the edge of the sea.

She cannot stop dancing. Her lust is exquisite and stronger than she. She feels compelled to leap into the sunset in the West as she sweeps closely past the railroad's garden of pleasure. Unable to stop moving, she continues to dance on the spot, her face turned upward, her ocarina circling above her head. Her legs are a delight. Time and again she feels a desire to caress her left thigh as her right thigh is leaping forward. The shape and agility of these legs is for tonight only. Their lithe power and their turbulent rhythm exist for this special occasion only.

There must be no darkness in the middle of June. Is not her dance proof enough that darkness does not exist? She must not disgrace this early June night. Should she catch the train at Västra Station? No, she smiles. No. The mountain hurries on, its cliffs exploding mightily against the sunset.

One to the right and one to the left solidify, become lampposts, spreading a red warning light as if danger surrounded them this June night. Only a heavy-set, tired old woman smiles and her smile becomes an axle angled so well that she remains unconscious of the effort it costs her to turn around. She looks after the light, lithe, spirited body, so gracefully leaping forward, its reddish-blond ponytail fluttering in the wind, her delicate, lively hands joyfully and playfully encompassing herself.

I'm running with my sister, it suddenly crosses her mind. I'm my own sister. I am two. I am my older sister. The little one may dance with the bigger. Cinnamoncandy dances giant leaps into the sunset together with Britt-Mari.

But can't Cinnamoncandy be a boy for all that?

Of course. I am running with my brother, she thinks. I am my own brother. I have always been two. My brother dances with his sister. What is his name? Dick, Jack, George? His name is John. No. His name is Arne. Who in me is older? I have always wanted to be both boy and girl. Both have always lived in me. My brother was strongest when I wanted him to beat up rowdies in school. My brother was always grown up when I saw Mommy needing him. He had a job and money. He was good and strict. Run ahead a step, then I can run better and we arrive quicker. Do you like clothes? Perhaps that new graduate does?

She thought of him last Wednesday when they found the right material. Her mother was real happy and said that it was exactly the way she pictured it, except that it was cotton. She had a different fabric in mind. But the colors were more important, and she had promised not to argue about the price. Didn't she sew all their dresses, the girl's and her own? That amounted to mighty savings per year. She made Britt-Mari stand before the mirror and draped the fabric around her. The saleslady helped and held it across her left hip and shoulder.

See for yourself. Just look at this.

Cinnamon-brown serpents curled and coiled on a pitchblack background. Cinnamon-brown serpents whose heads disappeared in the material's black depth, their necks veering back at that point. That was when she remembered that brandnew student. Her face blushed so deeply when she thought of him that all her freckles started swimming, like lice in the Red Sea.

She's happy; I can tell that she's happy, the saleslady babbled. Her long nails were rasping across Britt-Mari's back—long nails, grown for gliding sensually over fabrics and with lofty shivers of quality mark the threads and colors in the cloth.

Softly, like a caress, the mother bent forward to look in Britt-Mari's eyes. Britt-Mari nodded her okay.

That settles it, the mother said.

When fabric and thread were wrapped, the package looked very small. It seemed unbelievable that someone could transform the contents into Britt-Mari's most beautiful dress. But her mother did. Finished, the dress was hanging on a hanger in the closet. Tomorrow, Sunday, she was going to wear it for the first time.

I am dancing with my sister, she thinks, as she circles her ocarina above her head. She spreads her arms and whirls around as she transforms into three. She is her brother and her sister. They are three, whirling past the railroad's garden of pleasure, excitedly, in an ever increasing momentum. Suddenly they let go of her hands and disappear into nowhere. Her wrists pressed against her forehead, her ocarina like a crown in her hair, she dances on, alone and lonely, into the western sunset. An agile animal, she billows forward, her claws tearing in the sand, the dust puffing up in small, breezy gusts with every step. She shouts soundlessly, right and left, her mouth slashed, wide-open. She can taste the bloody artery and her hand suddenly wilts from her forehead.

She grunts noisily and lumbers forward like a pig, its rump swaying. Then she drops into the figure of a handpuppet, moving on invisible strings, its face suddenly that of a doll. Somewhere she gets heedlessly drunk. Another round of brutal blows pushes her constantly onwards. At some point she begins moving quickly to where she can hear a drowning girl's shrill screams.

She reaches the city limits. A hill, meadows, tilled fields; a house here and there, and groves. The shiny surface of a lake.

She stands still and signals to the sun. Having no valid signal system, she moves her arms to describe the letters she wants. Her eyes are tightly shut. It is happening in the northwestern sky. The sunset's radiance rises in miraculous tints, coloring the city a shimmering red. Elevators lead there. She wants them to get her. She is a stack of red bricks ready to be pulled up with a jerk. Come and get me.

Come and get me, she signals to the sun's last rays. I am a pile of red bricks and would very much like to be used. Please, fetch me. Lift me up. She signals over and over again.

Come, come. Please, do come tonight. Come now and get me. I am of no use around here.

She turns her back and whispers,

I rely on the elevator to come for me. I am turning my back because I am convinced that the elevator will come and lift me up.

She is waiting. Nothing happens. She waits a while longer. Nothing happens. She tries to signal with her back turned toward the sunset, trusting that this is the correct method. Again she waits, but nothing happens. A fit of anger overcomes her. Turning around, she sticks her tongue out. She waves her fist into the air, signaling: It's too late now. When the elevator gets here no one may take me along. I no longer care to be taken along.

Then . . . she forgets. She has seen the lake's nightpolished surface. She can see something reflected in it. She remembers other reflections mirroring in the evening waters. Finally she strolls toward the city, her eyes mute, but full of a vision that lead her inside her feelings and thoughts. A revelation, revived again. She walks down to the river, her heart listening, enclosing her secret, protected by the immense distance of time. She has seen it in the lake. She follows its contours that lead her sight all the way to the birth of the river. The Stadsberg rises in the waters of the lake. In its enhanced beauty, the mountain has been standing there since the dawn of time, painfully perfect, a blessedly complete form. A revelation, a true prophecy and comfort to reality's mountain at every suitable occasion.

10

I'm not functional. I love that word. Even though I don't know what it means. Not exactly. Funck-sho-nal. I'm not funck-sho-nal just now. Too bad that I never bothered to find out what the word means. I find it aggravating when I can't see anything in a word. I don't have to worry about the word when I do. Then I see, and that's better than just knowing. Now I know that he's at home with Mommy. I know it, but I want to see it too. I want to see him. I'd like to see what they look like when they're together. I'm going to wait outside Entrance A and watch Mommy coming out with him.

You're going to spy on them, like Gertrud.

Hush, I'm not going to spy. All I want is to get a peek at him. I do want to see him. I'd like to see him right now. I want to know what they look like together. That's why I'm not functional just now. It's not functional to sit here and complain. I whine and gripe because I want two things at the same time. It's impossible to satisfy two wishes at the same time.

Find yourself a third, then you'll forget.

I'm already in the middle of a third. I'm sitting here, bellyaching. I want to give in to temptation and see, and I want to retain my integrity and not see. Instead of doing any one of these two, I'm doing something else. I'm sitting here, complaining. I'm not functional.

Dance the way you did before.

That can't be done on command. Why? It's common knowledge—it's just not the same. Actually, I should find myself a job this summer. If Gertrud found one, it shouldn't be impossible for me. Errand girl, babysitter, nursing aide. Gosh, it all sounds so boring.

If we had a boat, we could drift with the current.

I'm not functional. We studied it just this last fall. "Sometimes neither birds nor fishes work functionally." What a simply wonderful and comforting thought. It provided me with many priceless insights. I must admit that I used to distrust both birds and fishes. I thought they were inhumanly perfect and that seemed, of course, pretty disgusting at times. Lord knows, neither birds nor fishes live in a perfect environment. Considering that they are now completely adapted to it is somehow a bit sickening. It would've been different if their living conditions were great. But, given that things are the way they are makes me wonder. The marks of nobility are lacking. That's why reading that sentence was like salvation. There are times when they are not functional. They may develop neuroses and therefore look miserable and pained. They go crazy, like me. And why do we behave so nutty? Why do we become unglued? Well, it's because we desperately want two things all at once. And why is that? The world is like that. Even the world of birds and fishes. There's no synch. We don't fit in. Neither the world nor we have shaped up to our final form yet. The work is in progress. It's good that we can signal the discrepancy with our heads, our hearts, our bodies. As conceited as we are, there's always the threat that the work is not progressing.

Now you're getting angry.

Not at all. I'm just sitting here, gabbing away. My thoughts keep on fluttering back and forth and my heart is panting. But certainly

I'm happy that I saw the essay and read it. The birds and fishes came closer to me, closer than certain human beings.

The yes-people?

Yes. It's horrible to see how some people adapt. It's even worse to see what it is they adapt to. Some become nasty, especially those who pretend to be satisfied, which is just a mask. Don't they know what love is about? Haven't they watched grown-ups? Love is beautiful, because it is so very fragile. God puts lovers on hold for a short while. They don't grow, but they don't shrink either. Encapsuled in their world of love, they are invincible. They don't want two things at the same time, and consequently they don't need to try a third.

If we had a rowboat we could drift with the current.

I'm considering a job. If I worked, I'd have enough money to rent a room. As it is, at home I'm in their way. They need to be alone for a while. They haven't settled everything yet, just the bare essentials. They love each other. But there's so much else. And all that takes time. Perhaps my existence bothers his conscience already, and he may need to work that out too.

You don't know a thing about him.

Mommy didn't look so happy night before last. She was very busy sewing my dress. She works best when she's dissatisfied. That's when she gets things done.

Dissatisfied? She has to be angry.

If I could, I'd sleep on Stadsberg every night. In some cleft. I could sew a blanket together to make a sleeping bag.

I wonder how long it'll last, their . . .

I've got to see him. I'll have no peace until I've seen them together. No way I can depend on Mommy. She doesn't see a thing. I've got to do that for her. It's happened so many times. I'm the one who can tell. I'm the one who sees. It hurts so often, to be able to see for someone else. To watch her ruin herself. She doesn't see. I do. I'd rather be carelessly blind. That's how it hurts to watch her.

Do you remember the fire at the paper plant?

I'm going there. I've got to see him. I have to see what he's like. It's not too late. If I run, I'll be able to see them leave through Entrance A.

I wonder what Pappa is thinking.

Me too. How much he must've loved her.

Because she's rather difficult too.

To die isn't the worst, she keeps on saying. It's worse for those who're left behind.—I'm not complaining. He helps me constantly. I know. If he had lived on a few more years I would have siblings! That would have been good for me.

Yes. As difficult as she is at times. And blind.

If this works out, I'll no longer worry on my account. I promise. Do you hear? I promise to wait. My body shall have all the time it needs. Just as Mommy says. When I carried you in my stomach I surely had to wait until you were ready to come. You weren't born because I used to cry: Hurry up, hurry up. You took your good nine months. Not a week less, not a week too early.

We aren't funck-sho-nal.

It's terrible to have to wait. But what are nine months! No, I mustn't say that. If only this works out, I give my solemn promise. Oh, I can feel already how calm I'm going to be. I'm not going to mock myself about anything. I'll wait, bide my time and wait, without getting tired. Just a little while—and I'll be there. I may never even remember how much I suffered while waiting. A little while—and then it's over. Then I can take care of some real job. I can fall really in love. It will no longer be ridiculous to love. A little while . . .

Several years.

A little while.

Several years.

A little while!

Do you think that a little while sounds better than several years? *A little while!*

Do you consider a little while the same as several years?

I'm not afraid. I've never been afraid of something that's really important. Not in my most secret heart. Only of stupid things. I've never even understood why stupid things are necessary. Can you understand why a body can't skip a few years? Like the years between three and nineteen? What are they good for? Why not simply sleep through that time?

Or lie in a skiff and drift with the flow.

I know that I'm going to be frightfully old. Oh, I'm going to live it up once I'm nineteen. Look at my hand. It's going to be a hundred years old. I overflow with tenderness and kiss it when I think of how long it's going to be part of me. I call this loyalty. It's unfathomable, this loyalty my hand is capable of. Look at it. It looks rather insignificant. Insignificant, but beautiful. This hand is the best thing I own. Right now, no one can comfort me the way my hands can. What would I do without them? Thanks to them, I can see what is going to happen to me whenever I want to. In whatever straights I may find myself, I can always lift my hands up and look at the beautiful forms I can create with them.

Magda Hagberg has hands too.

But what has she created with them?

Magda Hagberg.

Never for me. I'd rather commit suicide.

Never. We aren't like her, neither Mommy, Daddy, nor I. We fight back. We go our own way. We don't just sit still and lick our wounds. We don't kiss the foot that kicks us.

Functional or not functional?

Seriously. Don't forget that there's something called sincerity. When I notice that things are getting serious, I become functional. All of a sudden I know what needs to be done, and I do it.

Magda Hagberg.

I fight back. I go my own way. I kill.

I wonder what Grepp is doing tonight?

The water up here is much better than down where we live. You could even take a swim up here. The embankment is just wood, though rotting here and there. The piles over there are decaying, and the green stuff on the wood is as slippery as soap.

I seem to be hearing dance music.

Well, it's not too late yet. I can see the church clock from here. They haven't left through Entrance A yet. That Q should be dark-haired! A dark man would match with me, but not with Mommy. She knows it all too well and can never deny that she believes it too. She believes it. Still, she goes and falls in love with a dark-haired fellow. Then she tries to tell herself and me that things will turn out all right.

Couldn't she dye her hair?

Gosh. Dyeing hair and pretending happiness, how long will those last? If at least I could see him. Just watch his behavior toward Mom.

Foreman in the plant. She told me one night that there was a new foreman again. I didn't suspect then . . .

Neither did she.

Look. Finally a rowboat.

There are two sitting in it.

It floats so slowly along. The rower is not rowing. His oars are pointing up, one on either side.

I seem to hear dance music.

Gosh, the daily evening news hasn't even started.

The public park is not far from here.

Do you mean to say that the dance music comes from there?

Yes. If they haven't started dancing yet, they soon will.

I'm going to the public park—I'm not going to the public park. I'm going to see him—I'm not going to see him. Wonder what's in store for me tonight?

You're going to find a third alternative.

I can't.

Go home and go to bed. Sleep.

They haven't left yet. I can see the church clock from here. But look at those in the rowboat!

Now you've found a third.

Not at all. The third always comes of its own accord.

11

It was a dare, but Britt-Mari jumped directly from the high woodpile where she had been sitting and talking in dual voices. Agile and quick like a squirrel, she used to get the best grades in sports along with two other classmates. Considering the steep slope, she landed well. The sudden impact still in her bones, she looked up to the point from where she had jumped. There was a sudden flicker in her eyes and she gave a low cry, surprised and frightened at her own daring. She closed her eyes and stretched her hands out for support.

That's how it always was. Whichever way it happened, either before or after she felt dizzy. Leaning with her back against the birch-

wood, she waited for a while. Silly, she lectured herself. You little,
stupid goose.

It was not long before she let her emotions know that their efforts were totally inappropiate at the present time. She stepped forward and looked up again—the height seemed no longer that steep.
Just twice your measure, she mumbled, describing a measured arc
with her arm. Well, perhaps three times you, she felt obliged to
amend.

She waved her arm eastward. The ocarina retained its perfect,
anonymous look, but Britt-Mari's lips began to quiver. She could no
longer see either the church or the bridge. Her desire to jump and
her pride were again at odds with one another, and her inner, clan-
destine shiver threatened to reveal its black source.

She recalled now what had made her leave her lofty lookout.
The tiny couple in the rowboat. Or had they never existed? Had she
again perceived the ordinary with the intensity of her heart? They
were so unbelievably tiny, so unbelievably old, so unbelievably beautiful. As if they had just stepped out of a picture in a storybook for
children. The little old woman rowed while the little old man sat
aft. They must have been fishing. A newspaper spread over his knees,
the old man was cleaning the fish.

Britt-Mari watched the old woman turn, then row up to a dock
that broke the straight line of the embankment, and whose platform
steps reached almost into the water. The old woman tied up the
boat. Even standing upright, she looked unbelievably tiny, but she
did all the work. She pulled two baskets and a few red blankets up
the steps, while the old man waited in the boat until she could help
him get out. Even on the embankment they still looked tiny. He
wore a dark-blue carpenter's apron and fish scales glistened all over
it despite the wide-open newspaper. The old woman seemed to reproach him for that; at least he kept on pushing his brown hat further up on his crown as if he needed to feel free. The old woman
squatted down before him and tried to scrape off the scales with her
thumbnail.

Finally she got up, let go of the apron and complained with her
hands. Then she took one of the red blankets, put it over his shoulder and hooked the two baskets over his hands. Suddenly her hands
seemed frightened as if the thought had struck her that the old man's

beard could make him suffocate under the blanket. To save him, she pulled it out and spread the white neatly over the red. Couldn't he bend his back? Britt-Mari wondered as she watched these two traipse about.

The old woman put the other blanket over her own shoulder before she walked down again to the boat to untie it. It seemed that she wanted to pull the boat further upstream. Considering that they were so unbelievably small and so unbelievably old, Britt-Mari assumed that they were unable to jump directly onto the dock, but had to use the steps to get up on land.

Surely they were real. When she ran past the long woodbin, Britt-Mari saw them again. Stuffing the ocarina into her skirt pocket, she kept on running in order to help the old woman pull the boat. But the woman reached the ringbolt where the boat was to be anchored before she got there.

Britt-Mari watched them from a distance. It was clear that the old man was unable to bend his back. With his knees he pushed his baskets on a box that was just the right height. Rattling with the chain and pulling hard, the old woman had a difficult time getting the boat into the right position. She got angry and yelled. The old man walked over to her, but he could not help her. He even laughed about the way she handled the boat and she hit his leg so that he had to back away.

When the boat was finally chained and locked in place, they started fighting. The old woman wanted to go home. The old man wanted to stay. Britt-Mari stepped forward. Getting closer and closer, she realized that they were not as tiny as they had looked from where she had first seen them up on the mountain. In comparison to her they were at least a head taller than she, and she was by no means as little as she often imagined.

Finally the woman gave in, but not without stipulations. He had to consent to getting himself wrapped into the red blankets. They sat down, each one on a box, the third box with the baskets between them. The old man pushed snuff into his mouth. Pulling a tobacco pouch from one of the baskets, the old woman took a short pipe out of the pouch and lighted it with a match. The old man ogled her like a mischievous boy and moved furtively so that the blanket slid off his back and shoulders. The old woman did not notice, but kept on smoking, exhaling with small, quick puffs. The old man looked up at the Stadsberg.

Britt-Mari loved everything and everybody in that instant. Her heart moved outwards, reaching ever further. She looked quickly to the side, hoping to see where the taut curve that emanated from inside her and expanded into an unlimited beyond would finally settle. Her heart ached. What was happening to her now was too beautiful. Something fragile, deeply rooted in her, as slender as a straw, as soft as a blade of grass, was sweeping across the world in an ever widening, boundless sweep. Singularly solitary, it floated in the unfathomable expanse, bent, bent over the earth and ablaze with flaming roots.

Without a word Britt-Mari sank down on the box between the two old people. She took part in their silence. But she could not take it for long.

Say something to me, she begged, turning to him.

He is deaf, the old woman declared.

Britt-Mari looked into a pair of childlike, porcelain-blue eyes struck with wonder. A fine net of bloodvessels spread like rosy make-up over her cheeks. Her hair was as white as untouched snow. Her shawl, halfway folded up, cast a lightblue hue over it. Her cheeks puffed in and out, resiliently flexible with a life of their own under her gaze.

Say something to me.

That's not as easy as you think. I've been sitting here, looking at you. I can tell that you don't want me to ask for your name. No. But may I ask how old you are? No. Shall I ask where you live? No, not that either. What then shall I say to you? Well, let me tell you that this old fellow is full of batty tricks. She smiled as she puffed on her cutty.

Myself, I'm not much smarter than he. Would I put up with him if I were? At heart I really don't mind being the butt of his jokes. What do I do? Well, I rent a boat. I rent trolling spoons, fishing rods, and extra fishing lines with bait hooks to sit and roam around in the water. I dig for worms and fish with him for hours. His body makes him suffer for the pleasure. Pain. He'll be in pain tonight. It started already. He can't lie straight in bed ordinarily. He has to sit up. Sometimes on a chair, all night. He sits in front of the fireplace and keeps it going through the long winter nights. Snuff in his mouth and wood in the fireplace. He's as strong as a bear and never gives up. Sits and yaps and barks about the pain running riot in his insides: take off, inhabit numb rock, leave meat and bone alone. And a gent like this gets up one nice day, wanting to prove that he still belongs to those who got the message: may they be masters over the fishes.

She took the cutty out of her mouth and held her head between her hands. The mouthpiece shot upward, soft as a bird's neck.

What color hair did you and your husband have when you were young?

I was blond. He was dark.

That's what I figured. Was it difficult for you to get each other?

I was shy. And he was just as silly at the time.

Were you born in this city?

Oh no. We moved here when we were old. We have two married sons here and a daughter who married a gardener.

He gave a big laugh. Britt-Mari glanced at him. She wanted to catch him because she did not believe that he was deaf. She preferred to think that he just played deaf out of mischief.

Give him a poke, Britt-Mari heard—and she did.

She looked at him. His large beard grew out of every possible pore in his face. It was as white as her hair. Only below his mouth there was a golden-brown spot.

That was nothing, he said. I was thinking of thunder and lightning. He did not speak any louder than people with ordinary hearing. He sat quiet for a while. Then he cried out, his voice shaking with indignation,

I want the thunder to rumble and roll. The day is too good, and the night following it is too. It's aggravating not to hear it.

He can still hear thunder. Explosions too. If he should disappear one day, I'd know where to look for him—somewhere near a blasting site.

Lovisa, do you know what I came to think of? he said, his voice softly descending to a milder key, his face turned into space. Do you remember when lightning struck Dolk's cottage?

It isn't worth it to try and shush him, Britt-Mari heard while he was talking.

The entire village could've burned down. Every farm could've gone up in flames. Everything could've burned to the ground before the end of that night. We didn't know a thing. We were at home, waiting for the storm to pass. Then. Do you remember the scream? I can still hear it. Lovisa must save the village, they yelled. Only Lovisa can save the village. They came rushing in, all talking at the same time. Dolken's house is burning! Lightning struck! Your mother took Erik away from you. Did he ever scream when he couldn't nurse on your breast. Poor wretch, he had seen you take it out, but he didn't get a drop. Your milk was to be thrown right into the fire to work a miracle. The strong, white milk from a first-time mother right into the gulch of a fire thrust down from heaven.

How did it go? You must tell me how it went.

The fire was crushed, Lovisa said. It lost its power and could no longer kindle ordinary, earthly flames. Water could finally squelch it. The village was saved.

Britt-Mari gazed reverently at the old woman's breasts. Of course, they were shriveled now. In her imagination the woman's black dress, cut high in the neck, transformed into a deep-green, satiny garment with a white flower on its left side. Britt-Mari felt a strong, persistent twitch in her stomach area. A dull unrest took possession of her. How could she leave them without anything tangible? She wanted a link to connect her with them. At least a button, she speculated. Remembering the baskets standing on the box next to where she was sitting, she slid slowly backward, intent on sneaking her hand down one of them. She reached a paperbag and her fingertips felt something that was splintersharp. Pulling it up, she looked at it.

My, what is this? she asked in surprise.

Sugar.

Is it really sugar?

It's sugar loaf.

Loaf? It's as hard as a shard.

I pry these shards off the sugar loaf.

May I taste it?

By all means.

Britt-Mari hesitated. Then she asked,

How did it finally go? Were you shy for a long time?

For three years at least.

For as long as three years! How did you manage? That you didn't frazzle out! Didn't it show on you?

Nothing showed on him.

But how did you manage? For three whole years!

I carried my head high, above reproach from anyone.

Above reproach from anyone, the girl whispered, lifting her eyes up to the Stadsberg and then even higher than that. The sharp-edged shard melted in her mouth and filled it with sweetness.

It was difficult. It is difficult when all you want to do is to fall.

She swallowed, swallowed away the sweetness with a feeling akin to a miniature, but fiery impetuosity.

You must get up pretty high before you take a fall. If you stand very high up, your fall is going to be very steep. Only, you mustn't fall of your own free will. Because then it shows how you lived up there. Someone has to call you down. You need someone who catches you in your fall.

Britt-Mari looked with a sense of grief at the old couple, her mouth wide open. The tip of her tongue was hard between her lips.

You want to know how I managed the fall? I'll tell you, Lovisa said, pressing her extinguished cutty against her underlip.

Britt-Mari sighed and shaded her eyes to hear and see better.

At that time a pauper was wandering around in this area, making his living in a way that's unworthy of a human being. For a twelve-shilling piece he permitted anyone to give him a box on his ear. I saw him, the poor wretch, when he drifted into our parish. I had been working as a kitchen help at the local inn for about six months. It was a beautiful autumn day and I was polishing the silver by the kitchen window. I remember looking through the window at the countryside and the lake far below. Everything down there looked so painfully unreal. He who made me carry my head high above all reproach was just passing by my window. I thought it was just by accident, figuring that he had some urgent errand in the parish. He didn't look up. He never even looked at the window, though he kept walking back and forth past my window. The mountain ash by the gatepost shimmered a rust-red in the clear September air. Every time he disappeared, the lake and the village below seemed to vanish further and further away into the distance. With respect to my

surroundings I felt that kind of sad tenderness one usually feels toward
a fatally sick relative. That night they set up the chopping block in
the middle of the big room at the inn. The pauper sat down on it;
he always needed a chopping block, an ordinary chair would not do.
Only a chopping block could help him with his pain. But what about
his disgrace? Who helped him with that? My answer is: Those who
hit him. Those who threw him a twelve-shilling piece and then gave
him a box on his ear with their flat hand. There were a lot of people
that night. I had to carry glasses on a tray. Dirty in, clean out. They
kept on hitting, one after the other. The poor fellow took it, box
after box. Then one came forward and hit him real bad. It was offensive. I had just put down my tray with the glasses. A rixdollar is
not too much for the way I am going to hit you, said he who had no
business at all to say so. The poor fellow on the chopping block set
his face ready for the box from a braggart or a strongman. How could
he know? Then he who should not do so hit him; hit him so hard
that the poor fellow flew off the chopping block, spun around and
fell flat on the ground among the others who stood there to watch.
Blood was gushing out of his nose and mouth. Someone made a wild
dash for the door. I could never figure out how I got outside, but it
must have been through the kitchen. I ran between the outhouses,
looking, until I came to the barn. There I turned around and saw
him, running straight into the wall. It felled him to the ground. He
got up and bumped himself again and again, smashing his head against
the wall. He was as strong as a bear and fought that terrible wall
with outstretched arms. It was the wall, that terrible wall. His head
kept on thudding, his fists hitting, his knuckles banging. It was that
wall, that immovable wall. He kept on hitting his head and screaming. The wall hit back, until it penetrated all the way through to his
throat. He didn't want to live on this way. No one should have to
submit to beatings for pay, no one should be permitted to beat another for pay. Nobody should be so shy that he cannot open his
heart to someone else. It was then that I fell from my pedestal, visible to everybody. I rushed into his gaze between that hard wall and
that desperate body.

Again Britt-Mari became part of their silence.

Is that all? she asked with bitterness.

Why would music have to end? Why does it desert us? Music exists only for the strong. The strong listen to music and learn many tricks. Strengthened, the strong can leave the music and put the tricks they learned from it into practice. He who hath shall be given unto, so that he hath more than he needs; but he who hath not, from him shall be taken even that which he hath.

All's well that ends well.

For Britt-Mari it had not even begun. I'm so stupid, she thought. How can I be so stupid after having heard . . .

On the other side of the river, the dock cast its velvet-brown shadow into the water. A motorcycle sputtered up a series of shots behind the greenery. The sky stood brass-yellow behind the crest of the Stadsberg. Time for the lovers to be dancing. If she could but see them. If she but knew their hearts. If she but lived on the other side of her difficult, meaningless years. If she could but live her life above reproach from anyone.

She needed help. She needed support from wherever she could get it. She needed something steadfast to hold on to at times when she was faltering. To punish the bad and in the process to find out that she was part of it, along with everyone alive. To punish herself against the naked wall of evil and find love in the process. She needed to take along something tangible from this old couple. At least a button, she mused. She slid her hand again into the basket. Her fingertips were groping for something more durable than sugar. They stopped for a light tin spoon. Without looking at the coffee spoon, she stuffed it down her pocket. Then she got up and bowed to the old couple in a quiet, formal manner, lifting her skirt slightly as she bent the tip of her toe backward, hardly touching the wooden dock.

She walked straight to Storgatan, meeting many people on her way there. She carried her life high above anyone's reproach. But when she saw the church, she started running.

12

It was the new dress and the scent in the room of the lovers that changed her. The halfway lowered curtains and the flowers in the room told their own story. As in a dream, she watched herself in the mirror lifting her arms. She dusted her smooth armpits with talcum powder and she felt how wonderful it was to be alive. The mirror reflected her happiness. She smiled and beamed at everything around her. Everything was feast and enjoyment. She used one of her mother's discarded lipsticks. With an unexpectedly quick and dexterous hand she reshaped her lips. Where was the nailpolish? She could hear a frightened, chirping voice,

My evening is going to be ruined if I can't find my nailpolish.

Really, she was like someone possessed. She no longer walked, she glided forward. The cars seemed to stop when she stepped off the sidewalks. When she stepped up again, the throng of people absorbed her. They pulled her along and she became part of them. There was no difference between her and the others. She heard laughter, rippling and gurgling voices. People looked at her as they brushed against her. It was blessedly crowded. Bodies were everywhere, right, left, behind her. Everything was soft, kind, natural, mysterious. Never just superficial, and never really very deep. A dreamy, exciting importance filtered through everywhere, unexpectedly, and yet expected, just as fishes that are close to the water's surface may suddenly turn around: may they soon return.

They came. The excitement was light and stupefying at the same time, containing one thing only, but forever shifting. The return was as natural as it was surprising. How wonderful life was on a Saturday night in the middle of June! For grown-ups it was always like that on Saturday nights. Everything exuded freedom, everything was festive. No working week seems a waste of life in the excitement of a Saturday night. All faces come alive. Hands can only caress, lips only smile. There is room only for happiness and fun.

Her craving for illusion was simple. Who was I on Storbron bridge? How did I get past the city blocks of Norrmalm? As yet, she did not even ask. She did not realize that she was quite alone and the hill she was facing long and steep, its concrete rising like a flame, nakedly white. Sometimes she lifted her hand and pressed it against her neckbone. Then she would pant softly, oh, oh. She held the ocarina in her hand, its anonymous bird's head pressed against her neck.

Three young motorcyclists swung up behind her, like a welded patrol sent on an important, dangerous mission. Squatting like horsemen, they dug in their heels. They laughed about their noisiness and gurgled with happiness in their strength, their faces immobile and anonymous like birds in flight. They were ageless, their years panting underneath their masks which were fused tight in ecstasy.

The patrol dissolved behind the hill. Their combined noise rockets separated in three different directions, chasing ever further, their voices gradually thinning out as they separated. Eventually distance silenced them. But before she had time to reach the top of the hill, they suddenly streamed together again, once more a compact patrol on dangerous assignment. Britt-Mari stopped. Her body stiffened when the patrol dashed past her. Why was she here? The hill led further up into the Stadsberg. Who was she on Storbron? How did she pass the city blocks of Norrmalm? Which road had she taken to get here? Pain stung in her eyes.

She turned around, ran ahead, then stopped short to run in several directions, hesitated. She tried all over again. Her manner of moving looked like an attempt to gain acceptance into a lost dream. How can I fall asleep again the easiest way? Which is the best way for me to lie down? Right or left side? Legs pulled up? Head low or raised? The action needs to continue. How can you forget your most mechanical habits? Now I know. When I lie like this I sleep best. No, that doesn't work. The dream mocks, its luster is broken. Where the truth would have led I'll never know.

Another morning lay ahead. She fought against the inexorable clarity of dawn's power that forced final decisions upon her. If she could not keep on dreaming, then at least she wanted to remain lying in the bed she had bedded for herself. With a look of defiance she decided to go to the public park.

She looked at the entrance lights, a rainbow of colored lamps arched below tall trees and tinting the leaves an irascible, unreal greenish color. Cars lined up in tight rows on the spacious parking lot. She could hear the music, coming in thrusts like strong scents a capriciously fluttering wind might waft along. But nothing brought relief. She was incapable of mellowing. Everything seemed ridiculous. She carried the ocarina along. What was she to do with it? There was no pocket in the dress she was wearing. How could she get inside? She had no money. Just a key in her handkerchief that she carried, crumpled into a ball, inside her sleeve.

She walked up to a wall. There was a garden behind it. She could throw her ocarina there. No, she could not. Ridiculous. How childish she was!—Further down was a fence. She squatted down quickly and pushed her ocarina between two slats of leaves that seemed to belong to a currant bush. Everything was ridiculous. No way would she abandon her ocarina for good. She counted the slats from the wall to her hiding place three times.

Pressing her lips defiantly together, she walked up to the entrance. The lamps and floodlights did nothing to create sentimental feelings below June's dawn-light sky. They seemed in bad taste, overdone like cheap jewelry. Everything was ridiculous.

My mother works in the cafeteria, she said, smiling self-assuredly at a young man with a uniform cap.

She was not surprised at being admitted so easily. Her walk was full of purpose. Her aim was clear: to go on in spite of it all, there was no purpose, everything was ridiculous.—Up on the hill, she pulled away from the road and jumped into the bushes. She crossed over from one protection to the next, stopping where the shadows had settled in a smooth balance. The music came no longer in waves, but in a steady rhythm. The stillness under the trees was oppressive. There was pain in every step she took as she moved on. When she came to the other side of the hilly landscape, the shadows of the trees stood out ever sharper against the fiery green of the grass. There were bushes too, and she stopped between them in order to listen. She noticed a faint scent of lilacs. Had they already arrived? Were they really blooming? Was it a lilac bush in whose shadow she was squatting? She took a step forward. Branches pressed against her face and hands.

The rhythms clattered to a halt, and silence drifted up like a giant wave on the move. At the same time a lesser noise died down as well, a sort of hum, a soft scraping, a tuneless, unremittingly flowing sound. The dancers had stopped their dancing, their movements gone to rest under their heels and soles. The couples came streaming out. Other couples stood in line to get inside.

Jackets off! someone said. Jackets off!

A gang of bareheaded boys jumped forward, screaming and hopping noisily between the trees. Their arms and legs seemed to be unnaturally long.

Jackets off! Jackets off!

They acted as if they meant to take off their outer garments and throw them on the grass to begin a fight. But only their white shoulders in their shirts became visible. They glowed in a strangely perfect form. Were these shoulders? In the dark, the shoulders broke into a gallop, like white-hoofed horselegs, their shape appealingly precious and as strong and secure as horse's hoofs. Their owners, conscious of their worth, suddenly threw their jackets over their shoulders and folded their hands tightly around the lapels. Then they fled, screaming, to save their perfect, glowing shoulders.

The truth about this strange place pulled her out of the bushes and led her to the naked light across the grass. There was something enormous, something difficult for her to comprehend, that ruled behind these black walls, concealing from her a powerful, transformational force that in a miraculous way turned humans into dreamlike, airy beings with blissful faces and endowing even the most unpretentious bodyparts with an aura of glory.

She glided forth between some pale-green walls. The music came swelling forth again. The hum, the tuneless, everflowing sound permeated the air all around her. A smell of hotdogs and mustard and waffles hovered between the walls. Britt-Mari glided on to where she perceived the very soul of this remarkable spot on earth to be.

Then she stood still, did not dare to take another step. She was not disappointed. Her desires for illusion were easily satisfied. The many people crowding in front of her overwhelmed her. She had not expected such a multitude to be there. Now they obstructed her field of vision. All she could see of the dance floor was the bright tin roof and the yellow ball seemingly floating above its top. She remained standing on the same spot for two dances. Then the unbelievable happened.

May I have this dance?

She got frightened at hearing the words uttered right next to her. Her hands flew up to her cheeks. She pushed her nails into the skin, loath to take the necessary look to her side.

Aren't you a little young to dance, Miss?

She recognized that voice immediately. It was the new student. Looking up, she could see that there was less irony in his face than in his voice. He was without his cap. He was very dark. His black hair sported a French haircut, he told her later.

Mama takes care of the cafeteria here, Britt-Mari lied, regaining her self-confidence like a gift. What time is it?

Almost eleven-thirty.

Then I have to hurry to my Mom.

Just a moment, Miss. I have really thought of you several times since we last met.

Really?

Despite all her pretense, she could sense how real she became under his gaze.

13

That you didn't dance! How could you help not to? You were there and had permission. Nothing was in your way.

Her tone of voice made it clear that she felt sorry not just for him, but for herself as well. He watched her hand moving in the air between them. Her hand characterized her. It had just been on its way to him. Did she consider it not worth her while to touch someone who had not danced? Her hand closed up before it disappeared.

I simply can't understand, she sighed.

But I told you that I didn't come here to dance.

Then what did you come for? Throw arrows? Drink coffee? Shoot airguns?

I came here to study.

Simply looking?

To find out what it is that so strangely stimulates the multitude.

The music? The dancing?

Well, that's nothing more than framework.

What do you mean?

I mean that people go there to . . .

You are stupid, boy.

He spread his light coat on the incline. She had led him to this place because she liked its view over the sleeping bay. The long expanse of an island blocked their outlook with its green darkness. The dove-blue body of the water rested calmly between the dark shorelines, its ashcolored neck extending in a south-easterly direction. With a quick, uneasy glance he measured the distance to the houses on the side, embedded like dabs of preserve in green sugarcones and lifted by crane uphill to form a voracious, childish giant whose pale-yellow lip squashed against the black silhouette.

It's as fast as the beat of a wing, she said and sat down beside him. I have seen it only once. It's hard to follow. Before you know it, the shoreline lies before you, as clear as a mirror. And there is the sun.

As if probing, he began to lift his arm behind her back. They sat very close to one another. Pulling up one knee, she folded it under her skirt, then wrapped her hands around it as she leaned slightly forward. There was his arm. He caught sight of her ocarina. It turned a few somersaults down her skirt's softly slanting fold before it came to rest on its side, its head leaning against a fold in his trousers. And there was his arm. He let it drop again behind her back. A shiver ran through him. He investigated. The fist lay still like a dumb clapper. His body shook potently, but then it stiffened and he squatted down, listening to the warning calls that rang in his blood with icy tunes. An invisible car on one of the roads below them fought a severe cough attack.

Finally she opened her mouth and confessed without smart,

I'm a liar, through and through.

Her words calmed down the brittle horror in his body. Her voice cured him. Looking up, he even managed a smile,

In your case it doesn't do any harm. Not even to yourself, I dare say.

I shouldn't need to lie. It's really quite unnecessary. You mustn't think that I intend to tell lies. It's just when I say something, they somehow flow through my lips.

That's just why they don't hurt anyone, and it may even charm those who are wise to you. You lie because you're happy. You feel so full of life, that's what makes you tell these lies. Am I right?

Perhaps. Well, most of the time. But it isn't right. It's not good to be too big for your skin.

What do you mean?

She did not hear his question. She was listening to a motorcycle suddenly exploding a string of sounds through the leaf-turgid, water-hushed silence. But distance had hardly silenced this firevaulting clatter when a new round started up from another side, soon followed by yet another set of hot, lively, propulsive blasts. She could distinguish between two runs rushing at each other from opposite directions.

They're finished dancing, she said while waiting for the soundlines to meet.

It happened suddenly, like bumblebees on the chase.

Yes, they're finished now, he said, consulting his watch.

Perhaps it was extended time.

Do you know the term extended time too?

Well, I'm not a deaf kid walking through the world.

She did not like his laugh. There was something frightening about him. She could not really pinpoint what it was. Like a scent, it was hard to describe, but she could feel it, sometimes stronger, sometimes less pronounced. She could see it in his brown eyes whenever she looked at him. A steady presence of something that never changed seemed to be lurking behind every aspect of his behavior. He was never spontaneous. He was never carried away. He turned cruel instead. Cruel against himself and cruel against . . .

You should have danced, she said sternly.

It's not the dancing that's most important to them.

His unbending front became markedly evident. There was something unforgiving about him. He was always on guard, bitter, opposed to that which is constantly reverberating between human beings. Denied it to himself and others. She rebuked him.

How would you know? Did you go out and dance? Did you?

No.

Are you going to?

No.

Why?

I won't answer that.

How about some future time?

Never.

I feel sorry for you.

Not wanting to look into his eyes and full of pity at that moment, she put her hand on his knee. His steady composure was even uglier and full of hate when it was not lurking in the background. He wanted to get at something that permeated life on earth. Why? His notion of perfection was strange. Perhaps he was like her? She too was sometimes hostile to time. She too hated all these humiliating preliminaries. But he had almost reached the other side. He had reached his format and would be that way for many years.

Maneuvering her hand so as to be able to watch it, she suddenly perceived around her hand's outline something that struck her with wonder. Never before had she noticed anything like it. Night vanished around her hand, though the hand itself remained night-rich beautiful. She made her hand quickly sculpt another frame. Still, there remained the same phenomenon—night faded a slight distance away from her hand, leaving a stark void in between. The hand itself remained night-rich. Did her hand steal night from night? Adults appropriate music from music. They can live a musical life. What did music appropriate? What void could it emit?

She knew by experience how it was to live in the void that surrounds perfection. To some extent she knew what happens in it. She knew also that there were many different perfections. That accounted for the many kinds of voids, and why their horrors were legion. Those who approached perfection without being perfect themselves would always be victims of the horrors of the void.

Talk to me, please, she begged.

He said something, but what he said remained inconsequential. The happy motorbikers had caught her interest. There was no void between her and them. Like invisible, fantastic insects, they continued swarming in and out of the stillness. They were flying spark-trumpeters; they were two intersecting grassblades tautly stretched against winged lips.

During the summer only one public open-air dance floor was open in the city. But there were many, perhaps an entire dozen, in the surrounding districts. The roads were congested with people on motorbikes in a hurry to get out there. Did they want to investigate yet another dance floor at this late an hour? Had they not yet found what they were looking for? Perhaps they were just out of luck? Had someone spurned them? Their hopes were now set on roads and bypasses. Somewhere someone was bound to be left standing. Someone somewhere would be the right person. Or was it just the fun of riding around on their bikes? Were they homeward bound? On their way home in an unknown direction with a female conquest?

The girl must have a good figure. That's uppermost in the minds of these young guys. Just as important as the tenderness of Sunday roast for the housewives in the meatmarket.

She listened to what he was telling her, but did not want to let on that she did. Her hand continued breathing serenely against his knee. As if to test her, he took her hand and lifted it slightly toward his lips, all the while keeping a steady eye on her. He could feel her arm vibrating in a gentle movement toward him, but her words crushed his lust.

You could very well be different, she said, dreamingly hopeful. He pressed her hand against his kneecap.

I'd rather hang myself, he said. He meant it as a joke, but it failed. His voice got stuck and turned a husky bass. She shook her head sadly.

What's wrong with you is that your name is Arnold. She was resolute now and gave him a serious look. How could your parents be so mindless to give you a name that is as dark as a gateway, as solemn and gloomy as the entrance to a railway station. Forget your name and find yourself another one. That's my advice. Say . . . Her interest was suddenly aroused,

Perhaps you have a special name?

Have you?

She nodded.

What is it?

I was the one to ask first.

I have no special name.

A nickname?

In school. Not just one. They changed it in . . .

Hush. Don't tell me. I don't want to hear it.

She looked away, no longer happy with the motorbikers.

Don't you want to tell me yours? he asked after a while.

She turned toward him and scrutinized his face. Her gravity struck him with a force that denuded his features all the way down his pupils. In vain he tried to make faces. Trying to disguise it made his mask even more conspicuous.

I'll tell you, she said finally. But you may not use my nickname whenever it strikes you. Remember that. Only if and when you like me and want to make me happy. My Mom made it up, see. And so far no one else has ever used it. It's a wonderful nickname and it has helped me many times. It's as illuminating as when the sun lights up a bay. Sometimes my Mom needs to say it only once and it brightens my day.

She hesitated for a moment and he turned his face aside. She was no longer afraid. There was nothing in his steady gaze now that she needed to fear. He needed to be on guard because he was arrogant enough to be his own enemy.

Cinnamoncandy, she said and turned away.

You too are corrupt, he said quickly with a cutting fury. I didn't want to believe it at first. I walk about, watching. I seek and search. What am I looking for? Someone innocent. Where did I get the notion that you were? It's so obvious that you have already started the chase. For what? I'll tell you. You're hunting for qualities. You have come to understand that you are lacking something, and you are hunting for it. Your innocence is a false front.

I'm sorry. I am sorry indeed because what you're telling me is nothing new. And I'm glad too that it's not. Something is evolving here. Some day you'll calm down.

Her gaze, searching for a soft stronghold, found it down in the bay below them where the water was resting its dove-blue body.

There's one who is not false, she said.

Who could that be?

God.

Not even you can utter this word without it sounding nauseating and repulsive.

Don't you ever pray?

Not even when I was a child.

You should have. It's children and unhappy people who need to pray. Prayer exists for those who are deprived of something vital. How else could we manage? There would only be hate. I know how it is for someone unable to pray. He comes to hate life. He hates his very own existence. It is his hate that becomes his sole strength and fills him with importance. It becomes the source of his pleasure. Even though he is an invalid—and he who lacks something vital always is—he is proud of being an invalid because his innate hate keeps feeding his vitality.

And those who are not deprived?

They don't need to pray. Lucky adults do not pray. Prayer makes them look ridiculous. They don't need to be informed why they are on this earth. They already have enough of God. This earth is good to them, and they fit into it. How I long to be there! To be a person so rich that the question of continued existence never even comes up. The sign of being grown, free and happy is that of not being aware of God's existence. He fades from the world, as it were, and so the individual can fill the void with himself. He is no longer treading water. He walks on this earth as an adult, ready to live as a human being among human beings.

Are you treading water?

Of course. And it's good that I do walk over water.

How come?

That's not difficult to understand. When you give up and let go and then fall. What happens when you walk on the ground? Inevitably you get hurt. No one can help you then. If someone is able to help you then the fall was not inevitable. At its worst, you have made yourself ridiculous. I know how that feels, becoming ridiculous. But it's different when you tread water. Then you fall into the deep, right into God.

Has that happened to you?

Yes, of course.

Why didn't you stay in the deep?

How can I do that? It's only the weak part in us that falls, not all of us. Our body remains immobile, unable to either walk on or turn. Whenever our feeble will regains its willpower, God takes it up to the water's surface. Walk across to the shore, He commands. Be brave, and you will reach solid ground.

Which life is better, life on solid ground or down in the deep?

What a question. On earth we can be happy. But it is blessed to live with Him.

Then I don't understand why we need to be here. Why doesn't the best thing happen to us right away?

How should I know? All I do know is that you are not happy. You can't even feel water under your soles.

Those who are happy don't care a fig for unhappiness.

What does that matter? It's important that you feel the water and the deep beneath your feet when you become unhappy and weak, helpless and old again.

Are old people included as well?

Of course.

You skipped the aged before.

Did I? I didn't mean to. God tells everybody: Leave the shore. The earth no longer belongs to you. Be brave and walk out to the deep.

He is gruesome, the one you're talking about. Because everything seems so meaningless.

You don't feel any longing. Those who yearn for something know what they're yearning for. They know that their lives are not without meaning because whatever they are yearning for exists on this earth and they're making every effort to reach it. Their very suffering signifies their knowledge that this earth has its glory. It's a long road to this glory. It's a long road to the shore. It should not be so long. God should free people from having to grow. He should eliminate the distance.

Do you complain?

Yes. Often.

Why do you complain?

I'm hurting. I feel a hurt inside me not to be nineteen years old.

You're not innocent. You've started the chase already.

Yes. And I'm not ashamed of that.

No. You're not. But I am. I hate. I don't want to.

What is it you don't want?

I don't want to be confined within the hell of adjectives. He was breathing hard against her ear. She did not pull away. Life is a constant chase for what one has not, a perpetual muddle to satisfy our desires. We're all sold on our own colors and we hunt recklessly for more color, more color, more of the right colors.

Yes, you're so right, she complained in a faint voice.

Still, that's not where the problem lies. What does it matter which colors we carry? It's not the colors that make us feel miserable. Others have the same colors we have, though in different combinations and possibly more lustrous. The general chase for colors mollifies us and lets us forget our essential misery. But once you unmask the chase, your tongue begins to taste the moldiness, and the very desire for the chase becomes a counterfeit that smells of rare deceit. The cynic tells us: the chase is a mercifully shameless party. I thankfully decline and refuse to be led on. Our misery consists not in having too few colors, but in not being able to get out of one's skin.

You're talking with such enthusiasm as if you'd suddenly found happiness.

Hogwash! I'm not talking about general things. I'm talking about the basic evil of life.

Some spark has set you afire and now you're all aflame.

Perhaps. In that case I'm comical. How can I avoid being ridiculous anyway? We're all sold on our own colors. It's the colors we chase as if it were a matter of life and death. That's comical. Our happiness is as ridiculous as our unhappiness. It's a question of either finding a coin or losing one. That's the stuff we fuss about. And this is where we're looking for fate's various destinies. Still, our capabilities can never make a distinct difference between one human being and another. No color can ever differentiate in a definite way. Our loneliness is no quality. It's a state. Our quality is in the state of loneliness. To be alone is to exist in place. And as long as we exist we are always in a place. No one can keep us alive out of our place.

He who loses his life, he shall gain it.

Who says so?

Love. You have never loved. That's why you don't believe.

How can you command yourself to love?

She could not resist her impulse, did not even try to stop it. With a quiet, compelling resolve, she turned ever so quickly, looking away from the water through boundless space and, heaven gathered in her gaze, her lips plunged against his mouth. Happy or un-happy. To him the sheer existence of his lips was an affront. Their presence made him lose his insight. But to her they were objects of a mistake, a poverty that knows no love.

She kissed him.

He jumped up, his tense body tottering in a move to step away from her, in its very action a perpendicular, weaving, dark mast. He fled. Fled without a word. The image of the dark mast pressed heav-ily against her face. She lifted it nevertheless and looked after him. Upright on her knees, she looked after him. Nothing happened to him when she sank down. It happened to her, something that pressed against her face. Something happened and it happened in her face.

When she found her ocarina, she took hold of it, lifted it be-tween her hands so that the bird's anonymous face could see out over the water. A sudden fit made her shoulders shiver. She draped his coat around her body. The invisible motorbikes were still firing their explosive salvos. Of course, she kept on whispering to herself. She turned over on her back and faced the expanse of the sky above her. I'm going to be happy, she whispered. I know that I'm going to be happy.—She felt a hard object pressing against her back. In vain she tried to evade it and finally concluded that it must be in one of the coat's pockets. She managed to retrieve it.

It was an apple. A foreign kind, big and green and hard because it was unripe. She took a small bite. The image returned while she was chewing, again pressing against her face, its pressure even stronger than before. She could no longer remain lying where she was. She had to get free. And she too fled. Not far. When she regained her strength she looked back. He was standing by his coat. She hid behind a tree. She saw him bend down over his coat and find the apple. He lifted it against the light and examined it carefully. The apple and the bite taken from it. He's going to throw it away, she thought. But he did not. No, he himself took a bite, right at the edge where the first bite ended. Then, his coat over his arm, he started down the path that led past the tree. He lifted the apple and bit. She wanted to stretch her arms out to him when suddenly she became aware of her own strength because she refrained from doing so.

Are you in love? Are you in love? she whispered.

14

Startled, Britt-Mari sat up in her bed, still half asleep. Two sun-rods, their tiny dust speckles dancing in the luminous brightness, cut across her darkblue comforter. Her body started swaying lightly in the hushed light of the room. Usually a sudden transformation of sound and peace would announce that her mother was up. She listened for the well-known rhythm right through her drowsiness.

Not a thing could be heard. Quiet lodged in the crack to her mother's room. Her intuition told her that quite soon she would become the object of her mother's concern and the truth would quickly arise in her own eyes. No, there was not even the tiniest sound. She exhaled deeply, then followed it with a deep smile. Her dreaming intuition told her that everything had gone well. Her mother had nothing to fear from him. Everything was all right. No need for any more secrets. Her mother was reassured. She knew it now. Britt-Mari no longer had to see for her. Her mother now saw it on her own. All had gone well. Britt-Mari was again a happy partner in her mother's existence.

With a sigh of happiness Britt-Mari slid back down into her bed, settled her cheek comfortably and went on to further dreams.

It was Sunday morning. No alarm clock was set to awaken anyone. It remained idle and dreams were allowed to drink as deeply as they could. When its hands drew near the week-day positions, there was no more than a mere click in the mechanism, the catch nodding its head like a fool. It was one of life's great liberties to have nothing extraneous infringe on a good sleep and it was life's delight to let sleep tumble its waves against a capriciously curved shore, its clean surface glittering like a damp skin, and its boundaries dashing to escape dry land until the shore again became the marginal ground for its onrushing waves.

When she woke up again she heard the sounds of church bells. One dark sound, one light sound, the high and the sonorous harmonizing in a dignified festival of rhythm. Quiet reigned still in the crack to her mother's room. Britt-Mari made an effort to get out of bed, but sleep overwhelmed her again. Her dream permitted her to live in her mother's gaze. There she could come alive. Dream and fantasy permitted her to live a life ruled by a pair of large eyes.

Eyes are powerful. Setting their stamps on landscapes and life's facades. They are mightier than even that.

These eyes were gorgeous and brilliant, their sparkle precious and wonderful. Life's grand affirmation lived in them. In their gaze Britt-Mari was born in beauty and love and allowed to live an incomprehensibly beautiful, ardent life.

How could all this vanish? Suddenly there was a flash in these eyes. A cruel, soundless explosion destroyed their brilliant sheen, and from then on the same eyes reflected a totally different life, an irreparable care in deep quietude. Britt-Mari had to live under these eyes. She stood in their dark gaze. How white shone her arms! How clearly outlined were her raised hands!

Suddenly something happened that was worse than dying in the bottomless darkness. She was thrown out. The eyes rejected her. The eyes flashed. She was caught in a fire that did not consume her. Charred, she looked back and met a still, harsh coldness. No path left to return into these eyes. No life in them to share. All her attempts were cut off when the sharp axe fell into the center of that eye. The paths still in existence led away from these eyes. She walked them without ever getting anywhere. Frustrated, she returned to the eyes time and again. Her only way to cope was to remain still, nonexistent within herself. What kind of wonder was waiting for her when these eyes would recover their brilliance? What had happened? How could the entire world suddenly change? Nothing but happiness had existed. The well of the stars had adorned all that was alive, had conferred on every second of life a lofty sparkle.

Gazes meant so much in her life. With their fine nerve threads they stitch the cloth of heart's experience, piece by piece.

When a leopard-spotted something emanating from the sunrods leaped into her eyes Britt-Mari finally decided to get out of bed. She held her breath and stiffened her body to resist its backward pressure. Her head tipped over the yellow bedframe whose edge cut into her neck. The memory of her dreams and fantasies was so strong that it almost choked her. She fought hard to get rid of its invisible grip.

Sitting on the edge of her bed, she stroked her fingers through her hair. There was the stove. It was Sunday. Quiet stood in the crack to her mother's room. Were the flowers in the lovers' room still fresh today? She ought to take a shower. She ought to make coffee.

In her mind she had relived the looks of these eyes a hundred times before. In school, walking on a street, waiting in the dairy store, well, anywhere she might suddenly feel a body inside her own body. Which body? For example the drowsy body her mother used to carry upstairs, draped over her shoulder.

Her mother had gone out to have fun. Now the fun was over. She had to go and get her, then carry her home. The girl was asleep, of course. It was not right to wake her at this late hour. Even if she did, the girl might walk a short distance, then start clinging to her legs again and fall asleep. Even though she was four years old, it was impossible to make her walk upstairs. While she was busy closing the gate, the youngster would simply collapse and had to be carried anyway.

Her mother chose her female friends with an eye on their usefulness. She went out with co-workers who lived with their parents. They could easily take care of Britt-Mari. No trouble at all, she assured them. The girl was used to playing by herself. Just listen at the door occasionally. She had been fed already and a few cokes and snacks she had along. Afterward Britt-Mari was pulled out of bed in the middle of the night, during the winter months a rather difficult and time-consuming effort. While her limbs were pushed and pulled through gaiters and coat sleeves, she would hear whispers and sudden peals of laughter, turning to roars so loud that they often made her cry.

She could not recall one single face of that time, but she remembered the different voices and their laughter. It was frightening to remember just the voices. It was like in utter solitude imagining wallhangings at any given moment to burst forth with wild roars of laughter, or pictures to whisper, table legs to giggle, tablecloth fringes to bustle about, mirrors to smack forth kisses, or vases to sing.

The co-workers changed often and the rooms with them. There were rumors that her mother was certainly a jolly person, but oh, so fickle. It was easy for her to get new jobs and make new friends, but she tired of them quickly. Britt-Mari remembered hearing her mother sob many a time as she was dangling over her shoulders. Her grip holding the girl was harsh, and when she let go of her she fell hard on her bed. She would leave her there, still dressed in her outerwear, and walk the floor restlessly. Britt-Mari had the feeling of lying like that for nights on end. The piercing clicks of her mother's high heels never ended. Words her mother muttered in her despair spooked in the darkness surrounding the little girl on the bed: Why? Why should I have to live like that? Why me? Will there never be any change in my life?

The eyes branded her. Britt-Mari was the culprit. Her existence was at fault. Her little body blocked all the roads to a new life. That gaze hit her as if she had shattered everything that made life worthwhile. That gaze crushed the little girl, frightened her, made her unable to move. She began to have suicidal thoughts. She had a feeling of lying prone. Only blood and death could remove that hideous repulse showing in that gaze. It was bitter to be in the center of that gaze and still live on. Her back began to freeze. A heavy cold shook her shoulders. She reached a wall with a window, without being able to cut through. A giddy feeling remained in her back, its skin covered with goosepimples from inner pain. It was disgraceful to live on under the terms of this gaze. At an early age she learned to live this life of disgrace and shame.

There was a milder variation of this heavy gaze that did not totally reject her. While not excluding her totally from existence, it pushed her off into the future: If you were but a little bit older. How easy it'll be when you're grown up.

It was the gaze of these eyes that pushed her against the door one morning after her mother had disappeared through the door. Britt-Mari pushed her body tightly against the smooth wall to conjure up its growth. With balled fists and straining muscles she commanded her body to grow with such vehemence that eventually the grace of this growth materialized according to her will.

Her forehead first, then her entire body moved up higher and higher against the smooth door. Her delight exceeded any previous experience. A wave held her and carried her upward. She saw herself. Her wonderful growth stood white and perfect against a receding blue background. The warm movement in her soft arms encompassed the lanky girlish body, tottering across the floor and dropping in a chair, exhausted, still enraptured, still beyond the reach of shame.—Thus the secret was born that was able to cast a swift smile at her directly from her blood without concealing the darkest moments of her life, providing her with the symbol and key to her life.

It was Sunday morning. Quiet lingered in the crack to her mother's room. Carefully she padded over and closed the door. Let her sleep on. She would fix the coffee and prepare the tray. Her mother loved to have coffee in bed. The coffee should be hot and strong. Her mother would look so happy when blowing the steam away, inhale deeply and drink in heavy, big gulps. In these moments she exuded such a powerful, strong will to live, capable of lapping up the day's first hours with glorious lips.

A wild desire overcame Britt-Mari to scrub her face completely clean before seeing those lips.—The first washing was not enough. She lathered her face and throat three times and rinsed them three times. The first towel got sopping wet and she needed a second towel to rub her skin. Her freckles appeared like rusty spots on a mirror.

15

Her mother was inaccessible that day. Most of the time her mind wandered off somewhere into a distant wild blue yonder where things of importance were settled. At most she pretended interest in things around her, and that only to get time to pass. Something inside her seemed to be anxiously waiting. But suddenly she could wait no longer and settled the issue within herself. Envisioning the outcome made her chuckle quietly to herself, raise her hands and drop them again. Quite unexpectedly she stood up straight, her body full of energy and strength.

At times her face took on a cruel look. She raised her chin and it stiffened at a commanding angle. It was impossible for her to be impassive, and she constantly interfered in the things at hand. But the drama itself took place on a different plane, and its outcome was her major concern. Although absent from the scene, she acted in it.

She simply moved the scene, internalized it and pulled the strings. It has to go my way.

Leave me alone. Really, the way you chatter and carry on.

Britt-Mari had to hear her say that several times. Then, at one point the mother turned wonderfully mellow. The dismal present vanished. No longer was she just having a good time on Stadsberg one Sunday evening, but she saw herself living in some future time where all resistance had dissipated. Having reached her goal, she wanted suddenly to cradle Britt-Mari in her arms, or a few hairstrands at least. She twisted them between her fingers and held them up against the light.

You can't believe how happy I am. Cinnamoncandy, you want me to whisper a secret in your ear?

Sitting between her mother's knees, Britt-Mari pricked up her ears.

It's wonderful to be alive, she heard.

They smiled at each other in common agreement. Britt-Mari sank back, finally relaxing and feeling wonderful and mellow. The city below them was alive in a distant, heartfelt, dream-blue hush. They watched cars flitting past, saw people moving, soccerplayers run across the lightgreen grass of Idrottsplats field. Not a sound reached them from below. Down in the river two canoes were gliding past and a few motorboats lay bobbing in the bay. Only an observant eye would detect that they were moving. The waves looked like undulating, lightblue silk ribbons arranged like ploughs whose tips dived under the white rose floating closely behind the boat. Flocks of sails played in the sound in ever new combinations. Beyond the islands and the lighthouse on the bare cliff was the open sea.

The mother's arms rested on Britt-Mari's shoulders and her folded hand against her breast. The girl felt her warmth, the fresh, living heat of her body, the beat of her pulse, the safe, creating pulsation. She was surprised at how many soccerplayers would stand still during the game. A fickle wind seemed to make the decisions for whatever was happening on the field. She never saw any feet kicking; a windgust, seemingly mocking the players, would get to the ball ahead of the feet, rolling it off somewhere else. Such short distances. A hopeless hither and yon. The cheers and shouts of the spectators below them sounded like mosquito swarms on the rise. The rising ball floating in suspension and the air weighing its bulk before permitting it to fall made her shudder several times.

We're going to have a miserable midsummer holiday this year, the mother declared. This kind of weather won't last another week.

It might last for several weeks yet.

Not so! It'll be a hopeless midsummer.

How can you be so certain?

Certain? I'll tell you why I'm certain. This kind of heat isn't normal. There are all the signs.

I can't see anything abnormal. I simply love it.

Her arms separated from the girl and became shadows across her face.

This heat is a young cuckoo, the mother said. It chopped off for itself that which other days should rightly have. She pulled a dry gingerbread cookie out of the bag. It crunched in her mouth.

Well, what does it matter, after all, what the weather is like at midsummer? There are more important things to do during midsummer.

What would that be?

Britt-Mari managed a cringing smile. Her mother stroked her with her fingertips and chuckled from deep within her throat. Having heard it somewhere, Britt-Mari remembered a vulgar phrase. It reverberated like an answer in her brain: a friend in the bay, to have a friend in the bay is the most important thing at midsummer. She caressed her mother's round knees and finally made an attempt to find out what happened the previous night.

Did he like the beefsteak?

He sure did. He's a real glutton. Gobbled up three pieces, I think.

Did you get to dance a lot?

Every single dance we were there. Even a Hambo, that was the best of all. It's an eternity since I last danced Hambo. Those youngsters nowadays can't dance the Hambo. Just as well, as far as I'm concerned, especially when the music gets real lively. You have the dance floor almost entirely for yourself and you can go off flying, I should say. You should've seen us.

Britt-Mari happened to look at her hand while her mother was talking. There was a ladybug resting between two of her knuckles.

She was delighted. Carefully she picked up her hand and counted the bug's black spots. Ladybugs carried their lucky number right on their backs.

Did you and Daddy dance a lot?

The question simply rushed out on its own. Still, she did not regret having asked. She felt her mother's knees shifting as she stretched forward to reach for the bag with the gingerbread cookies. They crackled in her mouth. Britt-Mari prepared herself to receive no answer to her question. But then it came, in a careless tone of voice,

You know, your Dad couldn't dance, and there was certainly no fun doing it with him.

He couldn't? Britt-Mari expressed her amazement.

He had no style. He strutted about, trampling back and forth.

He strutted about?

The mother cooed like a pigeon on a tin roof. But not even her caresses could bring Britt-Mari any closer to her.

You have inherited his body build, so it's lucky that you're a girl. Otherwise it would have been a pity. You know well how it used to be when you tried to take the lead. It doesn't work. It doesn't amount to more than trampling and strutting.

But Daddy wasn't any taller than I am now. And you can't very well compare our kitchen with a dance floor.

Sometimes a dance floor leaves less room for the dancers than a kitchen and then it matters how good the partner is. Can he lead, then he can lead, and neither crowd nor elbow-room matters.

The mother chattered on, lightly and without feeling, not realizing how hard Britt-Mari took what she said.

A fellow should be able to lead. It's embarrassing for a woman to be stuck with a fellow who can't do more than shuffle back and forth. It's even worse at times when you feel like crying; it just depends on the mood you're in. A date like that can ruin your evening if you're crazy about dancing. You can't even call it dancing, and there's no fun. And I never had fun when dancing with your Daddy. No fun. Of course, I don't blame him for that. He couldn't help it. His body and my body on a dance floor. No, it was an impossible combination. With an elf perhaps.

The mother giggled. Then she yawned. Britt-Mari felt hurt, about the one as much as the other.

I still believe that Daddy could dance, she said stubbornly.

Why yes, when I took the lead, the mother said, yawning again behind her hand.

There are times when you remember wrong. I should know.

Following certain arguments this phrase was usually Britt-Mari's last resort. If it accomplished anything, it would provoke her mother's anger. But not today. She was beyond reach. She had already forgotten what they had been talking about. Her raised chin stiffened in an angle of determination. The cruel expression of her lips was not directed at anything in her immediate physical surrounding.

The mother became again the center of importance and Britt-Mari forgot too. The girl wanted to feel recognized and be part of her mother's life.

What are you thinking of?

Britt-Mari received no answer to her question. Her insides started wailing: you are blind, Mommy. It's always up to me to look out for you. Between the two of them, who took on the responsibility for her mother's life? It's me, Britt-Mari, because I have to look after her, whether Mother realizes it or not. She had to watch out, as always. And now her mother was waiting for a final decision that was not even up to her, but for someone else to make. What was it? Never before had her mother been secretive about her successes or failures. She couldn't. She radiated the triumph of being loved by her lover ever since that morning. Nothing else. Beautiful to watch, it was terrible at the same time. It was frightening to sense the void the beautiful surrounded itself with. Even now that the dread was somewhat mitigated, the girl grieved. The beautiful looked beautiful no more.

Tell me, what are you thinking of?

There was no answer. The mother did not even hear the question. Britt-Mari saw her mother lift her hands, then let them drop immediately again. Watching her chuckle quietly to herself did nothing to relieve the girl's distress. In a fit of spite, the mother knew that somewhere someone was suffering because of her. It gave her a certain sense of satisfaction and she reveled in her feeling of revenge. She got up with a sudden burst of energy and determina-

tion. The exploding inner strength made her look proud and dignified.

This heat is unbearable, she said.

Her words did not matter. What she said was as inconsequential
as the blinking of an eye. Neither her bearing nor her voice sup-
ported what she said.

It's impossible to stay in here, the mother declared. I'm pooped.
Let's clean up and go for a walk in the woods. We'll get relief in the
shade over there. Britt-Mari got up and stood next to her mother,

I haven't climbed the mountain today yet, she said. May I? Just
for a little while.

The resentment showing in her mother's face was toward her,
which should have comforted her in spite of everything else. But it
was too late for that. Her mother's attitude had obliterated her own.
She needed to get away from her mother and in solitude regain her
lost individuality.

What's that good for? I don't like you to run around on that
mountain. I never did. She bent down to pick up the bag with the
remnants of their food.

Just for a little while. I'll be careful.

You heard what I said. I don't like it. The mother was on her
knees, repacking. A few soda bottles clattered around. A spoon
dropped out of a mug and fell into the open brown bag.

I'll be back soon.

Go ahead, then. But be careful.

Britt-Mari ran off. She soon reached one of the many crags from
where she could take a jump. In her excitement, she landed flat on
the ground below, a slippery carpet of bearberries in bloom. She slid
down a little further where she could grab hold of the carpet and
finally came to a stop. She turned to look, but her mother had disappeared. All she could see was the naked mountain. But when she
got up on her feet again, she saw her mother sitting right where she
had left her.

Be mindful of your slippery sandals, the mother called.

Britt-Mari ran on and took another jump. When she turned to
look, her mother called down,

I'm going ahead to feed the squirrels by myself.

Her tone of voice sounded nasty, though not malicious. Britt-Mari turned her back. Lifting her arms, she pretended to fly. She wanted to be a bird. A lightning-fast swallow, a spool-shaped thrush, a globular, twittering lark, rising ever so high until it came sailing down, veering in from the west, like rain. She looked straight down.

She ran on again, following the mountain's strange, wonderful trails. One sloped slightly eastward, then stopped abruptly. From that point she took another jump downward and walked another trail that sloped slightly in a westward direction until that, too, took a sudden end—the trail possibly cutting further into the mountain. The third trail led upward, and the fourth trail no longer just slanted slightly to the east. No, it was a steep slope. Here she lay down and looked for their attic window on Storgatan 33. Then she followed the river up to the lake. Quietude settled in her eyes.

16

Half an hour later Britt-Mari finally returned to the mountain-crest. She did not expect to find her mother right away, and to start with she did not worry. She followed the general walkway in the direction of the outlook tower, which looked like a pagoda and had a metal flag on top. Many years ago the flag used to be yellow and blue. By now the metal was a rusty brown and the cross had almost disappeared. There were many people up on the mountain thanks to the beautiful weather.

The outlook tower was bolted and blocked. It was dangerous to climb its dilapidated stairs, their decay and state of disrepair visible through the broken walls. An article in the local paper had expressed the hope that a donor for their repair could be found. But that was several years ago, and no donor had shown any interest as yet. Britt-Mari resented the donors' great ability to exist in retiring invisibility. She guessed that the wealthy refrained from looking at the lookout tower to avoid embarrassment.

The cafeteria was open. So were the museum and all the other old buildings moved here from their original sites downtown or in surrounding districts.

Every table was taken both inside and outside. All the windows were full of patrons. Her mother had been correct when she decided not to sit there: On a day like this you can wait for hours to be served. And when you finally get something, there are all the other people looking at you to leave your table as quickly as possible. That's no fun. You just sit there on edge, afraid that you might swallow your coffee the wrong way, and you have to chew so well-manneredly and crook your little finger to lift your cup.

Britt-Mari lined up with the others. Her objective was to look and admire. The green chairs and the tables with the round, white table tops looked rather pleasant. Sparrows felt free to flutter around and pick up the fallen crumbs. The most daring among them even settled on tables where they could find left-over pastries and other goodies. Music sounded through the open doors from a radio, or perhaps a phonograph.

Most of all she liked the many good-looking people around her and tried to pick out the most beautiful. Since most of them were bareheaded she could easily examine the couples for their haircolor. Her survey pleased her. Most had chosen correctly. Dark men sat with blond women, or vice versa. Above all, it was the younger couples who had made the correct choice, so they should come out happy. In the future marriages will be happier than they are now, she thought.

Something caught her attention and she stopped to admire. It was a white hat of the type she had always dreamed of. Diminutive in size and brimless, it had on either side a pair of slender wings that looked like flattened horns.

The young lady wearing this dream looked very happy. She seemed very witty, because whenever she said something, her company around the table laughed out loud. Her pretty face was full of life, exuding a smiling self-confidence and a charming independence. The hat well underscored this attractive picture of lustrous volatility and pointed ease. It did not take long for the girl to notice Britt-Mari's obtrusive admiration. Like a naughty little child, she cut an insulting face at Britt-Mari. It all happened so suddenly that her company hardly noticed. But Britt-Mari felt deeply hurt by the contempt she saw in the girl's face. Blushing, she ran off. She tried to think of a good revenge and decided that the little white hat with the small, flattened horns would have looked far better on her. It was obvious that her haircolor was much better suited. This hat quite simply demanded her haircolor.

The hat and the grimace forgotten, Britt-Mari ran on. She had to find her mother. She wound her way through the crowds who were milling around and blocking the paths between the old houses. She jumped over low fences and took shortcuts, soon overcome with the feeling of having covered the entire area. She tried to calm down. Perhaps her mother had gone home? But she doubted that. Her mother liked the mountain, once she got up here. And she enjoyed stopping for a look at the old cottages.

Continuing her search, Britt-Mari walked on through a terrain of sparsely growing pines, interspersed with an occasional spruce or mountain ash. Further down by the highway the coniferous forest became denser and taller. She knew a tarn deeper inside the forest where water-lilies grew. A short distance away from the road was a lumber mill once driven by running water. She decided to walk past. But before she got there, she heard a noise that sounded like the call of a squirrel. She stopped, guessing that her mother, who enjoyed feeding squirrels, must be near.

In an effort to surprise her, she sneaked from tree to tree, becoming more careful when she finaly saw her mother sitting on a grey bench in the sunshine. There was a woodshed among the pine trees. Forgetting her plan to surprise and giving in to a sudden urge to watch her mother without being seen herself, Britt-Mari stepped behind a tree.

She saw her mother holding out some hazelnuts as bait. She never failed in these attempts and, although she could not see any, Britt-Mari assumed that she had already lured a few squirrels. Her mother had a way with animals. Dogs, horses, birds, cats—she always made friends with them without even trying very hard. They would rub against her, or ruffle their feathers, or wag their tails. Strange horses often came close to let her kiss them on their tender, pretty, smooth snouts.

Suddenly Britt-Mari saw a red squirrel jumping elegantly down, then sitting up on its hindlegs not far from her mother. Its forward-stretching paws softened as they slid down its white underbelly. Quickly circling around her, it looked at her, its nose sniffing intently, perhaps even nervously, at something that merited attention—something edible lying close by on the ground. The squirrel leaped over and caught it between its frontpaws, its bushy tail wagging. Her mother continued holding her bait out and stretched her arm further still. In a flash the squirrel jumped over to her, grabbed the nut and disappeared behind the woodshed with its handout. But not for long. Presently it was back again to capture another nut.

Her mother took several nuts in her hand. Already shelled, they were easy bounty. Becoming ever more daring, the squirrel continued its expeditions. Britt-Mari lost her desire to watch her mother. The squirrel was more important. Seemingly tireless, it was full of spirit and quite a number of lively, funny, entertaining tricks, such as running up the tall fir tree, to return dancing, head down, around its trunk.

A smaller competitor arrived, but it was soon checked and driven off. Becoming ever more daring, the first squirrel now ventured up to her mother's hand and sat there, dining daintily on the nuts offered. Intelligent enough, it quickly found their original source. After that it was no longer content with less than the entire inventory. Smiling, her mother let it have its way. The bag with the nuts was in a smaller handbag, made of tiny leather pieces stitched together, a leather string running through the eyelets at its outer end. The squirrel stood beside it, scratching. To make it easier, her mother pulled several items out of the bag and put them beside her on the bench. The squirrel took a mouthful of nuts and jumped off to its hiding place nearby. Every time it came for more nuts, its body disappeared in the bag and Britt-Mari could see no more than the tip of its tail bobbing up and down outside the rim.

Then it happened. It seemed obvious that this had been planned long beforehand. Still, Britt-Mari had no prior inkling of it. Not before the squirrel was caught inside the handbag did she comprehend her mother's gradual arrangement. With a muted cry of triumph her mother suddenly took hold of the leather strings, pulled the handbag shut and took it off the bench. She let the handbag dangle back and forth in front of her knees.

Calm down, my sweetie-pie, she hissed, rather excitedly. Calm down, my cutie. Now you are mine.

It was her mother's face that made Britt-Mari furious. She saw not pleasure, but malice. Not desire, but a craving to inflict pain. Not pride in achievement, but relish in trapping a live prisoner. Her will was too primitive and brutal, and her face showed it only too clearly. Worse yet, involving her entire body, her mother now intensified her brutality. She rose up and started swinging her arm, handbag and squirrel turning in a wild roundabout. Triumph was circling, and degradation along with it.

Ohhhhhiii, ohhhhhiii, she whizzed between her teeth.

Britt-Mari came rushing forward. She wanted to cry out, but something prevented her. When her mother caught sight of her, she stopped swinging her arm. But by no means did she feel caught and exposed in a hideous act. No, she even bragged about her cruelty.

I've caught me a squirrel, she called.

Britt-Mari turned blind in fury. Throwing herself over her mother, she hit her and suddenly found that she could scream too. Her mother pushed her away with her other hand.

What's gotten into you? Calm down, sweetie.

Britt-Mari stood still, shaking. Dumb again, she stared fixedly at the handbag, alive in her mother's cruel hands. She threw herself over the handbag. Her knees hit the ground and her body, twisting, fell backward, still holding on to the leather strings.

Are you crazy! her mother panted, huskily rusty. Let go, kid! Let go immediately, I'm telling you!

Blind with exasperation, Britt-Mari neither heard nor saw. She tugged and pulled as she kept on kicking with her feet. Her mother was stronger and Britt-Mari found no brace to steady her feet. With her entire body she tried to dig into the ground. Then she had to let go and her torso flew up in a jolt. She made herself as heavy as she possibly could when she fell backward.

Then the leather string broke.

Britt-Mari did not look up to see what happened then. Not wanting to see or be seen, she rolled over on the ground to find a hiding place. Her capacity to see became a terrible burden to bear. All her sensibility collected in her pupils. One single look could bring about an insurmountable pain. Another look would make life unbearable and not worth living. She was worn out. Her lungs were torn.

She heard the strange, miserable cry of the squirrel, whimpering, his cutting and mewing squeaks sobbing forth his distress.—Her mother did not touch her. But she stepped over and, standing next to her, she said from above,

What's the matter with you? Acting like a stupid idiot. What on earth did you think? Britt-Mari heard her mother's steps as she walked away. You, of all people, should know that I love squirrels, she declared from a distance.

Britt-Mari remained lying on the ground, her face pressed against her arm.

Do you hear what I'm saying? I love squirrels and all other animals. You know that. Get up now and brush the dirt off.

Suddenly Britt-Mari heard the squirrel, no longer in distress, but clicking his tongue. Her mother triumphed. See, she said. He even wants more nuts. Just look. He's coming for more.

Her mother sat down on the bench. Britt-Mari did not move, though her anger, despair and pain were gone. An incomprehensible peace let her rest on the ground. She felt totally cleansed on the inside. Flushed and tumbled clean. When she finally rose up, she saw that her mother was still the same way she had been all day long: inaccessible. She continued to exist somewhere far from where she really was. It was all right, Britt-Mari felt. As for herself, she felt clean to live where she was and not with that terrible, dirty suspicion.

There are some sandwiches left, the mother said calmly, a smile concerning an entirely different matter on her lips.

17

A power struggle ensued the entire week that followed. When early on Monday morning the mother stood holding her mirror in one hand and her translucent, crimson comb in her other, she had no inkling of the difficulties in store for her. But a superstitious fear overcame her all of a sudden as she looked at herself. She sensed a certain danger lurking in her presumptuous self-confidence. She was challenging the future, not the course of events, still convinced that there could be just one outcome. She had accepted a new element in her life, and now she expected him to tell her that. No, the problem was the threat to her peace of mind and her reactions to receiving news she would not want. She must not be surprised, was not allowed to feel this delightfully fresh transformation. She had to take the news as a matter of course.

Watching her mother, Britt-Mari was surprised. Her mother began trying to behave humbly. She tried to act tenderly happy and softly receptive. She tried to exhibit a quivering expectation and a childishly great happiness.

How could I be so stupid, she whispered one time, pressing her fingertips against her temples as if she needed to hide the powerful, massive curve of her forehead.

Then she expressed doubts about her red turban. It looked provocative. The red color was too indulging. Its form was not chaste. If she had the time, she would have exchanged it for something more appropriate. As it was, she did not have the time. On the other hand, thus far she had matched her make-up to go with the turban. She intended to change that, for sure. Her looks became more important than ever, especially in the morning. She hardly took the time nowadays to glance through the newspaper, thus allowing more time to spend on her make-up. She was no longer young and needed to take more pains. All this, even though officially it was to read the news in peace and quiet and preferably in bed for which she always sacrificed half an hour of her sleep.

Nowadays Britt-Mari needed to run to the door to get her goodbye hug, and it became a hasty affair, as impetuous as the whiff of a windgust. Afterward the girl would quietly turn and walk back and forth in the apartment for a while. An element of life died in the room every morning when the mother left it. The very air was mourning and all the scattered objects remained lying wherever the mother had thrown them. The newspaper lay spread out on the kitchen table, one half hanging over its side. Britt-Mari went over to look for the news that had elicited her mother's commentary. One of the engineers was celebrating his fiftieth birthday. His photo stood like a round ball above a pillar of text.

Her mother had expressed scorn for the engineer and dissatisfaction with the newspaper editors. She never read the article below the photo, but she was angry about his deceiving picture. In the newspaper he came out like a normal human being. But in reality he was a ridiculous little runt. In this case, her mother suggested, it would have been better to print a full-length photograph and place a matchstick box at the bottom for comparison. That would have given a truer picture of the man's size.—The thought of that engineer preoccupied her mother all morning long, and time and again she grumbled with indignation.

Once he even condescended to take up a discussion with me, she said. About discipline at work. Of course, it was he who decided on the topic. A supervisor needs to stand on his rank, he told me. Everyone ought to do that, I said. But he didn't even listen. He never does when he is condescending. Without respect there's no discipline. When the rats dance on the table even though the cats are in, that is anarchy and not industrial democracy, he said.—That silly little runt, making us out to be rats and himself a cat.—Of course, I gave him tit for tat, even though I could have died laughing. And while he pretended to listen to what I had to say on the subject, he pouted his mouth until at last it looked like a thimble with a burned-out cigarillo in its middle. A little one that's called Kolibri. Because he needs a cigar smell around him. That inspires respect. He thinks. But who cares about what he thinks about our behavior. Certainly none of us girls.

She had not heard anything yet. Britt-Mari could see it as soon as her mother came rushing in after work. Nasty misgivings passed by like shadows. No, not shadows. The misgivings were alive, stronger than everything else. Her mother did not want to exist among them and tried to evade them by haunting her body. She seemed to dangle within her own movements, because her will was more violent than her body could stand to be.

She was not going to have dinner at home tonight. Absolutely not. She had to leave immediately. He was waiting for her outside. She had to change. That's why she had come home, to change. She shushed Britt-Mari. Nothing but certainty must interfere. She did not want to concern herself with anything but certainty. All of it, complete.

Why are you standing there, staring? she screamed. Help me, for goodness sakes. I can't find a thing.

Not the right stockings. Not the earrings she had in mind. Not the stylish handkerchief. Her eyes jousted around the room until she gave up in despair, staring straight up to the ceiling with a face as if the very room was at fault. Contradicting herself, she then declared that he was supposed to be waiting outside the entrance door in as much as ten minutes. She was even contrary to her customary habits, because she never started changing before everything she would wear was laid out next to her. Now she was struggling out of her work clothes as if they were shackles. She was not even present in her room, but was hurrying forth on her way to her date. There, and only there, reality existed. And there, only there, was she going to find herself.

You could very well have brushed my shoes, she complained with a whiny, strident voice, cognizant of only a mere fraction of what she was saying. What are you doing all day long? It doesn't take more than two minutes to shine a pair of shoes.

Literally throwing herself from one place to the other, her body thrashed around like a scatterbrained jumping-jack. The rooms surrounding her presence here were just as unnatural for her as for a butterfly. Nothing inside the walls was like a meadow, nothing looked like flowers. The colors and scents here were a mistake.

When are you going to be back? Britt-Mari asked as the mother, finally ready, was on her way out. All of a sudden the mere question was insolent. Flapping around, she gave a sudden jerk and screamed in a nasty voice,

I'll be back whenever it suits me. Do you understand? Whenever it suits *me* and not a cheeky youngster.

Then she slammed the door shut behind her.

When she opened the door again it was with the utmost care. The time was past 1.00 A.M. She crossed the floor carefully, trying not to disturb her child. But Britt-Mari was wide awake, trying silently to interpret the sounds and the behavior of the person who darker than darkness was moving past. The well-known strip of light streaked forth, settling in its customary place. She heard her mother rummaging around. The alternating sounds and silences now differed from those in the mornings with regard to both speed and force. Softer sounds and more time were allotted to the silences. Suddenly her mother returned to the kitchen, still moving carefully in consideration of the sleeping girl. Britt-Mari understood that her mother was trying to find something to eat and sat up in bed.

Go ahead and turn on the light, Mommy.

I'm completely famished. I can't understand it.

Didn't you have dinner?

Of course I did. He took me to the most elegant restaurant in town. And what I ate should've been more than enough. Still, I'm as hungry as a wolf.

There are some meatballs left over.

Great. Exactly what I want. But how about you? Why aren't you asleep, my little girl.

She lit the lamp above the stove. Already knowing that the mother was pleased with herself, Britt-Mari could now see it too. Her mother was calm and collected. Her face exuded a beautiful satisfaction, and it made her smile glitter. She continued to smile as she spread butter on a piece of flatbread. Britt-Mari assumed that this was all she would be hearing tonight. Satisfied with the smile, she slid down under her blanket, thinking: thank goodness for that. Suddenly she saw her mother looking at her.

You won't believe it, she heard her say.

Nothing more. Her mother continued preparing her food. At least five meatballs went on top of the sandwich. Then she took the tallest glass they had and filled it with milk. Britt-Mari never expected her to sit at the kitchen table. As if she were working at it, she ate with great appetite.

You won't believe it, she repeated.

Suddenly she put the glass of milk down and bent forward across the table.

I didn't give in, she said. It was he who had to give in. Oh, the way we kept at it and talked tonight. Talked? That's a stupid word for what we did. We fought. We wrestled. No surprise that I'm famished.

She ate and drank all that was left over, then wiped her mouth with her hand. Suddenly she broke out in a sparkling laugh.

He didn't even get a kiss. He was hardly allowed to touch me. First you must make good on your promise, I told him; I don't accept any excuses. It's going to be finished between us if you don't keep the promises we agreed on. What d'you think? I asked him. Just stop, no intimacies! After what has happened between us, you can't act like that. I asked him, Where is your sense of responsibility? Don't you understand that love between the two of us can be the most beautiful thing that life can ever give a person here on earth?

What did he say to that?

He agreed with me. There's nothing wrong with his love. He lacks courage. And that bothers me. Bothers me a lot. That fellows can be such cowards. The love that does not dare shall not get either, I told him.

What did he say to that?

He swore that he'd do whatever we had agreed on.

What is that?

That we're going to be married.

In that case he would need a divorce first.

Of course. That's where his daring becomes an issue. It's true that I was overly anxious, and I could certainly have waited a little while yet. But I don't think that's the right approach in his case. He needs to do it on the spur of the moment. And that must be while this affair is still fresh. That's how things stand right now.

Is it a dare for him if it's you he gets?

That is something you don't understand, Cinnamoncandy. It's true in his case, unfortunately. He must have the courage.

But what is it he's afraid of? Is he afraid that I . . .

Gosh no. Not at all. It's the way I explained it: you can't understand that yet.

Could it be that he still loves his wife?

Oh no! He doesn't. I'm absolutely certain of that. But there's something he does like. To have his comfort. To be somewhat better off than others in his position. That's where the shoe pinches, and I've told him that too. You can't understand it, but I do. How could I help not finding out? Most of these fellows get that way as soon as they get over their first, romantic youth. Some are this way their entire life. Guys above all. Security and comfort become crucial factors in their lives. His present wife has some money. That's the obstacle.

My poor Mommy.

Oh, poohh. He promised me. I know that I'll get my wish. Besides there's something else I haven't even discussed with him yet. If push comes to shove I'll do it. Actually, why not do it anyway? She gave a low and crafty laugh. I'm really not that anxious to get married on the spot. We can very well wait. If we move in together I can retain my pension. It may be small, but it's always good enough for something. No, the important thing is that he gets his divorce and that must be done immediately. His wife has a house and rakes in the rent from three tenants. Also, they don't have to spend money on rent for themselves. That's how things stand. At the moment she's busy trying to sell that house. She intends to buy one here in town.

And I thought they were from here.

No. And she's not going to move here either. She'll have to stay where she is. Do you understand that now? That's why it's so urgent. She needs to get wise to the truth as soon as possible. It doesn't make sense to put it off. She might lose out if she really starts up with her business. So, it's best even for her that this thing gets out in the open. After all, money is so damn important.

Pounding her fist on the table, her mother got up. Her pride brought a look of contempt to her face, but her anger overpowered the disdain and pushed it aside. Only her pride remained.

Money, money, her mother said. Sometimes I feel like clubbing one of those moneybags.

She went to turn the light off. Then she stood still in the darkness as if brooding over something.

It struck Britt-Mari that she still did not know his name. She called him Qtwo, because there had been a Q already. So far he was only "he" in her mother's vocabulary, and that was really enough for Britt-Mari not to confuse him with someone else. "He" was the new foreman. "He" was dark. "He" was the person her mother was in love with. Why didn't she tell her his name? A name is like an illumination. You can see a face in its glow. Britt-Mari became uneasy, feeling that her mother's secrecy about his name threatened the future her mother was now building up in the darkness. Britt-Mari had heard of many a "he" who never amounted to anything more than "he," only to gradually disappear to join all those who existed outside her mother's interests.

She did not find out his name now either. She postponed the question when she heard her mother coming toward her, and when she felt her mother's hand on her forehead she forgot the entire question.

Forgive me, her mother whispered. You understand. Am I right, my Cinnamoncandy? You are smart enough not to imagine stupid things. You aren't, are you, Cinnamonandy? You know how I really feel about you in my heart. Isn't it so, Cinnamoncandy?

Mommy.

I'm listening.

Mommy.

We know now that we have each other.

Mommy, there's so much that's uncertain.

But not this, Britt.

No. Not this.

That's the main thing for us, isn't it?

I wish it were.

Isn't it then?

I don't know, Mommy. So much is happening. There ought to be no uncertainty, but there is, many times.

No, there ought to be no uncertainty.

There's one more thing still, Mommy.

Tell me.

If this works out, I don't think that you should move in together. The money we're getting comes from Daddy, and you know why we're getting it. If it works out you must get married. It has to work out, that too.

But if?

It has to work out.

But if it doesn't?

Then Daddy is going to help us. We must not forget that.

18

All week long the same scene repeated. The man promised to go ahead. He promised every day, but when it came to taking action he lost his courage. He never wrote that certain letter. He asked for more time to consider. He asked every day, and every day he got more time to think about it. Of course, he ought to be able to think about it. Go to your place and think about it. She was not going to influence him. Think about it in solitude, be alone and shoulder your responsibility. Yes or no. He did not have to say more.

The person he loved removed herself from him. Every day she went her own way. He was not allowed to touch her. No, he would not get a kiss. He could meet her again after having made up his mind. Have you written the letter? Yes or no? If it were to be a No, he would know the outcome. She would go her own way. What would he have done? He knew it only too well. If it were to be a No he would have sold his love for a mess of pottage. She would know his real worth then. She would rather do without a guy like that. Would rather suffer. Didn't he understand that a love like theirs demanded that he renounce all his old affiliations? Of course, he understood. Every day he repeated that he understood that. He would have the nerve, he promised. He'd go to his place and write that letter, he promised. Or wouldn't it be better to put it off till Sunday? You don't settle things like this with a letter, he said. It isn't fair. I'm going to see her on Sunday and tell her the way it is. He promised that he would discuss next Sunday all the things he had failed to bring up last week. No, she said. Every day she said No. He was not allowed to kiss her. Go and see a lawyer, she said. A lawyer will surely write that letter for you. But that wouldn't be fair, he said; after all, she has been my wife for all these years. I'll write that letter tonight, he said. Do that, she said. It would be terrible if she would get that nice house sold now. Go home and write it. Then come back and say Yes. Yes or no. You know the outcome. If yes . . . if no . . . You know the rest.

Her mother was strong in everything she did. Britt-Mari could not match her strong willpower, which manifested itself already in simple things, such as lifting her eyes to the window. It would happen that her mother saw a giant trap closing up in the air outside her window, causing a strong wave of fear to run through her body. At other times it was as if hopefulness were opening an entrance into the air outside her window. Then her inner vision kept on wandering forcefully in that reality she so strongly willed. She bid good-bye to him with the same willpower as she welcomed him.

While all this was happening, she managed to prepare her vacation outfits. She sat at home, sewing every night. Altered and sewed a vast number of new garments. She worked tirelessly. As soon as the dinner dishes were cleared away, she set the light electric sewing machine, its installment payments still not fully paid off, on the kitchen table. After that its quick, irascible spin took over, pushed on under the pressure of excess vitality, its hum vibrating with hard, familiar pathos, stinging and healing at the same time; leap followed leap, hissing and stopping in an alternating rhythm.

Britt-Mari stood with her back turned. She did the dishes, she listened, unable to match her mother's strength as she conquered old, reluctant remnants, outwitted old seams. Her scissors annihilated the resistance of old-fashioned designs. Shreds of material jolted exhaustedly over the edge of the kitchen table down to the floor, gathering there in useless heaps. Other remnants were unexpectedly elevated to fill honored tasks.

Britt-Mari got the impression that nothing in this power struggle was taken seriously. It was all a game, a show of strength, and in her own way her mother actually enjoyed it greatly. The essential remained. Whatever would happen concerning his yes or no, her love remained. Never for a moment did her mother doubt the fact that she was loved and that she was in love. What was it she was fighting for? She fought for her trousseau. Just as she now fought with her old dresses. She wanted that her love should emerge with a certain kind of trousseau.

Was this the reason for which her willpower geared up to such forceful action?

Repetition became the order of the day. Fear and hope materialized in never-ending recapitulations, both feelings equal in their striking power. Neither one was able to get the better of the other. Alternating back and forth, neither one would dissolve just by hitting its lowest point. All it did was to collect new strength for another rise up to its highpoint. Neither hope nor fear could surpass that peak it had reached the very first time. Drawing their strength from the same source, neither one could establish predominance. Strength, this unfathomable, vigorous source, spanned the same heights for hope and fear alike, but gained in strength for itself in the course of it. It endured time, covered the sky with a compact cloudcover. Weakness had no chance except when there was an opportunity to slip through a crack of one kind or another. On those days weakness was heavenly, arriving like an exhausted bird forced down to take a rest before continuing its flight.

The process was strange to watch. It caused the moment to glow.

One moment the strong hands of the mother held up the garment, surveying the result with satisfaction as she held it at arm's length away from her. Then it fell down. Her arms drooped. Her body drooped. Her gaze drooped. Weakness became a burden that made her back cave in. Her heart beat in vain because space was empty and love gone.

I think I'm dying.

Her eyes stopped short. She squinted. Dizziness surrounded her. She bent over and pressed her arm over her stomach, then took some steps with feet that hurt because they distrusted the floor they stood on. She could find nothing solid and concrete. The world consisted of bodily pain. But where was her body? Life consisted of feelings. Where was their origin? Sitting on her chair, she moaned with a feeling of total abandon. She held her hair as if afraid of losing it, her arms knotting around her head. Her feet came off the floor as she pulled them up. She rocked on one vertebra, uttering small, naked shrieks. She looked terrible. An ugly sight, it was beautiful at the same time, like the process of giving birth.

Nothing in all this was weakness. Though she was close to the breaking point, she was full of strength still. Something came down and settled there. Her willpower could carry itself. Left was her weakness, frail enough to look for a hold. Her eyes no longer imprisoned, the mother looked around. In a flash she discovered Britt-Mari beside her. She smiled as she caught one of the child's open arms and hid her mouth in the fold of its elbow.

Darling, everything about you is lovable, she whispered, pulling the girl's arm under her chin and visibly enjoying its smooth skin and warmth.

Like the talking animals of fairy tales, she asked to be scratched, stroked and caressed.

I feel ever so miserable. Here, Cinnamoncandy. You understand that it's finished between him and me. That's it. No, don't move away. Just go on doing what you did. I've been an idiot. But now it's finished. Britt-Mari, blow over my forehead, blow across my eyelids. Never more. Do you hear me? No more. Oh, how lovely you are. Everything about you is lovable. Cinnamoncandy . . . learn from my example. Oh, blow, blow on my eyelids. If you can avoid any of the problems I've been through then I've not lived in vain. You learn from the mistakes of others. That's the way it goes. Keep on blowing and stroking with your arms while you're at it. It feels wonderful. I am worse than disgusting. I'm a ninny. Lift your arms, pump, up and down, up and down. I'm so stuck-up. Listen to the truth, Britt-Mari. I am the worst pleasure-seeker. Nothing else. Looking for pleasure. That's the whole secret. The pleasure-seeker. You don't even know the word. You are still too untarnished. And someone like that makes her demands, no less. Marriage. She wants a man who not only works so that she can have it easy. He has to work for her stylish security as well.

She giggled. Pushing away the girl's arms, she made room for her giggles, showing that her energy was still very much present underneath it all. Then she shifted and, not even wanting to carry her body, she leaned against the table. She put down her head, extended her upper torso and stretched her arms forward in her desire to rest against a stronghold that was different, different entirely from her indomitable strength. Her arms expressed her wish: this is another body, not I. And her head declared: this is something other than my exhausting vitality. This is a table. It's made for persons to rest on.

Britt-Mari went to the gas stove and put on water for tea. She picked up the half-finished dress from the floor and hung it over a chair. Some pins with red and yellow glass heads fascinated her because they looked like part of an animated color cartoon. Her imagination turned them into drumsticks, beating on a skin that was a wall, that was a door, that was an entrance to a heart.

Her mother lay across the table, gasping for breath as weak people do. An inert atmosphere surrounds the weak and the easiest thing in the world, breathing, becomes an effort. Their exhausted strength can hardly keep up the most necessary function of breathing. The tea water began simmering, its steam puffing up in the thin air.

It's clear, her mother said with one of those fleeting weak smiles that leave no imprint, her reaction a result of the reviving power of the hot tea. I've thought of it before. I am saying it now. We are both going on vacation, together. Two measly weeks. He won't have any vacation this year, he's too new. With him around I won't have any vacation at all. Where are we going? You and I. The both of us together. Say something. Make a wish so that I may know.

Britt-Mari tried to think of something.

It has to be cheap, her mother warned.

Let's go to an island; the words escaped Britt-Mari's mouth.

A little island and little money. That should go well together. Water all around. The sea. And the sky above. Everything in blue. Warm and blue and friendly.

A boathouse that's no longer in use. That should be cheap. No window, no fireplace.

What good is a window when you're outside all day long anyway swimming and laid out in the sun.

And eating. Prepare food in a cleft over an open fire.

Great. Grilled fish is the best there is. Chimney-sweep. God, yummy-yum-yum. Come to think of it, I don't envy people who have an electric stove, you know. Never to see fire. Not even the flame of a gas stove.

Boathouses are beautiful.

Yes, they are, with shingled roof and grey timber. Smelling tar and nets and freshness. And think . . . before going to sleep you can lie and listen to the water gurgling against the poles. It gurgles even under the planed flooring you lie on.

And if the door faces west . . .

Britt-Mari saw that her mother's cup was empty. She got up to fill it.

There was a knock at the door. The mother knew immediately who was knocking outside. It was a Thursday evening that he knocked at the door. Without transition she turned strong, as quickly and invisibly as the sound reached the ear. Suddenly she was permeated with vitality, feeling so strong that she did not even care what she looked like. She got up, went to the door and opened it. Britt-Mari could hear the man's voice like a soft murmur, but could not make out his words. Not that he had the time to say much. The mother interrupted him.

Tell me yes or no. You know what I said. Yes or no.

The male voice took over as monotonous as a fan.

Yes or no, the mother cut in.

"Unreasonable," "pain," "enjoys," "inexcusable," "easier to die," "sale," "price," "put off," "sick," "angel." Britt-Mari could make out these and a few other words in the monotonously mumbling rhythm between the two. Then her mother cut it off decisively. She closed the door and turned the key.

What time is it? . . . She returned with a springy gait and strong arms.

Seven minutes before eight, she said with satisfaction. Let's see. . . . She stopped and stroked her hips with strong hands.

Actually, what did we do with that yellow material? She took the halfway finished dress and held it up against her body, lifting her knee to better see it hang.

Not so bad, she said. I'm going to wear it. You must help me, Britt.

Pinning the length of the skirt was a commission of trust for Britt-Mari. She got the T-square from its place in the closet while her mother struggled out of her dress and pulled the half-finished garment carefully over her head. To make it easier for Britt-Mari, she climbed on a chair and from there on the table. The proper length she had already marked with chalk. Now it was Britt-Mari's job to pin the correct length all around with the help of the T-square. Britt-Mari remembered how proud she was the first time her mother had asked for her help, but so afraid of not doing it right. Time and again she returned to check the earlier pins to compare the overall length at the chalk line. What a disgrace if the skirt had been uneven somewhere along the hemline afterward.

By now she was more self-confident. Even though, she was still extremely careful and never set a pin before having checked the last pin set in the material.

You don't need to set the pins so close together, her mother said, turning slightly to correspond with how far Britt-Mari had come. Taking her task too seriously, Britt-Mari tended to use more pins than necessary. She looked up to her mother who tried to look casual, but the effect was about as casual as that of a window dummy or a mannequin on parade.

There was another knock at the door.

Just ignore him, her mother said, standing strong in her summit. Really, she said. Is he stupid too? How can he think of getting anywhere, behaving like this?

She ordered Britt-Mari to finish her job. Although convinced that everything was going wrong, Britt-Mari continued. She could see it. Her pins were curving in a windswept line, she thought, not taking into account that the material was never even all the way around. There was never a parallel line between the pins and the skirt's edge.

After a short pause the man started knocking again. Britt-Mari glanced up at her mother and found that the knocks failed to make the least impression.

This is Stellan, the man called softly.

Britt-Mari was surprised. It seemed unbelievable that "his" name was Stellan. She had imagined a much darker name, or one more colorful. Perhaps one with more syllables, commanding admiration, or related to sports.

His name is Stellan, she announced upward, hardly able to digest her amazement.

I have to prevent him from unlawful breaking and entering, that's committing a crime, her mother said and climbed off the table. It's almost 8:30 P.M., she mumbled, looking as if she were computing something in her head . . .

The skirt never got finished that night.

Sylvia, listen to me, the man called through the door. Sylvia, I need to talk to you.

Sometimes a guy feels no shame at all, her mother said to Britt-Mari. Then again there are times when he acts like the princess on the pea. Oh, how terribly scrupulous he is then.

Sylvia, you have to come out, the man called.

Don't be insolent, the mother yelled through the door. But she got herself ready and was even prepared to repeat her argument with him.

Sylvia, open up!

Calm down, she called. I'm coming.

She had nothing new to tell him. She would not budge. She could only reenforce her demands and toughen up, so as to get him going a little faster.—She put a dress on and fixed her hair. The man thought that she took too long. There was another knock.

Yes or no?

He turned quiet, but this competition in strength only stimulated the mother. No new words and thoughts were necessary. She needed strength, and it was pouring forth. She was ready for a debate. Her willpower would give her the pertinent eloquence necessary to drown his cowardice and arouse his courage. She opened the door slightly.

Yes or no?

He grabbed her hands and pulled her outside. She let it happen and pushed the door shut with her hips. They stood whispering outside the door for a long time. Britt-Mari sat down and stared in the opposite direction. Then it turned quiet. She tiptoed to the door and put her ear against it, but still could not hear anything. Carefully she opened the door. Not finding anyone outside, she tiptoed to the stairs. Now she could hear them again. They were standing further down the stairs, talking with low and intense voices that hardly sounded human. Britt-Mari tried to make out what they were saying. She worked her hands to get a similarity, but she could not. Her hands were too cool and fine-limbed, unsuited for caricatures. They were good for building up the configurations of pain, evil and anger, but not this, not these abstractly hot, abstractly hoary, abstractly intimate and abstractly hostile vibrations. What talked down there was a mixture of steel and meat, a combination of machine and animal, a blend of gasoline and blood.

They continued further down the stairs and Britt-Mari followed them. When she got outside, she saw them walking across Allén in the direction of the church, silently and stiffly, with long steps, a gap between them. Her mother led on. They climbed the corner steps leading up to the church, one on either side of the iron hand-rail in the center. Taking the lead, her mother chose the nearest path and he followed her up the slope to where the lindens stood, their dense, luxuriant, leafy crowns forming a roof that created a constant, greenish twilight underneath.

Grepp, Grepp . . . Britt-Mari called into the yard. Presently the caretaker's dog came running. His tail swept the ground in front of her feet and his nose pressed wet spots on her bare knees. Grepp kept her company to Kyrkogatan, the street where he found an old-fashioned streetlight, originally lit with gas, though now it had an electric bulb. Because it was June and the time just 9:00 P.M. it was yet unlit. Behind the church and the school the sky stood close and mighty. No building was taller here than either one, and space abounded around them, free and wide. Whereas mere air surrounded other buildings, heaven reigned around these two.

Grepp and Britt-Mari played around the beautiful streetlight. She never tired of casting an admiring look at the cemetery's high, wide main staircase. Grepp never tired of her hands and the way their signs guided his movements. Her mother and he whose name was Stellan never tired of each other or their debate as they continued circling the church building. Britt-Mari watched them walk past the grand staircase five times. The second time around they were al-ready walking arm in arm. But when her mother came home, she told Britt-Mari,

I didn't give in. He had to.

19

Her own tenacity slammed shut on her when hope died. The power struggle was no longer between her and the man, but solely within herself. Her eyes met neither disintegration nor fulfillment in the air just outside her window when she looked out. They met a barrier. There was no road to her any longer, and no one could break her strong barrier down. An iron blind stretched in front of the window, and before the door stood an iron gate that sent shockwaves with every touch. His roads to her were blocked. It was her own fault; she herself obstructed the roads for him. Her damned tenacity had run rampant. Caught in her own cocoon, she had no strength left to break free.

Watching, Britt-Mari interpreted the rigid, harsh power in the grip of her mother's hand as it encased her eyes in darkness and forced her mind, the most agile of all, to stand still. She tortured herself; her thumb and pointer pressed into her eye sockets with such force that all of pain's discolorations came to burn forth in what is most sensitive. Her hands rose and pushed an iron crown into her hair. Torment throbbed out of her mouth.

So began her wandering through the narrow cell she had built around herself with her own vitality. The power of her hand had turned the key, which disintegrated in the intense heat. The key, rendered worthless, was the lump that scorned her. She could not get out. Nothing existed beside her imprisonment. Nothing mattered. She kept pacing back and forth.

It was never like this last winter. Then it was not her own energy, but another's deceit that had engulfed her. Someone else's raw power had clubbed her down. Exhausted from the fight, she was too weak to gather enough strength to get out of bed. Even the pale winter sun became too strong for her eyes. She had fought and lost and nothing is more wretched than a hero in his first total defeat. The antagonist, stronger, more cunning, less conscientious and younger, left his indelible mark that renders him forever present. Especially at night imagination revives him and the miserable heart can do nothing but suffer the agony. Britt-Mari became aware of it when, in the middle of the night, she would hear the thrashing body in vain trying to escape from itself. She would rush over and try with her arms to constrain the invisibly present enemy.

The girl saw the difference between then and now in the way her mother's hair looked. Last winter her hair was dry, straggly and sticky with perspiration. Its sheen gave way to a dull grey that slowly spread over it. When finally permitted to wash the hair, Britt-Mari did it with a feeling of relief. After that she toweled it dry so thoroughly that every strand breathed again and brushed it until its former brilliance returned.

Now that hair was lifeless and scrubby. Its sheen was gone again, but the hair turned blacker than ever. Left without the nourishment it received during happier times, it became an ugly, naked, pitch-dark, greaseless black with static strands that tended to separate.

At first Britt-Mari was unaware of what was going on and when she finally noticed, it struck her with surprise. She had a feeling of seeing it happen right under her discerning eyes. By now the poor condition of the hair was conspicuous. The girl was happy. She knew the remedy.

I'm going to wash your hair, Mommy. It's terrible the way it looks. Oil, lots of oil . . .

The mother stopped her pacing, eyeing Britt-Mari without interest. The girl was busy hemming one of her mother's altered skirts. Her hand rested on the nougat-brown fabric, her needle between her fingers. Not more than a few centimeters were left of the thread she had threaded.

Just go on with what you're doing now, the mother said.

But you look a fright, Mommy. Just look in the mirror, you'll see. It must be weeks . . .

So what? It doesn't matter anyway.

I happen to know that you like to have your hair washed. Makes you feel like a new person. You told me so yourself many times.

You're talking nonsense.

Let me do it and you'll see.

I really don't feel like it tonight.

Tonight would be a great time.

And you think . . .

The mother resumed her pacing. Britt-Mari continued her sewing. Her eyelids, pale pink like rose petals, slid down. Her light-red eyelashes were too short and hardly visible, much to her chagrin. Last fall she bought the various ingredients at the drugstore for a miracle recipe her mother had found. She remembered with happiness the good time she and her mother had mixing the various ointments and drops, her excitement every morning when waking up and checking in the mirror the effect of the hidden power that was supposed to darken her eyelashes and make them grow. But then the day came when her mother suffered this betrayal. After that her own longing to be a knock-out with filmstar eyelashes waned.

The jar was still there, but the cream smelled rancid. Even though her desire had returned, she refrained from acting on it. Every time she unscrewed the lid a sense of lurking danger overcame her and then she quickly put it away. This goo should never be allowed to start a new round of grief.

When Britt-Mari finished the rest of her thread, she put the skirt away, resolved to go through with that hairwash. She knew a trick that would make her mother do what she wanted. This was not the first time she simply ignored her mother's refusal and prepared openly everything she needed. Without saying anything, she boiled lots of water and took out washbasin and towels, including two of terry cloth, one large and one small. The shampoo bottle was still halfway full, and there was enough oil in the cupboard. She poured a cup of oil in a saucepan and heated it.

The mother did not seem to notice the girl's preparations. She continued her pacing, back and forth, locked in her own tenacity.

It's ready, Mommy.

Her mother looked up. She shrugged her shoulders to show her indifference, but voiced no objections. Improving the looks of her hair would not improve her predicament. Of course, it would not worsen it either. Britt-Mari accepted her victory with a humble smile.

Britt-Mari was full of trust and confidence. Washing her hair had cured her mother's distress many times before. There was something soothing about the very act. It drove the soreness away, step by step, though it was hard to tell which one of the steps was the most efficient: rubbing in the warm oil, the deep massage, the hot, steaming towels or lathering in the shampoo. At any rate, with the first rinse a slight improvement was undeniable. Then, already beyond the turning point, the process of recuperation visibly intensified. By the last rinse, containing much more cold than warm water, it was obvious that the cleansing act was on its way to completion.

Britt-Mari allowed vitality plenty of time to regenerate. She enjoyed working at different speeds and did everything with reverent hands. Overcome with a ceremonial solemnity, she started pouring the oil. After that her resilient fingertips massaged the scalp with rotating movements; then her supple, intense palms took over. She tried hard to be quick with the towels, dipping them in hot water and then wringing out the excess. The steam rose up her arms right into her face. Inhaling the mist, she could feel vitality at work. Quickly she wrapped the towel around her mother's head and pressed hard with her palms.

Repeat with the oil . . .

One of the highpoints in the alternating tasks her hands performed was to have the water rinse the hair absolutely clean. The water was literally drawn out of the hair to make each hairstrand as sleek as silk. Though she did not know it, the quality of the hair was such that it could shed water without losing its supple smoothness. The hair looked so light as it floated in the second rinsewater and felt ever so soft and pliable when Britt-Mari took it up in her hands. Water droplets rippled down and bounced off its blackness. Pulling a strand of hair through her fingers, she heard it whistle like a grassblade, as glossy and darkgreen as a laurel leaf.

To be sure, something happened to her mother during this careful treatment. When all was done, it was clear that her enclosure was broken. But the result was different from what Britt-Mari had expected. The large, white terry cloth towel folded double around her head, its sides draping over her shoulders like the veil of a nun, her mother broke into a fit of anger. It was anger hurled at the world outside her. It was not turned inside, against herself.

I could kill her!

These words were the beginning of her outburst. Pushing Britt-Mari's hands aside, she got to her feet, took a few steps, then stiffened up. She repeated the same sentence with the same violence, her voice blazing. Fueled with anger, her hate broke forth without touching her. Even though Britt-Mari knew who was meant, she asked,

Whom do you mean?

His wife, of course. Who else?

What has she done?

What has she done? No one can tell me that she's innocent. She's full of tricks.

Have you heard anything special?

Heard and heard. She keeps him back. She's more than just a trifle shameless, that one. She keeps her claws on him and won't let him go. I could kill her. Strangle her with my bare hands. That woman is disgusting.

Britt-Mari tried to think, but there was no time for that. Her mother's words came rushing out.

If she were dependent on him economically, if they had children together, then I would at least try and understand, perhaps not even say anything. As it is, she is independent financially, and there are no children. She's a vampire, a poisonous spider.

But what about him? Can't he . . .

She's spoiled him. With her he's a weakling, a jellyfish. That's her doing. It's downright criminal. To bind a healthy, strong fellow to herself in a way like this, that's more than criminal, there's no excuse. He feels sorry for her. Oh, my, my, my! So pitiful. It's so difficult for her, poor thing. That someone so nice and kind has to be so ill. Oh, my, my, my!

Is she ill?

Yes, she is.

Very?

It's as bad as can be.

Fatal?

Worse than that.

Her mother turned aside, though hardly in consideration of Britt-Mari, not even of herself. Anger was in command. On occasions like these, the daughter showed a maturity far beyond her age. The mother would talk to herself and the entire world at the same time. With a smile of scornful superiority, she now let out the fact,

Female disorders.

The entire scope of this information was beyond Britt-Mari's understanding. She kept staring at her mother's cruel smile directed at the window. But the smile soon faded under the impact of loathing and anger that pasted a dirty plaster across her lips. Her mother felt deeply hurt. Her mouth bled with wrongs suffered, and anger nailed shut the origin of her suffering.

It's pure meanness. That woman is as slippery and poisonous as a snake. Listen to this! He's allowed to have mistresses. She doesn't care. He may have a dozen, as far as she's concerned. But when the game turns serious, then she spouts venom and poisons everything as much as she possibly can. And then he hobbles back to her, his heels stung. He can't see that he ought to be pitied. Not she. These witches who build their power around their female organs don't deserve it. They always manage, and in a way that always makes it the man's fault. It's his fault that she's sick . . . and it's terrible to watch him put up this boyish expression when thinking of her and himself. She's inhuman, he should say. I'll suffer the dire consequences if I don't leave her, he should say. Instead he tells me, She's been so darned understanding. Another woman would hardly have accepted these habits of mine so easily. But the way she looks at me almost makes me feel honest in spite of it all. Can you believe that he's a grown man when you hear such mush?

Have you ever met her?

No. But I'm going to. Meet her face to face.

What are you going to do?

I don't know yet, but I'll have to think of something. I'll have to see her. I'll have to talk sense with her. I've kept my peace far too long already. Something needs to be done.

You're not going to travel there?

Well. Well, yes, I'm going to. Even if it has to be on Midsummer Eve. I'll go there.

You mustn't, Mommy.

I have to serve her the truth. I've got to. Pour back all the venom she's dished out.

You mustn't.

Oh, mustn't I! Is she the only one who'll have and have and have all her life, is it? I'll show her that it's my turn now to be allowed to have, to take, to fight, and to lie . . .

Calm down, Mommy.

I'm not going to calm down now. I'm going to put a stop to her tricks. And it has to be now.

Calm yourself, Mommy.

I could murder her.

Mommy!

Britt-Mari rushed over and pressed herself into her arms. Her mother's face was too real, too close to murder, the brutality of what her words expressed clearly evident in it.

Listen to me, Britt-Mari whined. Listen to me.

But, caught in her anger, her mother ignored her.

You must not kill that terrible woman. She's not worth it. Listen to me, Mommy. It's better to suffer. It's better to go under. So much can happen still. Listen, Mommy! Sometimes you see things in an entirely different light.

For goodness sakes, let go of my arms, the mother said. What's the issue? Let go. What's come over you, girl?

Britt-Mari let go. She was crying.

You're not listening to what I'm saying, Mom.

What's that you want me to hear now?

I'm so afraid.

What is it you're afraid of?

I could see that you can really do it.

What can I do?

I saw it in your face. You can do it.

What's that you're talking about, tell me?

You mustn't murder her.

You're crazy! Do you really believe . . .

The mother took hold of Britt-Mari's head, pulled her ponytail and forced her face upward.

Did you think that I meant it, literally?

Britt-Mari nodded. Her mother became angry in her ordinary way. She pulled her towel off and threw it down.

So very much like you! Just like your Dad. Head against the wall. All according to the letter. Just one way. Only one direction exists. Fish is Baltic herring. Pike is not fish. Meat is pork. Kidney is not meat. He was that way and you are too. Good Lord . . .

Britt-Mari was dumbfounded. Goosepimples covered her arms.

I'm going to give that woman a lesson. She truly needs it, and it's about time. It's going to be she, not I who's going to get the boot. Mark me.

Her mother pulled out her hairbrush. For the next fifteen minutes she either stood or sat with the soft body bend of a woman brushing her hair. Britt-Mari watched from her bed, her legs pulled up. She realized the coming turn of events when her mother took out her nice outfit. She would go to him, Stellan. Perhaps she might first go to the public telephone and announce her coming. He lived in a rented room. If he happened to be at home . . .

I do hope that you won't keep yourself awake, the mother said before she left. I don't know how late I'm going to be. In any case, it's silly for you to stay awake.

Thus prepared, she was ready for the stormy return. The mother discovered that during their power struggle she had disarmed neither him nor herself, nor lessened their love. Both had collected firewood for the fire that now flared up. Already the following morning Britt-Mari came to understand how well everything had gone and how superfluous she had become during the night. She, her feelings, her cares. Her mother needed not her worries, her views, her watchfulness. The danger was warded off this time around. Danger threatened Britt-Mari instead. She had to get away from the heat. Her mother was burning. Her mother's heat singed Britt-Mari already from afar.

20

Her teeth were chattering and that awakened her. She could feel her shoulders shaking and a tugging in her neck. Painful, it was yet without horror.

Something glorious was approaching her. A window stood open within the warm darkness. Something unearthly was flowing down, transposing the night.

Her body answered as well as it could in its insufficiency. A muted music of desire, a quivering trembling of her heart, an inner light filled with expectation.

The painful surface layer of quivering cold and agitation was the outer edge of the condition that had to be overcome, the last remnant of the all too familiar, the last dust that needed to be shed.

The glorious was near the point where it could be touched to effect her change. She felt a whiff of sheer fragrance. It was delightful to feel surprise waning and with it the lesson, whose profile consisted of easily explained and safe security.

It no longer existed.

Darkness was alive. Her mouth closed. The rumbling of her teeth behind her closed lips faded away and a soothing sensation spread across her neck. Something in the darkness smoothed her shivers. Her body lay absolutely still.

Her heart opened up and it contained nothing but the worship of the glorious that stood so near and shaped her into something whose form was readiness.

Something great was about to happen. Now she remembered. She was not afraid. She had bridged the chasm. Her readiness lit up that which was to come just as the moon's lightwaves light up the dark.

This had happened to her once before.

She would recall the experience, though not all of it. That was impossible. Only some. Surely not the most important things. But something for sure. The pure happiness that permeated her. The bliss of which she became a part. Her body that was borne aloft in such a strange way.

Her neck came first, then her shoulders rose up, and after that her entire back. Her body's weight disintegrated. She was lifted up from her crown all the way down to her heels. Only her heels remained.

Her body was floating free in the air.

It happened very quietly. She felt a gentle lift. Her blanket followed along, hanging down on both sides. But her hands did not hang down, even though she did not fold them. They were lying on top of the blanket, weightless.

When her body stopped, her head was perhaps one meter above the pillow.

She remained in this position, she did not know for how long. Pure happiness does not count in seconds. Bliss does not run through an hourglass.

She perceived.

She cannot remember how she returned to normal. She seems to have slept through the return. She felt dizzy at one point. It was as if someone with lightning speed was pulling out a spiral that was wrapped around her heart.

But her heels hurt. She touched them in the morning before stepping into her sandals. She smiled. Her heels hurt.

21

Of all the burdens, time is and remains the greatest burden throughout the ages of earth. Mountains crumble and the mighty rivers dry up. All the bodies weighing down the earth disintegrate into merest dust. But every moment is a stepping-stone on which man devastates his glorious strength.

Britt-Mari has no other reality than the one that exists underneath every moment's invisibly hard surface, whose sole conciliatory feature is that it can only reflect, if it reflects, her past life.

With closed eyes she lets memory restore the dead hours to a visionary life so that she may feel as rich as a fertile landscape whose soil bears many kinds of fruit. But she has iced over from want. The creature she finds in the picture is she herself, the way she was in the past. Who is she now? Can these two be the same person?

Turning toward the future, she can hear her opportunities murmur like a thickly populated city, and she heaves herself eagerly up on the stepping-stones so that she may ultimately reach the hour that presents her with the right harvest. This stepping-up testing continues until she is eventually crushed and the invisible shows a gravestone.

But what blissful lightheartedness awaits man when at some time during his slave-life time's pull relents!

Beholding this lithe flame that is love enables her to test that which on earth is the most burdensome. Weighed down by the burden of time, she feels the stepping-stone's true weight pressing against her, and she begs and pleads to be spared seeing it in its nakedness.

Passion, this famous sensation, only haunts those best endowed, it is said—those who are in possession of the brightest weapons. Passion haunts her too. She tries to escape. Yes, she would love to escape its grip. If she but had some shiny weapon, but she has none. All she can do is to raise stepping-stones, and she has raised the stepping-stones with her bare hands for a devastatingly long time.

She begs and prays to be spared. She tries to escape. She has the nagging suspicion that she lives in a world of her own imagination. Perhaps pure, unadulterated childhood is still a part of her. If so, she wants to experience it. Simple reality should exist somewhere here. And she ought to be able to find it.

She begins to look for it.

All summer long she keeps looking for a friendly shadow. But the people are burning under the July sun, all burning, mostly the adults, her mother most of all. Wherever she looks she finds only people in flames.

22

One night she began sleepwalking. She walked over to her mother's room and took the red fabric that every week-day morning transformed into a turban around some black hair.

She returned to the kitchen, went to the desk and pulled out one of its two drawers, the lower drawer, hers. In that drawer she kept a light yellow box with two red-lacquer roses and two green leaves. The key to the box was in her little girl's handbag she hardly used nowadays. She took the key, unlocked the box and crumpled the material down in it.

The box contained her various mementos. Stolen mementos. Love mementos. Veneration mementos. Worthless items, all stolen compulsively out of veneration or love.

The last time she had opened this box it was to put in a tin coffee spoon, stolen from the old couple who were returning from a fishing trip and who told her about the power of mother's milk on fires started by lightning and the time when the old woman used to carry her head high above all reproach.

Britt-Mari locked the box and returned the key to her handbag. She did not forget to push back the desk drawer. After that she returned to her bed and went back to sleep.

23

One day she overheard some people talking about someone who had become a shadow of herself. Her curiosity aroused, she stepped closer, careful not to disrupt the conversation, but to hear as much as possible.

Two women were talking in the portal. Britt-Mari happened to be there for the shade it provided, because of her personal problems, and because iron bars feel cool even in the heat of summer. Leisurely she observed passersby who had a set goal, because also those who want to escape need to choose the direction they want to take. So far Britt-Mari had not found a way that would lead her away from the fire of adults. These last few days, more than ever before, she was outside, on the streets, down by the harbor, on the docks along the river, in the public parks. She listened to many conversations and looked at many faces, hoping that the experience of others might show her a way out. So far it was all in vain. She was standing in the gateway, depressed.

A tall iron gate led into the backyard and the custodian locked it every evening. The poles on its sides were shaped like halberds, their tips pointing at the rounded arch. As a rule, one side of the gate stood slightly ajar, a rod, anchored in the wall, holding it in place to bar unlawful entrance. The children in the building used it to turn somersaults. Britt-Mari remembered the time when she had done it.

Grepp lay in the portal, panting, his jaws open and his tongue slobbily rolling back and forth. Off and on he gave a jerk and licked up his drooling saliva and then his ribcage, pumping hard otherwise, stopped moving.

She doesn't have much time left, one woman said. Britt-Mari knew her because she lived in the building. About half a year, the doctor thinks.

And she still goes on as if nothing had happened. How can she?

Gosh, she believes in God. It's not a big deal for someone who believes that Paradise beckons the minute one lies down and dies.

Any way you look at it, death is death, after all.

I think that cancer is terrible. That doctors should be so power-less with that sickness! Considering that they've gotten so far with so many others.

I went in to get some buttons. And she sure looks like she's dying. Just terrible; I don't know how to describe it. Her face was full of dark spots, like shadows, I thought. But that was from inside, at least I got that impression. Sort of like beautiful apples that are rotten inside, you know.

Britt-Mari understood that they were talking about the woman in the fabric store and pulled back into the cool shade of the portal. Without transition, the women went busily on discussing different matters, such as the impending navy visit. According to the paper, smaller units of the royal navy were coming to town. Well, that'll get the local girls going, said one woman. Yeah, all the teenagers will be on their feet, said the other. Yep, and a lot of screwing here and there. Mostly there, they agreed.

A tiny flicker of hope shot through Britt-Mari, a feeling closely related to curiosity, a strange curiosity similar to longing. She had never before seen a "deathdoomed" person. Now she knew that she had. It was not so long ago that she had been in this fabric store, but without noticing anything special. Of course, she was more concerned with her purchase and had not looked so carefully, she reflected. She hesitated and then decided to go there.

It was an old store, still looking the way it had looked before all the world wars. Perhaps the store was older than the woman, and she was already very old and had white hair. The store was without one of those modern store windows, one that was large and wide and reached almost down to the sidewalk. Here, if one wanted to, one could put his elbows on the window ledge and look in, though one could not see the customers inside because of all the merchandise hanging in the window, a sweater, a blouse, or a smock, some-times even an embroidered tablecloth, or a runner with Santa Clauses and Christmas trees, or else with Easter bunnies and Easter eggs. Opening or closing the front door started a bell ringing over one's head. It was usually so dark inside that fussy women went to check the yarns and threads by the open door in the daylight to see their true colors before buying them for their projects.

Britt-Mari stopped outside. Looking inside the store window, she tried to peek past the sweater, today a blue-white knit. She looked up at the store sign of metal that went from the door all the way across the window. It had several rust stains and it buckled away from the wall, but that was on purpose because it was nailed fast that way.

Britt-Mari knew that a pair of doves had built their nest between the sign and the wall. She used to watch them climb through the opening on the right and see them standing absolutely still in the crack. Once, when she was nine years old, she had seen a baby dove fall to the sidewalk, unable to fly back. Britt-Mari watched it crawl up to the side of the house, shaking with fear. She knew that grown-ups rarely liked doves; they sound terrible and make everything dirty. But even though this was a dove, the woman in the store came with a ladder and a boy climbed up and put the baby bird back in its nest.

All these memories ran through Britt-Mari's mind while she stood outside the store, undecided, looking. She wanted the door to open and give her a chance to see whether there was a customer inside, hoping that there was none because she preferred to be alone with the woman, at least to start with. Luckily, it was not long before the door opened. The bell tinkled and an old woman came out, her shopping bag bulging with packages. Seemingly the kind that is afraid of having forgotten something, she stopped and rummaged among her packages. That's when she dropped one, though without noticing it. Britt-Mari saw it and wanted to go and pick it up.

She never made it. Bitterness about her harsh fate suddenly overcame her, making her body slowly turn stiff and rigid. People were burning, people fired up their lives, unafraid of the heat. Britt-Mari became afraid. Her body was hard and numb. Her life had come to a halt because she did not dare, because she thought that it was not proper for her to dare. She had nothing to dare with. All she could do was wait.

The round package remained lying on the sidewalk behind the woman's feet as she shuffled away.

Britt-Mari turned her attention to the fabric store window, waiting. Nothing happened with her. She turned to see whether the package was still lying on the sidewalk. It was thin, round and grey, tied with a flat string advertising the store. Presumably it contained some fabric. Perhaps for a girl's dress, perhaps for a blouse.

Nothing was happening with her. She watched the woman disappear around the corner in the distance.

To enter the store and see the old woman became meaningless. She had no business in there. What was she to do, feeling, as she did, that she had to get away from people?

Grepp had followed her. He was a sorry sight with his wrinkly forehead, his melancholy blazing eyes and the dribbling tongue flopping about.

You and I, we'll find something that suits us, Britt-Mari whispered and she suddenly bent down to grab his ears. We have to live in style. Both you and I love style. What shall we do? I know. We'll go and drink the world's best water there is. Not from the faucet. Oh, no. Not even from the well at the Sandsbergska farm. There's water better than even theirs. Are you coming along to the creek that flows past the hydro-electric power station?

Grepp did. They followed the brook deep into the woods. Britt-Mari drank at twelve different places. She insisted on the figure twelve and tried to make Grepp understand the importance of that figure. Even if it could be no more than one gulp. Even if it was just a few drops on Grepp's tongue.

She took different positions when she drank and tried to vary them each time. Sometimes she lay prone and stuck her mouth into the water; that was the most peaceful. She could lie there for a while and enjoy the coolness of the damp earth and of the water as it rushed closely under her face. Other times she squatted down and scooped the water up in her hands. Grepp waded for long stretches up the brook. Britt-Mari took off her sandals and stalked around in the water, carefully avoiding the many stones. After that she walked barefoot, following the path next to the brook and remembering that one summer she had gone barefoot every day except on Sundays. That was when she was a child, a little girl still.

The brook scuttled through terrain that made it easy for Britt-Mari to vary her positions, and she refrained from repeating them. The most fun was to stand in the middle of the brook, bent forward and trying to catch the water that came spurting through the crack between two closely-set stones, the fine spray rising and falling without any definite pattern, which made it impossible for her to know beforehand where to hold her mouth. At one time the spray jolted against her teeth, and she felt with delight its cool purity spreading over her teeth. They felt lovely for quite a while afterwards.

For hours they roamed through the woods on top of the mountain. She learned to distinguish between the various degrees of shadows. She sat in the leaf-scented shadows of trees and the dry shadows of cliffs; the crevices' cool deep with their drifting acidy odors; the coquettish web of sparse foliage and the veils of wide trails that made their mark on her as she impressed hers upon them while wandering forth; the shadowy stillness of plaited lacework on the footpaths; and the green-blue darkness in the fonts of dense leafy groves.

She tried not to detach the city and the people from her thoughts. But that would not work. She had her back turned. All her undertakings and bright ideas were ceremonies carried out with her back turned to the city and the people.

24

I'm home, the mother called as soon as she entered the door. She sounded false and her enthusiasm a sham. It was apparent in everything she did that she had been contemplating Britt-Mari's reaction and expected a few unpleasant moments. To have as few as possible, she tried her hardest to shine and overwhelm.

Britt-Mari was still in bed. Listening to and watching her mother, she was happy about one thing. She had not given in to the temptation of letting the orderliness in the kitchen go. The dishes were done, the floor mopped, and the place dusted every day just as if her mother had been at home and everything was as it used to be. She was especially proud of having exchanged the dirty dishcloth for a clean one just the day before. There were freshly gathered flowers in the bowl on the table.

Her mother had not been home for five days and nights. She was at Stellan's place, eating, sleeping and living with him. They were lucky. The family where he rented was away on vacation and they were alone in the apartment. It was really to their advantage that Stellan did not have any vacation this year, the mother said. She could rest at her leisure. And if someone needed to rest, it was she, she said. She took her beauty sleep every day and had finally the time to spend on the care her body needed so badly. There was a bathroom in the apartment where Stellan rented. Everything modern. Her mother had never lived in a modern apartment and found it enviable to have all the conveniences. You can't believe how much easier your work gets, she said. And just think of winter. You needn't light any fire. No chimney smoke or gas smell. The electric stove is wonderful. Hygienic and safe. And there's hot water always, as much as you want and need.

I sleep, she repeated. I don't do anything but sleep. Time and again I wake up, hardly believing that it's true. I can fall back asleep and can stay asleep as long as I want. And stay in bed, lazing. And lie in the bathtub as long as I want. You can't believe how wonderful life can be. Water, sleep, food and . . .

She giggled, pulling her body backward as if someone quite unexpectedly had caressed her very gently. Then she smiled her beautiful smile, straightened up, her hands against the table, and everything was well. She was here to get clean underwear, had not taken along enough of one thing and another. Suddenly she needed to display her presence and make an exhibition of the luck that had come her way. It was not a discreet, well-modulated disclosure. Britt-Mari squirmed, well aware that her mother's unnatural behavior was her fault.

Her mother came over and stood next to her bed.

You aren't bored these days?

Oh.

You don't look too happy.

I'm happy if you are.

If? If I'm happy! You can well see that I am. You know what I'm thinking right now? That we should think of some fun. You and I together. Go swimming, for example. We could go to the public beach today. Take the bus and lie on the beach for a few hours. What do you say?

Don't worry about me, Mom. You know that I like to be alone.

I know that, though I've never liked it. I could never get it into my head that it's good at your age.

Are you going to start that again now? I know how much you need your vacation.

But I haven't planned anything. I'm just lazing around. All day long. Go out and buy some food and have it ready before Stellan comes home. That's all. Of course, the days go fast. That's how it goes, always. When one's really happy for once, time flies far too quickly.

That's true.

Not long before I'll be in the harness again, and then . . .

Is it going to be the way you want it to be, Mommy?

Her mother laughed. She started pacing back and forth, displaying her well-rested body, her elegant bearing, her smiling self-assurance, her comfort in existing. She wore a lemon-yellow dress with white appliqué and a daring, wedge-shaped neckline. Suddenly she remembered something and, lifting one leg, she showed her new shoes. A present from Stellan. Never before had she worn such elegant shoes, she said. Real crocodile. What do you say?

You are beautiful.

Britt-Mari knew that lemon-yellow was one of the most difficult colors. Not many can wear it without looking drab. Fat women look fatter. Pale women look anemic. But her mother looked even lovelier and younger in yellow, more resilient and dignified.

That's all you see?

I can surely see that you're happy, Mommy.

Finally, it comes out.

Oh, I do hope . . .

What?

That everything is going to go your way.

Good Lord, girl. You look real sad.

That's not true. It can't be true.

I have eyes. I can see.

Then you shouldn't worry about me. You know how I am.

Her mother sat down on the chair beside Britt-Mari's bed. She was about to say something, but then it was as if a hand were stroking across her face, eliminating all seriousness and replacing it with a dreamy expression. It was nothing enormous that moved, no brilliant, inconceivable happiness. Rather, it was a quiet longing, a picture of simple serenity. Britt-Mari guessed that she was thinking of him, Stellan, who had no vacation and whose Sunday trip to his wife she had managed to undercut. No longer did she demand of him to get a divorce. She no longer mentioned it out loud. She considered other expedients. It was a triumph for her that he had not visited his wife last Sunday. She provided the proper excuse. That he had to work on Sunday. Production was down at the plant during vacation. Instead the machines were to be overhauled. And several lesser improvements, yes, even some new installations, and he was busy with this type of thing at the moment.

Do you have an idea where my red scarf could have disappeared?

Britt-Mari was surprised that her mother took up the subject again. She thought that her mother was dreaming of the future.

I haven't found it, she answered, though I've looked everywhere several times.

Strange. I don't usually lose things.

Well, it has happened. Do you remember those brown gloves?

Gloves, yes. But a scarf that is worn around your head. No, I can't imagine that I should've lost it. If I had worn it around my neck, then perhaps . . .

Her mother bent slightly forward and looked Britt-Mari straight in her eyes. Suddenly she smiled a quick, shrewd smile.

He likes children. Actually he would very much like to have his own child. And why shouldn't he get one?

Britt-Mari saw a disfiguring expression in her mother's face as she slowly turned her profile. Something sharp and calculating spread over the corners of her mouth and eyes. A little groove, indicating calculation, stratagem, cunning.

You understand . . .

But a glance at Britt-Mari's face stopped her mother short. With an irritated wrinkle between her eyebrows, she looked jumpily across Britt-Mari's head.

Shall I fix breakfast for you? her mother asked and got up.

Do you have the time?

Of course I have time—Britt-Mari . . .

Changing her mind, she sat down again.

With a quick stroke through her hair, she tried to smile at the girl and look calm and friendly. Before folding her hands she straightened her skirt and took a deep breath.

Cinnamoncandy . . .

The physical distance between them suddenly became too wide. The mother moved over to the bed and Britt-Mari cuddled closer to her. They kissed and then sat quietly, their hands on each other's cheeks, retaining behind their closed eyelids something that felt like a quiet river of unity.

You know that I love you, the mother whispered.

Mommy.

Just now I didn't like you, Britt.

I could feel it. Sometimes you hate me. I can understand that. You must hate me. For your own sake you must hate me.

Now, don't exaggerate again. It's just that . . . You are too strict and moral.

They put their arms around each other, with averted faces, each chin resting on the other's shoulder.

It's going to be all right. Just have some patience with me.

And you with me, Mommy.

Good Lord, you have always been my pride. It's just that you are too fine, too refined for me to have. Sometimes you look at me so that it hurts all over. Then I think: she ought to have a different mother, totally different from me.

Hush, Mommy. You mustn't say things like that.

But that's the way I feel. Often, often. And that's why sometimes I fly off the handle. Then there's something else too. I'm afraid for you. You'll have many difficulties because of the way you are. And that makes me mad too because I feel that you should have learned from me—and you seem not to have understood—that life isn't so great that it would give anyone a reason to walk around with a face like yours.

I don't know, Mommy.

But that's the way it is at any rate. You ought to harden up and be more playful.

How could I do that?

I don't know. But now . . .

Now?

Now perhaps we can have it better. Oh, sometimes I think that it's for your sake everything happens. I mean, this, the latest affair. You can't imagine how much it hurts me when I consider that you'll hardly be proud of your mother once you grow up and can judge things. You'll . . .

Hush, Mommy.

I'm right. You'll act as if . . .

Don't say anything, Mommy.

All I want to say is that now I have some hope. You don't know what has happened to me these last few days.

The mother let go of the girl, not daring to look at her. She looked across the room.

I've never loved anyone before.

How about Daddy?

I was so young.

But you always told me how much you loved Daddy and how happy you both were.

Sure. Sure. But after him, all these years. I got the impression that I couldn't love. Love didn't mean anything to me. Life, for all that's worth, was nothing but amusement and pleasures. That's what I thought, Britt-Mari, and you must have known it. I was afraid. Often, often. All along I knew in my heart of hearts that I was wrong. A woman is not a woman if she doesn't love. That's it. She isn't mature if she doesn't love. She is nothing. She is a flirt, a beast of burden, a stupid idiot who drifts with every current. A pleasure automaton, getting rusty if she can't be in the swing at all times.

What about last winter?

That was vanity. I can see it now, nothing but vanity and fear. I was afraid, thinking that life would never come my way. It has come now, finally.

May it go the way you want, Mommy.

I love him, and that's something beautiful, Britt-Mari, even if it doesn't look exactly that way yet. I'll die if this ever comes to an end. Not in any ugly way. It won't be like last winter. Oh no. I would fade away, quietly and quickly like a grass blade. Without complaining. Perhaps in one single night.

Britt-Mari remained silent, contemplating. Suddenly displeased with herself, her mother showed a touch of anger.

I am happy, she said decisively. Days go by and I don't even think of the future. I haven't even thought as far as my nose reaches before I saw you. Well, by the way, wasn't it you who started asking questions? "What's going to happen? What's going to happen, Mommy?"

A thorn of enmity sat in the corners of her mouth.

Why always think of the future? she said, sighing angrily. Everything turns cheap if we constantly think of the future. And such strange things we speculate over. We can't accept the happiness we're offered and become part of. No, we think of taking advantage and looking out for ourselves so we can live safely and quietly and comfortably in a month, next year, for the rest of our lives.

She got up and now her lips trembled with a longing that still recalled the shudders of the cold in all its facets.

No, no, she said.

Without looking at Britt-Mari, she walked into her room. The girl could hear her mother starting to sing and suddenly her features turned serious and ascetic. Her lips took on a strict, introspective look. She put her hand across her forehead as if to seal a thought.

25

The bell tinkled mutedly above her head as she furtively slid over to the counter. No one else was in the store besides her. But it did not take long before the old woman came in from the inner room where she had been.

What can I do for you, young lady?

Britt-Mari did not answer. All her attention focused on detecting the shadows, those spots of something rotting below the surface like the rottenness underneath the outer peel of a beautiful apple. She looked for these signs of death with a cold flare of curiosity that showed in her tightly squeezed lips. Unconscious of what she was doing, Britt-Mari clenched her hands into tight fists and put them on the counter. The woman pulled them up playfully.

What is it you want, little lady?

I was just browsing a little, Britt-Mari answered with some difficulty.

Go right ahead.

I may not buy anything.

That's not necessary. But if there's something special you're looking for I may have to get it out. I'll be happy to do that.

There's nothing special.

Suit yourself and browse around.

The woman smiled, much to Britt-Mari's surprise. Caught in a fit of sudden shame, she pulled her hands back and looked away. Her sudden reaction would have yanked her clear out of the store if the woman had not said,

Sitting in there I felt very lonesome and longed to talk to someone. And suddenly you showed up. I think that I've seen you before, but I don't know your name.

Britt-Mari Månsson, the girl mumbled without looking up.

The woman started moving about the store and picking out things here and there. Britt-Mari listened. It took quite a while before she got over her shyness, or rather a feeling of shame, and she could look up. Not that she was doing anything illegal or forbidden, but her behavior was inexcusable. Her own sensitivity did not tolerate her mute obtrusiveness and what she was doing made her feel depraved.

She changed her mind when the woman started talking to her. Obviously she liked to talk and had no difficulties in forever finding new questions and comments on Britt-Mari's answers. It did not take her long to learn rather intimate things about Britt-Mari's life. The woman kept busy as she talked and did it in an easygoing manner and without emphasizing anything special. Like a background accompaniment, she kept bending down behind the counter, stretching up to some shelves, dusting a carton, or straightening out a fichu over something standing on the counter top and turning it around while she tossed questions at Britt-Mari. The girl answered them all, though her awareness of the woman's impending death remained ever present. She had the feeling that the woman's every move and touch, so careful and calm, was a last good-bye from the objects in her store. Even the questions she asked Britt-Mari seemed a farewell, a last show of still being able to face that which she was about to leave.

Suddenly something extraordinary happened. The woman dropped everything she was doing and existed just for Britt-Mari. It was no more than a moment, but the woman was standing there with a bearing as final as a picture, looking at the girl, staring at her, and Britt-Mari met her gaze. The woman's searching eyes met hers and took part in her life. Without further interpretations. That was already done. The emanations from the old and the very young eyes met in confluence. Their gazes were related. For the first time in a long while Britt-Mari felt an indescribable calm, a peace that made her shiver in gratitude, although nothing had happened save the show of kindness in the grey eyes, the goodness in the pale face and this muted smile of secret understanding on the colorless lips.

Do you like to embroider? the woman asked at long last.

Yes, I do.

Britt-Mari noticed a bulge protruding from below the woman's right waist where her sleeveless jacket was pulling apart. Pushing out the black-and-white skirt, it was about the size of a baby's head. It reminded her of a baby skull that can't get through.

How nice that you like to embroider.

I don't know very much.

Cross-stitch surely?

Yep.

Featherstitch?

A little. Just a little.

But then I could teach you. Would you like me to?

That would be great.

That makes me very happy. You can call me Aunt Greta. You're going to be a skillful embroiderer. Your hands show real talent.

Does it show?

It sure does. In the shape of your fingers and your entire hand. The way you move your hands. Your fingers are so nimble. I bet you can bend your thumbs way backward. When Britt-Mari showed her how far back she could bend them, Aunt Greta laughed and Britt-Mari laughed with her.

I'm going to teach you knotstitch and twiststitch, petit points and mosaicstitch.

I don't even know what all that means.

But you know that you want to learn?

I sure do.

It was a momentous moment, so great that Britt-Mari began to have her doubts. The counter was oldfashioned, going from one wall to the other, on the left side one piece could be lifted to lean against a red iron stand for paper rolls. After that was done, a gate could be pushed open for entrance.

Please, come in, Aunt Greta said and stood ready to let her pass. Without really daring to believe that this was truly happening to her, Britt-Mari hesitatingly passed through the narrow passage, the dividing line to last week's loneliness. A patient fellowship stood waiting for her on the other side, a friendly shadow, a time of tolerance kept warm by a mellow, calm fire.

Britt-Mari sat down in the inner room by the window facing the backyard. Her chair had soft lines and a royal blue plush seat. It stood next to a round, slim sewing table with low, curved legs and a lace tablecloth on top. The scent in the room was like nothing she had ever smelled before—a violet-blue lavender scent, as violet-blue as the light filtering through the starched curtains.

Would you like a cup of tea? Aunt Greta asked.

Britt-Mari liked to have one. She minded the water in the electric pot while the woman returned to the store, alerted by the bell's tinkle to the arrival of a customer. It did not take her long to wait on the customer, who came for just two rolls of thread. Aunt Greta said that this was a quiet period for fabric stores. All the summer dresses were finished and no one was thinking of fall clothes yet.

I'm going to take out my finest cups.

I want to be sitting here, Britt-Mari thought, today, tomorrow, and the day after that. I want to sit here all the days of my summer vacation. Here I can wait for what is going to happen to me, to Mommy and Stellan and to all human beings . . .

26

The next few days Britt-Mari experienced a peace and quietude that were as far removed from happiness as from care. Something was resting, was almost asleep. It was her feeling of guilt, dormant along with her rebellious urges. They gave her a respite, a lull that touched her body as much as her emotional life. Her moods and various desires were no longer at war with each other. The peace she felt even undercut her premonition that something lay in wait for her in the room, biding its time and occasionally renting the very air until a net of maggots enmeshed it like the inside of a rotten apple. Was this peace the same as expiation and forgiveness? This feeling came to her often. Now I can wait until my time comes, she would think then.

There were other times too when she thought: I am guiltier than ever! I am neither cold nor warm! I am lukewarm! I am fit to be cast off.— But these thoughts never aroused any catastrophic sensibilites. At the most, she turned ironic. She looked at the world of adults with ridicule.

Many grown-ups, deluded by personal ambitions, talk a lot of nonsense. They are not satisfied with being whatever they are. Drunk with self-esteem, they think that they can speak for everybody and that whatever they have to say concerns all people. God gave them a wonderful form, the best created here on earth. But instead of talking about the things they know best, they babble a great deal about how all creatures, living or dying, should live their lives. Not that their talk is of any great consequence, but it is downright ridiculous. Somehow they have come to think that when they speak, they're not simply talking through their own throat, but a freely suspended, factual, impartial throat, hardly human and not belonging to any special person. Actually, this extra throat is a metal pipe.

The use of this extra throat is often ridiculous and sometimes so pathetic that the whole world should reverberate with laughter, and earthquakes of ridicule shake up mountains and cities. Job's friends as they visit to pity and comfort him are but one example. Here is Job, pious, honest and upright, edified at his own expense and suffering open, terribly painful sores. He speaks out of his misery, and his able-bodied, healthy friends, frightened, rebuke Job for his words. They give long speeches, seemingly disputing Job's suffering. Not once do they perceive that they're judging him out of their own prosperity. They use their extra throat.

Still, this throat may be a boon to this earth. Those who grow, who work on their development, who struggle to overcome their taxing façade, should not pay much attention to the wording. The metal pipe's rumbling is but a corrupted version of God's words. For the sake of the sufferer: How can we apply the words? Those in pain should not take them as final, but just for what they are: the product of work. And all work is done to be consumed. After the work is consumed nothing stands in the way of the continuation of the work.

Britt-Mari was sitting in the inner room of the fabric store, embroidering. The process within her lay suspended. She no longer felt longing for herself. At rest, she was waiting. She had learned something about the splendid state that puts its imprint on adult life for a while: love puts grown-ups into an elevated state of mind and nothing bothers them; they have reached a plateau beyond the reach of laws and demands. God has set them aside because lovers cannot take on anything else. Neither can they dispense with even the smallest crumb of love: the state of love is total and condensed, it cannot be wanting for anything, it does not get lost little by little. If it gets lost then it does so in its totality.

27

Britt-Mari spent at least five hours every day with Aunt Greta in the fabric store. Nothing happened, nothing else besides the constantly repeating regeneration of tranquility and calm. Well, let's have a cup of tea now, the woman would say. And then they would sit for hours doing nothing but chat with each other.

Aunt Greta's last name was Landberg, and she was Miss. Her closest relatives were nieces and nephews who lived in other places. They were doing well, Aunt Greta said. One was an engineer, one a radio officer on a big ship, one a gradeschool teacher. Two of them were married and had healthy children of their own. Miss Landberg had snapshots of them all and showed them often. Britt-Mari heard so much about these relatives that she soon had the feeling of knowing them very well, as if she had met them personally.

I hope that they are in peace with God, Aunt Greta said one day. Even though I know them pretty well, I don't know anything about that. It's so difficult to talk with young people nowadays about their Maker. I don't understand how that can happen. People today love the everyday, that much I do understand. And they prefer to live in peace with their everyday. Who doesn't? But knowing that all the other exists too . . . I think that modern people have it difficult. Everything beyond the everyday is one single confusion for them. No one can straighten it out, not even the most talented. It's understandable that most of them don't want to discuss anything but the commonplace. They think that God just complicates things further.

Britt-Mari liked what Aunt Greta said then,

Of course it's nice if a person's everyday face happens to be well-to-do. But everyday's face is superficial. It only shows the outside of a person's mundane status: merits, title, home, children, age and such. But we have also an inside face, the face we carry before God.

The woman in the fabric store was full of confidence. To her God was the good shepherd and the merciful father taking care of his children, now and at the end of their days. Full of trust, she committed herself into his hands. There will be an explanation to everything some day. Whatever is unclear to us, whatever pains and grieves us will be fully explained in Heaven. God is forever ready, holding his arms out to receive all souls.

Britt-Mari listened to this gospel of peace, feeling deeply its serenity and tranquility, like sleep. No strife, no demands, no antagonisms, nothing that incited; doom and humiliation ceased to exist. Every once in a while Miss Landberg said that all men are siblings. It reminded Britt-Mari of her mother, and suddenly she understood the meaning of her words "like siblings."

That was when Britt-Mari, haunted by her mother's loneliness, declared with a sigh, If Daddy were still alive, things would be different for us.—Her mother was by no means taken in by this impossible observation. With irritation in her voice she announced that when a marriage lasts long enough, the partners live like siblings, without excitement. When something happens then either they forgive each other, or they become indifferent. Routine grips them and the home becomes as dull as work on an assembly line.

It was her mother's "like siblings." Britt-Mari knew by now that her mother was wrong with regard to marriage. Couples do not necessarily act "like siblings" after a time. The old couple she had met by the river were not living "like siblings," even though they had been married for so long. But she knew that before. Her mother often said things not because they were true, but because they suited her at the moment. That made them true in a way, though it was better to understand beforehand what her mother wanted to express with what she said. Then one didn't have to take these roundabout routes, but would understand immediately what it was her mother offered as truth.

Britt-Mari was embroidering an oval coffee tablecloth with daisies not larger than one-cent-pieces that would eventually become a border garland around the cloth. Later she was to embroider a smaller garland in the center. Whenever she wanted to, she could take her embroidery home. One afternoon she did it, and from then on she took both cloth and yarn skeins home every night. That kept her quiet. Some particle of the atmosphere in the store's inner room followed along.

Britt-Mari did not see her mother for an entire week. She came once and left a small note, telling her, among other things, Dear Cinnamoncandy, everything is wonderful. Your mother is very happy. I hope that you are too.—Britt-Mari wrote a note too, explaining shortly that she was well and that the woman in the fabric store was teaching her to embroider and was terribly nice to her. And, she added in response to her mother's reminder in the note, she did not neglect her eating. Finally, there was enough money, twenty crowns and some change in the metal container in the pantry.

Toward the end of her mother's vacation Britt-Mari understood that she needed to find a scheme to leave home. She did not want to be in the way again at home. Her mother and Stellan would need to have a place where they could be alone.

She still had not met Stellan and did not know quite what he looked like. Once she had seen him. That was when he and her mother walked around the church in circles. But that was only from a distance. She had not seen his face.

Again Britt-Mari started her painful brooding. Aunt Greta was worried.

What is it you're thinking of? she asked.

Britt-Mari gave a start, but calmed down immediately.

You looked so unhappy, it hurts to see you that way. Is something wrong?

Nooo, Aunt Greta.

Are you sure?

Yes.

You were far away? So far off that you didn't know where?

Perhaps I was, Aunt Greta.

But you mustn't go off with things that hurt you. Girls your age have such lively fantasy. I do remember the way I was. Imagining all kinds of horrors.

Not here, Aunt Greta.

Britt-Mari looked around and was able to smile. When her eyes met Aunt Greta's again, the same thing happened as the first day. The old woman's gaze took part in her life. Their eyes were confluent, and their close relationship lived in their eyes.

After a while Britt-Mari wondered whether she should tell Aunt Greta everything. For a few moments she felt a pining urge to unload herself. Not to look for help. Who could help her? But just to be able to talk about things that were pressing. Everything seemed to depend on them. Talk about the pain of not being grown up, talk about her great distress when she . . .

No. She could not talk about it. It was impossible, even with Aunt Greta. She needed to do something else. Already tomorrow she needed to try getting a job as dishwasher. If Gertrud could be hired, then she should very easily . . . But she did not discuss even that with Aunt Greta. Looking around in the room, she bade a silent good-bye to it. When she left that evening, she told Aunt Greta that possibly she might not be able to come the next day as usual. There was something she needed to do, she said.

You are welcome whenever you come here, Miss Landberg told her.

28

When Britt-Mari sought refuge with Aunt Greta in the fabric store around three o'clock the following afternoon, she was unconscious of the despairing force with which she opened the entrance door. But something made her stop short and look up. The little bell was not tinkling. Her impetuous entrance had choked the bell's sound and its clapper now tilted toward the curved metal rod on which it was mounted. For the moment all she could think of was the people's smirking at her efforts that day. All the adults had been snickering, everywhere.

She closed the entrance door with exaggerated care. The bell, emitting two tinkling sounds, came down like a leadweight.

The smirks had started early in the morning. Hagberg first. Why did she have to take the stairs in D when coming down from her attic? Because she wanted to see Grepp. That's why. And she met Hagberg on the stairs, that old rag tailor, and he stopped, holding on to the handrail with both hands. Then he said something stupid to her, bent forward and smirk-laughed. She didn't answer, but walked past him, slowly. She owed her dignity to walk slowly. His greasy, hoary laugh reverberated in her ears for a long time afterward.

But Grepp remained invisible down in the yard. Instead, there were two women talking to each other. They had a very finely chopped laugh. First they said something, then they turned their faces in the opposite direction, and then came their smirky laughs. After that they said a few more words, and again their faces jerked each in its own direction as if someone had pulled them on a string or as if their lips had suddenly become a shameful organ they did not want to show each other. Then they devoted themselves to chop up a strangely longstretched happiness.

Britt-Mari did not look at the customer in the fabric store. She forgot even to say hello to Miss Landberg, who was busy taking care of the customer. She went directly to the counter, opened the side and disappeared in the inner room. She did not try to take out her needlework, but sat down on the chair covered with royal blue plush, waiting for something to happen to her. Nothing happened. The room betrayed her, holding back its power, refusing to affect her as it had done before. No calm came to her, no tranquility, no peace in the violet-blue daylight, not even the cozy pleasure in the lavender-scented air.

People were smirk-laughing all day today. Smirk-laughter kept them busy to an unbelievable extent. They smirk-laughed in a thousand different ways. They smirk-laughed about anything. They smirked at her too. Smirked at her on a running scale.

She did not get a job.

She was stupid and inexperienced, and acted that way. But that was not all. They had laughed at her appearance too. The way she looked, her voice, her hairdo, her way of using her hands, her slender body were all objects of amusement. Her solicitations seemed to make her body look even more fragile in their eyes than it was already. At first she tried in one of the biggest restaurants, entering through the kitchen door to get immediately to where she wanted to go. Of course, she had seen the sign: Only for Personnel, but that's what she was there for, to become one of the employees.

Temporary help. For a few weeks . . .

They laughed right into her face. The general amusement spread with the grapevine. A little, fat cook, holding her round fist against her chubby cheek, smirked, You're really someone. What an enterprising little go-getter.—Tall with words, but short on earth, tiny runt on the floor in the kitchen of a big, modern restaurant. Here, have a cookie and stick to sweets for a little while yet.—And then a pair of hands came, flapping with laughter against her shoulders, You're sweet, my gosh, so sweet you are. And then she got a wet smack on her cheek, and the same mouth snickered that it was moving, absolutely touching.

Britt-Mari went to smaller and smaller restaurants. Then she changed to diners, and even those became gradually smaller and less pretentious. Only the people's preponderance to snicker did not diminish.

Aunt Greta came in. Walking over to Britt-Mari, she wondered quietly and perhaps therefore more penetratingly,

You're not yourself. What has happened?

I don't want to be a child. I can't be.

Well, tell me. What has happened to you?

I can't be a child.

Britt-Mari, has anyone been stupid to you? Tell me. You know that you can.

It's me who's stupid, Aunt Greta. It's just me who is.

But something has happened to you, right? There's something that has hurt you.

Britt-Mari was holding her hands in front of her eyes and did not take them away. Shaking with embitterment, she was keenly aware of her demoralization, which conspired in setting her apart from regular human company. Though equipped like any other young girl, she alone committed the crime of hating her equipment and detesting its stipulations to a degree that skirted a longing for death. Disgusted with her lot, she demanded that nature annul its laws.

Miss Landberg checked her hands and straightened her back, sad because she felt at a loss. She knew that the girl had not met with some simple, concrete little mishap, that much she had learned about the girl this past week. The child had both worried and fascinated her. Those long lapses of mental absence when the girl's body became no more than an abandoned casing; her unconscious bearing when her body became the instrument of a deep, complicated pain whose meaning still carried an obviously naive badge; her complete presence thrusting from the center outward through her skin and surface, creating this special atmosphere around her.

I don't want to hurt you, Miss Landberg said. I'm afraid that I'm going to hurt you, whatever I may say. She stepped away from the girl, who was shaking her head in denial of her fears.

I could say some stupid things, Miss Landberg resumed after a while. Such as, calm down, all things pass. Have you ever had a toothache? I could ask. It's painful and sometimes almost unbearable. But before you know it, the pain is gone, and then you forget pretty quickly how painful it has been. I could say that. And I could continue saying that when you remember this hour, tomorrow, or next week, you'll smile at yourself, thinking that it wasn't that bad. Other hours followed, and right in the middle of that hour I still hoped that it would end soon, and even in the middle of that hour I was far from broken. Yes, I could say that, and I'm doing so too. Are you listening?

I don't understand how I could be so . . .

Miss Landberg looked up at the girl who had dropped her hands and folded them in her lap. She sat staring at her fingers, or her nails, or perhaps at nothing.

I do so love to live. I am so happy to exist.

Perhaps that's why? Those who feel this true joy in living are insatiable. They want life in full. They are not satisfied with less than living life to the fullest and black despair besets them when their goal keeps on moving beyond their reach and becomes inaccessible.

I want to be an adult. I pine for it as much as for Heaven.

What is that you're saying?

I long for it as for Heaven. Right now I'm neither child nor adult. I'm standing outside of Paradise and want to get in.

Do you think that grown-ups exist in Paradise?

Yes, grown-ups may love.

What do you mean?

They can love. That is paradise here on earth. I hate. I want to destroy myself. So how can I enter paradise?

Overwhelmed, Miss Landberg sat down, faint with her need to listen. But Britt-Mari did not continue.

Most people never grow up, Miss Landberg resumed suddenly. Some never even reach your level of maturity, Britt-Mari. Even though they may add one year to another, perhaps become more dexterous with their hands. Yes, their hands may become magnificent, though they may be coarse and rough, worn out, or delicate. But their heart? That stops growing. Look at me? Do you think that I, as old as I am, became an adult? Do you think that I ever was?

Britt-Mari looked at the old woman in surprise. For the first time ever she noticed that her cheeks were a pale pink and her eyes did not want to meet hers. Instinctively she looked down at the floor instead. The woman was hiding something under her arm as she held it across her stomach and pulled her jacket tightly together.

I can tell you the truth: I never grew up, even though I asked for it. Not as early as you. I managed to become twenty-two years old before I realized that I was still not an adult woman. Only then did I understand what I lacked. I was immature. I was actually unfit to live. Life went past me because I was immature.

Miss Landberg rose up and started pacing the floor, still hiding that something under her arm. She pulled her jacket together.

Many years passed before I finally gave up hope, before I settled with being the immature person that I am. I never had a man. I had no children. I doomed myself to living alone. I did not dare to love because I knew who I was. Believe me. If someone had fallen in love with me before I was twenty-two, I would have dared. But that never happened. No one met me with love. Now I could not meet anyone. I hid myself, withdrew. I could no longer tell myself that I was a Cinderella just waiting for the happy circumstance that would disclose the truth about my birth. Only after a long time, a very long time, my despair turned into happiness, an unpretentious happiness, but happiness nevertheless. And what did this happiness consist of? Look at my body! I had a body capable of work, and there was work it was suited for.

She stopped, stretching her hand forward to lean against her desk. The pink color on her cheeks darkened, tinting even her forehead a pale red. But she smiled. Britt-Mari watched her smile spreading and then slowly fading away.

That's the way it is for me, and so it is for everyone. No one is created to stand aside. Even the immature have something that enables them to do some of all the things that need to be done. Saints aim at perfection, but they end in black despair, with a feeling of total abandon. At this point a blessing may strike them in suddenly discovering all the small human needs that must be satisfied to enable man to live. The saints realize then that their services are needed and their task is to carry them out with perfection. To give a glass of water to someone thirsty is in its way perfection and cannot be surpassed. The same holds true for thousands of other ministries and acts. They are perfect. Nothing can surpass them. And the world is full of these wonderful tasks. Not one moment passes without such flawless acts. And should my sinful heart ever detect a surge of perfection passing through my life, I confess that where sin exists, it may receive something perfect from the heart: forgiveness. I have the strength to continue my work. My heart is not going to block the way. I no longer feel any hate toward my own imperfections, and the shortcomings of my fellow men do not make me unforgiving.

Silence. Britt-Mari sat in this silence. She turned away. The music had stopped. The wonderful strength was now molded, life's lovely devices brought out. Silence. The strong person need only take whatever suits him. Where there are the resources, all one needs to do is to choose the way of rounding out one's life.

Britt-Mari felt an urge to leave so she could grieve in seclusion.

Suddenly she felt a deep respect, a deference for the woman in the fabric store reverberating in her. The old woman had a beautiful body even now that it was about to fail. She carried herself with pride, with a dignity that did not deny her shortcomings. To the contrary, pride and dignity kept her shortcomings open and ready for change. Like a ray of light striking her heart, Britt-Mari recognized that she needed to find shortcuts and more daring ways, darker and much more dangerous.

That was why she felt veneration for the otherness. It was the underlying reason for her desire to leave and grieve in seclusion, now that she had reached the point where she could do this. She could stretch out, supine, and in solitude meditate on the three figures she had met once before—the two beings who assumed an ever increasing reality beside her, one at her right and one at her left, beings meant to be part of herself. But she had not acted on that. She had remained static in between them, neither schoolsick nor schoolhappy, a defiant truant. That's how it was and it caused her to grieve. The two others were so much simpler and, by the same token, so much more difficult to become. And she grieved for that. She considered it a proper homage and a suitable betrayal to leave the woman and the little room now. She curtsied to the old woman, her face echoing her deference. All she said was,

Thank you.

29

She left, but she never got a chance to grieve in seclusion. The time was not ripe yet. Magda Hagberg caught up with her on the street and let her know right away that it was strange how invisible Britt-Mari had become of late.

Mrs. Hagberg had been shopping and was carrying her shopping bag. She complained about the price of meat and the impossibility nowadays to get meat at a cheap price. It used to be that the poor could go to the open-air market and wait for the end of the day when farmers pack up. That's when they sold out everything that was left. There were no longer farmers selling meat in the open-air market. No one was allowed to sell meat there. It was unsanitary to sell meat in the open-air market. It won't be long and they have to brush the meat with toothpaste before they can sell it, said Mrs. Hagberg. The prices in the market-hall, where she had gone in the hope of getting a better price, were at least as steep as in the finest butcher store with tiles and marble counters and stainless steel, she said.

Britt-Mari always thought that Mrs. Hagberg was different outside from inside the house. Surely just an impression, because Mrs. Hagberg, walking on the street with a shopping-bag over her arm, talked the same way as when she sat in her kitchen, ripping old suits apart. For all that, Britt-Mari did not consider Mrs. Hagberg the only person to look different inside the house than the way she looked on the street. A good part changes when people are out on the street. She remembered a teacher she had only seen in the schoolroom and the schoolyard. Once she met her on Storgatan and the teacher looked like everyone else without anything special about her.

In contrast, Mrs. Hagberg did look different when outside. She looked conspicuous, diverging from current style and fashions. Her clothes were oldfashioned. The hat she wore was made according to her own ideas. Rather masculine, it made her eyelids look strangely refined and sensitive, and her forehead dignified and feminine. Her nerves never got used to the street traffic. Shocked and frightened, she would flee in spurts across every street. Never daring to walk close to either the buildings or the street because of the bicycles, she tried to walk in the center of the sidewalks. This was rather difficult and she often had to zig-zag her way forward.

Hagberg has really been pretty decent this past week, she confessed unexpectedly.

How nice, Britt-Mari said.

Don't think that I trust him for all that, Mrs. Hagberg hastened to add. I know him by now. I'm sure he's scheming on something. He's not about to drop his vices all at once. He's no pushover. Don't ever believe that. Not like so many others, where you at least have a reason to forgive and can feel sorry for them. No, Hagberg is planning something. Figuring on a fitting time, a time when it hurts most. And so he drinks.

Britt-Mari did not say anything. Suddenly Mrs. Hagberg stopped, her free hand pointing.

Look how terrible. The bloodstains are still there.

Bloodstains?

Yeah, don't you see them? Over there. Close by the gutter.

A car came driving over the spot she was pointing out.

Now can't you see them?

No. I don't see any bloodstains.

But I can. Because I saw them when they were almost fresh. The blood. I'm not going to cross there again.

Was there an accident?

Yes. About an hour ago. Right outside our place.

Was someone . . .

Yes. The dog died immediately.

A dog?

Yes. Luckily it wasn't a human. Though a life at any rate. He had no time to get away, they say. It's strange, isn't it? A dog that couldn't get away, though he lived here and was used to this. But he couldn't get away.

Was it Grepp? I mean. . . Was it Felix?

I don't know what his name was.

Was it the caretaker's?

Yes, of course it was. The caretaker was the only one with a dog in this house, except Mrs. Grafström in the A section, but that poor. . .

Britt-Mari left Mrs. Hagberg immediately, automatically knowing what to do. Her mouth felt dry, and her throat was like sandpaper. Her first thought was, Why did I never give him that bath? How could I? I meant to do it a thousand times.

The custodian's name was Janzon. Many thought that he spelled his name with a z because he wanted to be refined. Britt-Mari

knocked. Mrs. Janzon was sitting at the kitchen table, playing patience with her dirty week-day deck. Several cards had broken corners. On the table stood an empty beer bottle and a glass with a few
sips left. Mrs. Janzon looked discontented and bored. Her full, voracious lips had a look of disgust about them, and her large, black-blue
eyes stared at the world with indifference. Still, she saw most of
what was going on, people said. Her laughter would echo from the
garden walls during the summer months when the window stood
open.

Where is Felix? Britt-Mari asked.

Mrs. Janzon's lips cut a ridiculing smile while executing several
moves. Still looking at her cards, she finally said,

Haven't you heard the mutt has kicked the bucket?

Britt-Mari was silent. Despite her unwillingness to talk, Mrs.
Janzon continued,

Pure accident. Else it would've cost us a pretty penny—if it had
of been the mutt's fault and something happened. But see, it wasn't
his fault, just pure accident. I'm not saying a thing. It was Reuter
who absolutely wanted a dog. A custodian needs a dog, he said. What
bunk, he? A custodian must have a dog, of course, he said. . . A real
feller needn't work and be custodian, I told him. A real feller has a
job which he can support his family on. Specially if he, thank goodness, has no children to take care of. Either inside or outside his
marriage, I said. Where did he get the idea, a custodian has to have
a dog? He could never explain, and that even though I told him I'd
look in the telephone book and call any damn custodian that has a
telephone and ask, What about it, must a custodian have a dog?
Mrs. Janzon laughed a goodnatured, contemptuous laugh, amused
and bored at the same time.

It looked as if she did not have a stitch underneath her flowered
summer dress, sewn up like a duster with buttons in front. The dress
was sleeveless, and had a deeply cut, wide neckline. Mrs. Janzon was
fat, though her skin looked still young, solid and elastic. She heaved
backward against the back of her chair, scratching her scalp through
her light, frizzy hair and stretching her bare legs out. A pair of shab-
bily elegant slippers sat on her feet. Perspiration in her armpits made
her almost reddish-colored hair there stick together.

Confound it! Mrs. Janzon let out with a long-stretched yawn.

Britt-Mari was disgusted and angry.

Where is Felix now, his body?

The body. That one come in and asked. What'll I want do with the body? Was one who told him who the mutt belongs to. So he come in to me. Just a whipper-snapper, but rather smooth and good manners. Beginning salesman, I'd guess. He smelled toiletwater, and it wasn't just 'cause he works in it. Though of course he must advertise his stuff. Stood there in the door and bowed and was sorry as if it was a relative to ours that has died. Gosh, I told him. Don't bother me none, but it's too damn bad for Reuter. If he'd been home so perhaps you'd gotten a piece of his mind, I added. Reuter's so hot-headed about himself, I told him and had fun, for goodness knows, I haven't ever seen Reuter hot under the collar. And that there fair boy got the jitters and looked at the bedroom door and excuses gushing out of him. So, of course he was a salesman, for sure. Nice shirt and tie. His suit too, though his pants could've been ironed better. But he was driving a car, of course.

I've never before in my life been in a car, Britt-Mari said.

And you're still alive and in good health.

Where's the body?

What'll I do with the body? he asked. Don't concern me, I answered. The mutt wasn't mine, t'was Reuter's mutt. Is he in one piece? I asked, 'cause I thought that if a custodian has no living dog, so perhaps he needs one that's stuffed. I can't really tell you, says this goodlooking idiot. I can't even stand nosebleed, I howled, and so he bowed again, silent and pompous, and so he wondered almost whimpering whether he couldn't conveniently get rid of the poor dog in the garbage can, 'cause that's so close and good enough 'cause it's emptied every morning so there won't be no question of no smell. When he said it I screamed and put my hand in front of my mouth as if I'm ready to chuck up. Pure pretense. I wanted to see if sweety-pie would react. And he sure did. Madam, he said. How are you feeling? I directed him to the pantry. Pilsner and a glass. He poured and everything an' even wanted to know whether I could bring the glass to my lips. You ever heard the likes of a feller to be polite? My hands shook, of course, and he hung over me with one arm around my shoulders. I was just about to ask him to dip a towel in cold water so as he could towel me around my forehead too, but then I got tired of his highfalutin' mannerisms and asked him to beat it. What's that you're trying to do? I said. Don't you think I don't know what you wanted do with your hand? Beat it, I screamed. And I've never seen a face more yellow than his's. He ran, bump, against the door. And I took a gulp . . .

Did he throw Felix in the garbage can?

What do I know? D'you think I went and looked?

Then I'll do it. May I . . .

May? None of my concern.

I want to bury Felix.

Bury? Did you say bury?

Yes. If I can find the body.

But what in heaven's . . .

Mrs. Janzen got up from her chair. Her face, puffy and vacuous before, suddenly expressed a sort of supercilious, touched kindliness. She was very big. Her hair reached up to the lamp and it shone golden, towering in curly waves above her flat face. With a loitering gait she crossed the floor, her chubby hand moving forward as if she intended to play with an animal.

Seems as if you're very sof'hearted, she said. Looks to me that the little heart loved that there wretch of a mutt.

Her chubby hands were about to pull Britt-Mari closer and press her against her fat stomach and breasts. This was her way, extremely slow and extremely vital, extremely vague and extremely deliberate. Several buttons on her flowery dress were unbuttoned both at top and bottom. The white skin on the inside of her thighs above her knees and the deep cleavage between her breasts were visible. Britt-Mari gave a gasp, surprised at being able to tear herself away from the spot where she seemed to have been stuck. She disappeared before Mrs. Janzon had a chance to complete her close encounter.

Britt-Mari went straight down and checked the three metal garbage cans. There was Grepp, his dead body already halfway covered with garbage and discards. His front lay downward, his beautiful face and the melancholy drooping ears violated by lack of respect. Britt-Mari turned her face away from the sweetish, sickening fumes of decomposition arising out of the can and put down the lid.

A cold drive to act hardened her and made her feel unreal to herself. Numb and quick, she walked as in a dream. She did not need to think, she reflected later. She knew instinctively what she needed. First she borrowed a bicycle trailer in the store. Finding no shovel in the building, she took the dustpan from her home. She found her mother's sackcloth apron, used when she washed clothes, and one of her own outgrown nightgowns, the yellow one with blue flower clusters. Then she pulled the box with Christmas stuff out of the closet, knowing exactly what she needed to get out: the Christmas bell they attached every Christmas to the ceiling light in her mother's room. It was green and had red letters that said Merry Christmas. Her mother had told her that her father had bought it. That Christmas she was two years old and her father, dressed up as Santa Claus, came in and stood under the lamp, ringing the bell, before he opened his sack with Christmas presents. Finally, she took along the rubber gloves from the sink.

Then, her eyes closed, Britt-Mari pulled Grepp out of the human refuse and the odious smells. She wrapped his dead body first in the sackcloth apron and then in the nightgown, which she folded over like a paperbag. If Grepp's body was ever so heavy when she pulled it out of the garbage can, it was, now that it was dressed, light enough for her to lift into the trailer with ease. Pulling the trailer, she considered it fitting that it had rubber wheels. It should not rumble or screech. It should go softly and quietly to the place of burial.

The evening sun came flooding through the gate. Turning to check whether the body lay correctly, she saw her own shadow stretching long across the cement floor on a slant toward the wall. There it broke and the rest of her shadow rose up on the wall. The break went straight across her breast.

She selected a place at the foot of the Stadsberg surrounded by young birches and a good distance away from the road and homes as a fitting place to bury Grepp. When her dustpan proved unfit for digging deep enough, she went to the nearest home to borrow a spade. The woman wondered what she needed it for. She told her the truth,

I'm going to bury a dog up there in the wood.

She got the spade and dug a grave deep enough for the dog. Before she filled it up again, she rang the Christmas bell over his body, his head first, then without any special order. She rang, her body bent forward and without moving her arms. Only her wrists moved back and forth. Then she built a mound with the earth that was left over and decorated it with leaves and the flowers she found, wild pansies and red German catchflies, some harebells and speedwells, and lastly a few sprigs of rosebay. She started to cry when she picked the flowers. Not out of grief. Not only out of grief.

Afterward she sat down on the ground and looked around. Wherever she looked, she noted the singularity of everything alive and how enclosed everything was in its loneliness. Every tree, every bush, every flower, every grassblade. Everything that lives stands alone. She perceived the beauty of loneliness. Beautiful and cruel. Alone, all life exists in a world of distance. But we can go to the lonesome, we can stretch forth our hand and reach it, we can bend down to it and praise and love it. This is what makes loneliness beautiful: the fact of being able to bend down and touch is always something solitary and always carries its special imprint.

But how could she possibly reach every living thing when they all live alone? There was not enough time. There are too many of the lonely. Distance preoccupies most of our life's time. There was not enough time to reach every tree, or all the bushes, all the flowers, all the grassblades even in this one hill in the forest. Fall would overtake her, winter and death outstrip her. One lonely life's happiness, how rich it ever may be, is unable to touch each and everyone to show her love to each and everyone. Life flows out of us and our zest to live will never be satisfied. Even a forest hill presents us with a tremendous task—when we love.

30

It was shortly after 10:00 P.M. on Saturday when Britt-Mari caught sight of her mother. She had not seen her for over a week. The girl was sitting in the small park with the red maple tree she called hers. She was not sitting on one of the benches, currently occupied by people whose proximity irritated her. She had been sitting there earlier this evening, sharing the benches with many older people, retirees, out for an evening walk in the fresh air, as they said. They gossiped with leisurely longwindedness about trifles, observing obvious facts about the warm, humid weather and the visiting sailors flooding the city. Someone considered it impossible for so many to be housed in three or four vessels, let alone that these were warships. The life of the warriors, someone remarked, as if that explained the matter. The exercises teach them some discipline, two old fellows agreed.

They must have saluted from the *Vattenledningsborg*, one man said. He had not heard it himself, but a woman he knew had heard it. There was a battery of cannons by the *Vattenledningsborg*, small, friendly cannons that never had been fired against people or houses. Standing there since the time of the sharp-shooters, they were used only during royal festivities. The association of sharpshooters and their ladies had collected the money for the small cannons so that this city, like others, could manifest its devotion to royalty with some rumbling in the mountains.

The park benches were now anchorage points for sailors hunting for entertainment and girls. The sailors were young and cheerful. Their leave was young and so was this Saturday night. The city's beer joints and restaurants were as young as the city itself. The girls were young, and the sailors were young for the girls.

Let's go to *Folkets Park*, the public park, someone called with young enthusiasm. His comrades jumped up from the bench and left with renewed pleasure at their performance before the young. It was not long before a new group of sailors occupied the bench.

Britt-Mari sat perched on the banister of the wooden stairs that led straight down to Ågatan, the street by the river. The stretch below her seemed almost deserted. Only occasionally a belated motorboat came chugging downriver, usually full of adults and children on their way out to the archipelago for the holiday. Britt-Mari kept looking at the sidewalk in front of Storgatan 33. She did not think that her mother would return home this evening, but she could never be sure. Dusk was turning darker, the streetlamps came on. A steady stream of cars flowed across Storbro bridge, its sidewalks on either side crowded with people having the same goal.

"Are not two sparrows sold for a mite? And not one of them falls down to the ground without your Father's wish."

One day the woman in the fabric store had said these words. Britt-Mari thought about Grepp's fate. Aunt Greta had also mentioned something about the lost faith in Providence. Britt-Mari could not remember her exact words. Sometimes words act on us, sometimes nothing happens. Life is a gift, not our desert. Was it this way she said it? Words sometimes open up a world that is too large for us. We exist only where our feet are touching ground. The entire landscape disappears for us when we bend down to do homage to a flower. Aunt Greta had talked about the heathens' idea of fate. Britt-Mari did not remember what exactly. But she remembered something else she had told her.

People say that we mourn the dead, but that is hardly correct. It is not the dead we mourn. We mourn the life that remains for us who survive. The fact that we continue to live although the loved one is dead. That the sun rises just as before. That we still get hungry. Get sleepy. Get dressed and get undressed. That we work, we talk, we worry about the future, we still enjoy, we suddenly laugh, yes, we even catch ourselves at being interested in one thing or other. The dead man is not so important. His death does not splinter our limbs and does not even cross our hold on life. It is our impending treason that makes us cry at the sight of death.

Britt-Mari listened, feeling an ice-cold band settling on her shoulders. But she was not upset. No, not even for a minute. The truth never upsets us. Only our frustrations upset and cross us.

The sight of her mother suddenly appearing on Storgatan shortly after ten o'clock P.M. touched her far deeper. Literally bouncing and jerking forward at the outer edge of the sidewalk and thus sidestepping the crowds, she looked as if she were balancing on a plank. She carried a suitcase in one hand and a bulging shopping bag in the other. Suddenly her strength gave out. She turned toward the houses, set the bags down and stood for a while bent forward as if in pain. Then she pressed one hand to her hips to steady herself.

Under the impression that her mother was ill, Britt-Mari jumped off her perch and ran across the street. Her mother stood stiffly and halfway turned to the wall, looking at nothing but a stone wall.

Aren't you feeling well, Mommy?

With their deliberate turns—along with an unreal expression in her face—her mother's movements looked utterly stilted and artificially dignified. With uncomprehending, aimless irony she jeered,

Of course, I should find you on the street. For sure, you're out here.

Did you fall and get hurt, Mommy? For Britt-Mari the swollen eyes were the only reality in the unreal face.

Be quiet. You'll shut up, above all.

Tottering, her mother bent down to pick up her bags. Britt-Mari gripped her arms and got her upright.

Why didn't you take a cab if you're ill?

Shut up, her mother repeated and freed herself from the girl's hands. Keep your mouth shut, above all.

She gained a sudden strength. Decisively and with exaggerated power she lifted the bags, and they looked light as she carried them. She walked on in a brisk pace.

Can't I help you?

Her mother did not answer. Britt-Mari began to notice people staring at them. In a flash she understood that her mother was not sick, but drunk. Her mother's spurt of energy brought her around the corner. Britt-Mari ran past her, got the key out of her pocket and opened the door. Without looking at her, her mother wobbled straight ahead toward the stairs. There she let go of her bags, took hold of the banister and leaned sideways against the wall, one foot on the first step.

Britt-Mari patted her mother on her bare arms, unable to say a thing. The hall light hurt her eyes and the smell of alcohol made her sick. Her mother was preoccupied with something that was happening in her guts. Her eyes were pinched together, her face twitched nervously and her forehead was damp with perspiration. In but seconds it looked as if her very skin was fermenting and dissolving. Then her body grew limp and her skin sticky. She bent further forward.

Let me help you, Mommy.

Not one look, not one gesture revealed that she was conscious of her daughter's presence. When her nausea passed, she let go of the banister and stood up straight. Widening her eyes, she seemed to see something only her mind could see: the reason for her predicament, the origin of her present misery. Her left eye stared cross-eyed out underneath her swollen skinbags. The hall light went off.

Her mother laughed hysterically. She was hitting herself across her mouth. Britt-Mari touched her. Suddenly she voiced,

He was an athlete. He was the All-Swedish champion fifteen years ago.

Did he hit you?

He carried the banner for all Swedes. In soccer. But then his foot got bad and there was no more hope. The All-Swedish Lover Boy couldn't kick.

Her mother started going upstairs, uttering muted screams in the darkness,

Lover Boy. Lover Boy.

Britt-Mari wanted to press the light-button, but then she reconsidered. The darkness was better. It was better to experience her mother in the dark. That would prevent her from clashing with the pristinely yellow walls and humiliation before the quiet, wide staircase. The girl took care of the bags. All went well the first flight. Halfway up the second flight they became too heavy and she had to leave one bag behind. She returned to pick it up by the third. They proceeded in this manner.

Suddenly her mother yelled,

Damned Lover Boy!

Leaving her bag, Britt-Mari ran up to her mother. Not wanting anyone to come out and see them, she asked her to keep quiet. Her mother calmed down, but then stopped on the stairs, defiantly refusing to go further. Britt-Mari pleaded and begged, talking as if to a child. When her mother finally gave in, Britt-Mari ran back down to get her bags. She took both. She had suddenly gained in strength.—At the foot of the fifth floor her mother stopped, holding on to the banister with both hands. She did not cry but stood quietly bent forward like an animal. Britt-Mari did not let go of her bags.

Just one more flight left, dear Mommy, she said.

Everything is left. Everything in toto.

Just one more flight left. Go on, Mommy, and you can lie down in bed.

Her mother did not move. Britt-Mari had to leave the bags. Standing next to her mother, she tried with her hands to get her back to her senses. At long last her mother had an inkling, not of the things that had happened a few hours ago under a different roof, but of what was going on right here and now. She was moved. Her hand flew out to caress Britt-Mari. But coming so quickly and unexpectedly, it hit the girl lightly on her ear. Her mother did not notice. She grabbed hold of her daughter's shoulders and, squeezing them tightly, she justified herself in the darkness.

I'm not drunk. You mustn't think that I've been drinking. It's the shock. What has happened is sitting in my throat. And I'm so terribly disgusted. That's why I drank some. Because he left. But it's not the alcohol. It's the shock. That he took off. I don't understand a thing. No, I don't understand it.

Did he go to her?

Yes, that spider, that womb-sick dame. At nineteen twenty-five hours. I couldn't keep him back. He took the nineteen twenty-five. I . . . Mumps, he said. But I don't believe him. Couldn't it be a disgraceful sickness instead? That's what I think. That disgraceful sickness made him. . .

She started laughing. Britt-Mari tried to quiet her down. It was impossible. She tried to force her up the stairs, but her mother held tightly on to the banister and did not move. She threatened to scream, to shriek so that the whole house, the whole world would hear her shriek. She repeated it over and over again, though without going through with it, while Britt-Mari continued in her efforts to push her up the stairs.

On a sudden whim she changed her mind.

Take care of me, she begged. In her hand Britt-Mari could feel her mother's pleasure in having someone work and toil with her body.

The girl helped her mother up the last flight of stairs, unlocked the door, got her to her room and finally down on the bed. Her mother kicked her shoes off with a sigh of relief and said that it's all over now and she's her old self again.

Britt-Mari went back to get the bags, finally able to take one thing at a time. Indeed, she felt some pleasure underneath it all. The fact that things don't hit us all at once. That we can manage one thing at a time. That everything has its time. That she in the middle of difficult uncertainty and fear was able to bend down and feel the bag's simple and comprehensible handle in her hand.

Returning, she found her mother sitting on a chair in the kitchen, drinking milk right out of the bottle. She drank more than a half liter. Britt-Mari carried the bags over into her mother's room. Then she locked the door out to the attic. Her mother sat bent over her knees, in the process of finding herself again. At a given moment the overhead lamplight bothered her. Britt-Mari lit the little night-light by her bed, then went and turned it off.

Aren't you going to bed? she asked.

Her mother gave a jerk as if someone had hit her.

Shut up. You'll shut up, I tell you. With that she walked in to her room, slamming the door shut behind her. Minutes later Britt-Mari heard her mother's screams. Not words. Just naked, raw scream-ing. She had no other way to express her deep hurt. Britt-Mari went in to her. The room was dark, but the shades were not drawn and she could see her mother lying on the bed, still undressed. She had simply thrown herself on top.

Can I do something for you, Mommy?

Her mother's screaming continued with ever shorter breathing stops. Britt-Mari returned to the kitchen, not knowing what to do. She considered calling a doctor, but did not dare to call for help yet. For want of anything better, she ran some cold water, soaked a towel in it, wrung out the excess. Then she went in to her mother, whose screaming now came in ever longer intervals, her breast pumping hard. Snore-like rasping sounds came through her windpipe. Britt-Mari wiped her mother's face and pressed the folded towel on her forehead. Her mother let her go ahead.

Britt-Mari sat down on the chair a short distance away from the bed. It was quiet in the room, a blessed human silence. The night reposed softly and darkly against the window. The hum of the street did not reach up. Britt-Mari knew that, if she were to get up from her chair, she would be able to see a slim golden streak of light lingering behind the Stadsberg.

Her mother began talking to herself, off and on raising her hand and seemingly addressing her. Britt-Mari listened.

He wanted children. He loved children tremendously. It was his greatest wish in life. To have a child. It would with one stroke change reality for him. A child that was his. After all, it's a child that makes life meaningful. Generation to follow generation. It's a person's foremost task to continue his bloodline. He babbled about it continuously, long before vacation, before we moved together and lived with those Dahlins. Imagine having your own kid, he said. A boy. That would clear up a lot. Your own little guy to train from the very beginning so he'd amount to something both as a soccer jock and a human being. Methodically. Character and feet. Speed and focus.— I heard all this. Heard it so many times. That can be arranged, I said. There's nothing wrong with me.—No, there's nothing wrong with you, he said. You're just the kind of woman a guy wants to have a kid with.—That's what I heard. Was it so strange that I saw a way? But I don't seem to be wise to this kind of lover boy. No, I'm not wise to them at all. I don't understand anyone. I don't understand myself. Here we were, eating in a restaurant. It was so simple. Sure, it was simple. It was wonderful too. Then he says, I'll treat you even better coming up, just wait, one day I'll treat you to the most expensive there is.—It didn't change any that I said I had it wonderful as is. He would always surpass the wonderful at some future time. He included the future in everything we did. Better coming up, just wait. This here is nothing to what's going to be.—But everything is fine now, I said. I'm so happy.—Then you'll be dazzled with happiness one day, he said. Just wait, better coming up.—And it was as if he always had to warm himself with the future to get warm now. The future came to his tongue in some strange way, and he liked its taste. Just like that, whether big or small matters.—So when he suddenly says today that now it's finished between us, now I'll go home, I answer him, Stellan, there's something I have to tell you, a secret you'll be interested in. You understand, I say, it's so that I . . .

Are you with child, Mommy?

Not at all. But I said so. He would have liked to have a child. It was so important to him. And sooner or later there was bound to be a child, the way we did. He was never careful. You and I must have a child, he said. Just wait, better coming up. Why delay what is the most wonderful of all, he said. Just wait, better coming up. And he did it so it became better coming up for him.—But when I said that I was almost sure that I was with child—because what else could I say?—then he laughed and said then you've been sleeping with someone else because I can't have children, see, I've been sick and there's no chance in the world I could be the father. Mumps, he said, it's a dangerous sickness at a certain age, but sometimes it's good to have had it, I notice.—You and your future, I screamed and I didn't understand him and I still don't and I never will. Why, I wonder, why did he always go on about a future that he knew didn't exist? Why did he take salt and pepper out of the future and sprinkle it on, all mere products of his fantasy? Why did he have to lie?

If I had just seen him. Now I don't know a thing. I don't even know what he looks like.

What he looks like? Kind and gentle.

But he isn't.

But that's what we think. It's so exciting. His appearance is so strong and masculine. A bouncer, an ablebodied guy. And when he later opens up for you, see how good and kind he is inside. He's so sensitive. He's so noble and righteous when you talk to him. He knows how to say the most wonderful things so that you think they're true. And if you don't believe it, there's still enough good left to be satisfied if you just look at him.

Her mother managed a cynical laugh.

Yeah, he's kind and sweet and wishes everybody well. With words. It's just his actions are so damn rotten. Not the words, not the words. I don't think he really knows what he does. We fought. Yes, I tried to keep him with force. He hit me across the eye. The All-Swedish star hit me. He had two big scrapbooks. Hundreds of snapshots of himself in all kinds of positions. It's sickening to think of it. And snapshots of all those who've enriched his life and whose life he has enriched. And that's exactly what he said when I was lying on the floor, howling, and didn't want to get up and tell him good-bye, thanks for the good times. He stood over me and said, I'm glad for the time we've had, Sylvia. You've enriched my life and I'll never deny that. Thanks. A thousand thanks. You've been indescribably charming, Sylvia. Don't think that I want you to feel like me just now. No, not just now, he said. But I know that some day you'll see all this in a different light. Thanks once again, he said. A thousand thanks. It would of course be nice of you to tidy up in here before leaving. For the Dahlins' sake, I mean. Goodbye, Sylvia. Once again, a thousand thanks for everything that's been between us.

Britt-Mari got up from the chair. Standing still in the room, she listened, an absurd happiness slowly filtering through her. That she was she. That she was none else but who she was. That she stood totally alone. That every human being is totally alone with his life.

Try to sleep, she said and went to her place in the kitchen.

She undressed. Then she went to the sink and washed herself. Before she was through, her mother entered, leaping over to the side of the stove and holding on to it as if to avoid getting too close to the girl's body.

It's really your fault that things turned out the way they did for me!

Screaming at first, she repeated the sentence three times with a gradually plummeting, softer voice. Britt-Mari continued to rinse the lather off her face, then reached for the towel to dry. Without an answer, she went to bed. Her mother followed and started screaming again.

You look like a goody-goody, Britt-Mari. Always. Morning, noon and night your face is nothing but a sermon. I trust that you live a proper life, dear Mommy? You're not going to let yourself be dragged into the dirt, dear Mommy? Of course, I don't begrudge your having fun, dear Mommy, but, dear Mommy, you ought to consider there are other values in life.

She waved with her arms, then stiffened up.

D'you hear what I'm saying?

Yes. I hear you.

What's your answer?

Nothing.

Can't you talk? D'you think it's not worth your while? Perhaps you think that I'm unreliable?

Britt-Mari remained silent.

Do you refuse to talk to your own mother?

We can very well wait until tomorrow. Why should we talk now when you're so excited? We'll regret it. We'll say things that aren't true and we don't mean.

We? D'you want to say that I lie? You think that I'm flighty.

She waved her arms around, skidding in her own movements.

It's your fault that things went the way they did. I'm made to take one day at a time. I'm made to roll with the punches. But then

I have to face you every day. There's a higher life. O yes. There's a love that shines high above the earth. O yes. Everybody has an immortal soul, full of boundless love, o yes. But your mother is a tart.

Her body was slipping with the many fantastical gestures she tried to perform. She had so many faces left to pull in the air around her. One that deformed her face she liked above all: she took hold of Britt-Mari's ponytail with both hands and hung herself on her.

Your mother is a hussy. Do you hear? You mustn't ask of your mother to be anything but a lewd hussy.

The whole weight of her mother's body came against Britt-Mari. She reeled and would have tumbled if her mother had not slipped down on her knees first. Britt-Mari tried to steady her, but she could not. Her mother fell full-length on the floor. She started to cry, a cramp-like tearless crying. Standing stiffly upright, her arms stretched out in a helpless gesture, Britt-Mari could not understand why it was not she, Britt-Mari, who was crying.

Her mother was crying. Her mother lay on the floor. When Britt-Mari bent down and put her hands on her shoulders, her mother gave a start. Britt-Mari tried crawling next to her, but her mother shuffled off across the cork rug in the direction of the door to her room.

Britt-Mari got up, watching her mother crawl over the floor. It was slow. It was laborious, difficult. Deep weariness inside her breast held her back. Everything was gone from her except this shuffling, degraded body.

Not for one minute did Britt-Mari consider the scene in front of her of lasting consequence. Absolutely not. Life did not end here, not their lives. Her mother would not forever continue to crawl across the floor in her present condition. Britt-Mari knew that she ought not to have this certainty. Not now. She could not cry. She did not shuffle over the floor. She could not get herself down and do it. She had lost all need for grief and it frightened her. Coldly watching her mother crawl forward on the floor, she could feel something dying within her. Her love for life, her love for beauty was dying and she turned cold because of the great cost. She hardened at the thought that nothing remained. Our difficulty is not the cruel changes hitting us. The difficulty is the loss of meaning in what happens. It frightens us into a cold, hardened form from which life looks like a hallucination whose grandiosity and misery we don't share. Her mother was miserable. Out of her senses, she could not project in any direction that things were to change once she would fall asleep, change during this very night already. Britt-Mari saw before her an unreal vision of a dark, evasive figure carrying its skin, a skin surrounding organs and blood, through the passages of the thousands of transformations in human experience.

Automatically she followed her mother into the other room. Again the mother was willing to accept the help of her daughter to care for her miserable body, as she put it.

Don't polish the casing, her mother mumbled. Just throw a rag over the casing. That's enough.

When she finally rested between the sheets, her tears began to flow. Time and again she whispered that she loved so in the extreme. That's what was wrong with her. She always loved so tremendously. No one in the entire world loved the way she did. It was her fate to love in the extreme. She would continue doing so as long as she lived, because that's the way she was created. She no longer mentioned Stellan, gave no name to the man she loved. Britt-Mari realized that this was right. Her mother did not love anyone. She felt tempted to bend down to her mother and whisper, You don't love anyone. You have never loved anyone in particular. You haven't even loved yourself. You just wanted to love. You were willing to love. And when you thought that you loved someone special, it was a wrong thought, because you still only wanted to love.

Again her presence became too much for her mother. Again her mother accused her of being the cause of her present suffering. It was the girl who had duped her into going beyond her capabilities. As if she really wanted to live the life of a secure housewife! She would have cheated right away.

I cheated on your father. Do you hear what I'm saying, Britt-Mari? I cheated on your father, and he knew it.

Although Britt-Mari did not believe her, she made no objections. She sensed that her mother wanted the words to touch her, but she would not permit it. She let the words pass. Her mother would often come up with accusations. But she did not succeed now. Britt-Mari left her mother and returned to her bed. She was tired.

She was frightened. But when she was about to take off her slip, she knew that it was impossible for her to find sleep. She stood still for a while, waiting. Then she got dressed again, quietly and carefully and without really making up her mind about what she would do next. When there was no more sound coming from her mother's room, she walked out into the night.

31

She was surprised to find that the hand of the church clock had not reached the midnight hour yet and that the city streets were anything but deserted. Hardly two hours had passed since she had been in the park and seen her mother return home. The darkness was only darker. The brightness of the streetlights was more intense and, by the same token, more solitary. She posted herself in the far corner of Allén, from where she could see the roof. She inspected it as if her looking could control her mother's condition behind all the metal, girders and stones. But the darkness up there was total. Not even the window globes were distinguishable.

At some distance before her, where the city's main streets and entertainment centers converged, Storbro bridge's wide light path rose above a river of darkness, and parks girdled all this to both left and right, Saturday night's tomcatty spirits provided the plaza with its special atmosphere—a mixture of subtle indolence, gratification, and lust offered, peddled, sown; of unquenchable, indiscriminate aggression and thirst for abuse along with a flourish of green-dotted, galling arguments.

Britt-Mari turned the other way. She walked over to one of the trees on Allén and stepped behind it, hoping for regeneration. Nothing happened. But when she remembered her pictures, comfort came to her. They made it clear that coldness did not rule her. Her mind could still distinguish the important and desirable things in life. She lifted her hands, yet able to create the configurations she knew were beautiful.

The world had not changed. This new icy darkness did not dominate the world. The icy darkness ruled her. Not her memory, not her reasoning power. Not her hands, not her movements. Because look and see what she could do! Throw her head backward, fling her hands up, open her mouth and, with a ring of warmth in her voice, call faintly,

Love me, God, in this black night.

Her arms swinging, her body gyrated from her tightly locked feet rhythmically upward.

Make love come alive! Awaken my heart from death! Feed your lamb!

Heat spots blossomed across her body. Her wrists and neck were on fire. Mangled ribbons of heat burned her legs. Look at her ability to play! She felt a feverish happiness at being able to impersonate all that was exalted and desirable. In a flash she remembered her feeling of absurd happiness just before the icy darkness overcame her. That she was she, herself, and no one else. That she lived protected within solitude's solidity. She remembered this happiness and her play now performed the task of proving her uniqueness.

She started walking down Storgatan. The darkness was sated with warmth and humidity. Everything standing upright seemed to have a soft, translucent consistency. The thought of never being able to return home and, at most, to just correspond with her mother in the future occurred to her, but it remained meaningless. She needed to play. And she did. She walked thirteen steps on trial and under strict control, but felt only her own legs and feet. She stopped at a cigarette vending machine to listen, only to find that she had no double hearing. Then she tested her vision. In order to provide her eyes with a neutral starting point, she covered them with her hands, counted to seven, then removed her hands and looked carefully around. She had no power to see double. There was no way for her to fabricate a memory for anyone's life but her own.

Things turned hazier when she examined her thoughts and feelings. Thought rose up against thought and feeling against feeling. This state of affairs confused her to the extent that it made her take a turn off the main street. Holding her hand in front of her mouth, she ran up an alley. Which thought, which feeling represented her? The flow of various thoughts and feelings did not stop. To the contrary, it seemed that her interest gave thoughts and feelings special liveliness and regenerative powers until finally all degenerated into a gallop of sentences: I'm a widow, I'm a princess, I'm an Indian girl, I'm an eagle on a mountain top, I'm a lemming about to drown in the Gulf of Bothnia, I'm pregnant and the house of correction is beckoning, I'm a girl who has hurt herself badly, I'm a teacher, I'm a cook on a steamer, I'm a filmstar, I'm a star, fallen down to earth and crashed into pieces . . .

Then the tight squeeze of her icy darkness made her stop. She could play, but where was the secure reality she needed to play with, or on, or against? She could not transform the serious into play. She herself was the empty transformation. She was nothing. If there is a chair, it can be transformed to a train. She could do nothing but transform nonexistent nothingness in empty air.

Britt-Mari reached Köpmansgatan. The row of planted birches gave the street a friendly look in the nightlight. They looked neither dusty nor in poor condition under this light. The narrow band of grass the car riders wanted to eliminate along with the birches glowed lightgreen under the electrical lamps. A man on a bicycle without lights turned around Bethlehem Church. No stars were out. Britt-Mari needed only to call out that she saw a policeman to watch him jump off his bike and lawabidingly lead it further, perhaps get a nod of gratitude. But she never completed this performance and it occurred to her that most of the time we only consider plans without actually carrying them out.

Köpmansgatan lay almost deserted. She stopped and counted three cars besides those parked on the street. All three cars turned into an alley. Nobody seemed to have any reason to walk up or down Köpmansgatan at night. Even those who were outside only crossed this road. Britt-Mari too decided to turn into the alley leading to Storgatan. She stopped close by the coffee shop *Blå Lyktan*. Something was going on there. Five others, including two sailors, were already watching.

It was like a film clip.

Two gentlemen, dressed in summer suits, one of them bald and wearing a small-chequered vest, were tugging at a young woman and trying to get her to follow with them to their parked car. Facetiously they could not understand what had gotten into their little sweetheart to make her so rebellious all of a sudden. Everything was settled, wasn't it, and little sweetheart here ought to know by now what kind of noble gentlemen she was dealing with. Did she want their cards? Well here they are. Or did she want to see their aristocratic family tree? They could oblige with that too. Hoho, the gentlemen laughed, pulling sweetheart's arms with less funny jerks. If cash wasn't good enough, perhaps they could leave some industrial shares carrying six percent interest? Sexy? Hoho, the gentlemen laughed, blinking their eyes at each other while still holding on to the girl's wrists. With their free hands they were trying take hold of the girl's back and push her through the open car door.

As if fallen from the sky, an older, rather strange-looking woman suddenly appeared in their midst. Her clothes looked very distinguished. Slim figured, she moved with complete self-assurance. Only under her oval hat with dove-gray brim lived a face with weary features and doubtful glow.

Gentlemen. Gentlemen, she called. Her gloved hands stood stiffly in the air.

For shame, gentlemen. What are you doing to the child?

Raising her hands, she managed to touch the young woman's cheeks.

Let me look at you, she prattled as if talking to a baby. Let me look straight into your eyes. She needed not more than a quick glance to discover the secret. With a boundlessly moving voice she turned to the gentlemen,

She is a virgin. This lovely child is a virgin.

But that was more than the little sweetheart could take. Panic-stricken, she gave a long-drawn screech, pulled herself free and jumped right into the car. The gentlemen marked their pleasure with a "Hipp, hurray," not late to jump in right after her. But the older woman did not give in so easily. She called forth a long life's experiences, all of which painted the blackest future for the virgin if she were not careful enough to get immediately away from the lechers.

Look at me, she called pathetically. I know how things go. I too was a virgin once.

When no one in the car paid attention to her, she changed her stance. Wondering whether she could come along wherever it was they wanted to go, she assured them that no one would regret it.

Old is best, she said, her quivering lips smiling.

But the motor and the men were ready and the car glided away from the small crowd that had gathered. Suddenly indignant, the old woman called for the police against this white slave trade. But then she discovered the sailors and turned to them with a smile. The promise her smile contained aroused them. Wobbling back and forth, they thudded together. The woman kept on talking with elegant, controlled hand movements and suggestive facial expressions. One of the sailors slapped the woman's flat rear and another pulled off his white cap and placed it on the woman's tailor-made shoulder.

There's something special about a sailor, she sang with a feeble voice and graceful body movements. But ten bucks. Absolutely no less than ten bucks.

We'll have a ten together, one of the sailors said, wobbling and guffawing. They grabbed hold of each other and straightened their backs.

Are you completely whacky? the woman said, shaking her hands. What do you take me for? A Mrs. Consul or a businessman's wife?

What's it going to be? one of the sailors asked.

Take hold of my arms, boys, the woman said.

The sailors did, playing drunk as long as Britt-Mari could see them.

She left the plaza in a hurry. She knew now where she wanted to go. All rivers and creeks run out to the sea. Night and day, throughout the ages rivers and creeks maintain their course—seaward, to the sea. Britt-Mari ran in the direction of the harbor.

But when she came to the Esplanade she gave in to an urge to follow its course. The center walkway seemed deserted and far away from the streetlights. It did not take her long, though, to find every bench occupied. Couples were holding each other, talking in sometimes low, sometimes excited voices. She stopped in the darkness, trying to think of her loneliness in a playful, new way. She was standing here now, as lonely as the flower she had picked for Grepp's grave mound. Who would come to meet her? Who wanted to cross the chasm that loneliness dooms us to live behind? Who stretched out to honor her? Who was interested? Who found it worthwhile to communicate with her? Who would like to talk?

No one. Why? Oh, she did not exist. She was dead. The icy darkness prevailed. No, I don't feel a thing, she mumbled, considering the entire world a stranger to her. Her eyes moistened, and she had the feeling of her limbs locking tightly while her body stiffened, like wood. No one knew her. She was a stranger, she discovered. Wherever she turned she would learn that she did not fit in, that no one was waiting for her and that there was no task demanding her contribution.

My native city, my native city, she mumbled time and again without realizing that she was walking down the center aisle of the Esplanade. A man's voice was bellowing and she gave a jerk.

My country, my native country, she whispered, feeling a strange comfort that made her reel.

She discovered that she could stagger this thought, my earth, my globe, my God, my heavenly Father. Who are you? she asked herself. Swedish, was the answer. Who are you at heart? God's child, was the answer.—Then she perceived the bitter truth: to be Swedish is to be as lonely as she was; to be a human being is to be as lonely as she was; to be God's child is to be as lonely as she was. She reached out for one affiliation after another, tasting each one with her senses, only to return immediately to her own skin. To live in her native city, in her native country and in God's created world means to live in a kitchen in a small attic apartment or to walk along Esplanade's gravel path without anyone in the world who wanted to cross the vacuum that surrounded her.

Look, a child of her city, a child of her country, a child of her heavenly Father.

She started running again, leaving the Esplanade to take Kyrkogatan down to the harbor. She was dead. The icy darkness prevailed. She denied herself a chance to live. At some time today, this evening, tonight, she had stopped existing. She stopped outside a store entrance and walked into its darkness.

Where are you? she wondered aloud.

She repeated the question several times. Disguising her voice, she whispered the way she would when entering a strange room; she joked as if playing blindman's buff, she was strict like a mother calling back her straying children, she was angry, she was indifferent, she was sad, suffering.

Where are you? Where are you?

Here I am!

The answer surprised her, even though it was her own. Just like her pompous harangue uttered a minute ago, the words came with a painful, naked voice, so close that she yielded to the sublime. Someone had spoken through her mouth. The real Britt-Mari had finally come through. No longer surprised, she felt this real girl taking hold of her in a physical transformation. Stepping out of the store entrance, she saw her body casting her shadow on the sidewalk up to her waist. The rest disappeared in the darkness. She pulled her shadow out to see herself complete all the way up to her hair. Pulling her ponytail aside, she watched it casting its own shadow. Then, step by step, she withdrew into the darkness and lo, the shadow gradually broke up and eventually she stood without shadow altogether.

Finally she was herself, softly and sensitively real, full of pain and guilt and longing and reality. How could she ever have acted the way she did? Did she not love her mother? Of course she loved her mother. She realized it now. Cognizant of her real caring, all at once she knew where her place was.

She had to help her mother, had to think of something that would straighten things out. It was difficult. It was hard to know what was true and what was false about her mother. She hardly told things straight, the way they happened to her or others. Her versions indicated her wish to change the past, the future and herself. Britt-Mari knew instinctively the truth about her mother, and her tales could not deceive her.—The least she could do now was to be with her in case she needed her. If for nothing else, only to pull up the shades, get her the paper, make coffee, stroke her forehead.

Britt-Mari turned to go home.

But after no more than a few steps she had a change of heart. She stopped abruptly and recoiled as if sensing a lurking danger. She took a few more steps, trying to overcome her inner reluctance. Suddenly she felt her neck stiffen and strain backward. Hopelessness in her eyes, she stared ahead and her gaze, losing its focus, turned empty. She felt the bitterness of her predicament and her scorn turned on herself.

She spun around to walk down to the harbor, getting ever more excited on her way there. She had the feeling that soon, very soon something enormous was about to happen to her. Good or bad, she fantasized in the abstract and carefully avoided imagining particulars. Her premonitions were definite, as distinct as conventional words like native city or fatherland, words that provided human emotions with the same strange scope. To succumb, to succeed. Love, hate. To find, to lose. A meeting to alter everything. An energy to come charging like the powers of spring, igniting all, all . . .

Then it happened. She had not yet reached the harbor when they met. Arnold called her name. She stopped and turned. He came quickly toward her, holding one arm up and waving eagerly. But she felt sad because he did not look the way he did when she first met him. Was he drunk too? Had the tomcattish Saturday night spirits taken hold of him too?

He began to sing, loud and shrill.

Quiet, she called.

But he did not stop. He too was unreal, his movements, his face, his gaze, his intentions. He had cast off his image. Now he acted up.

Do you hear that I can sing? Can you hear my true song?

Hush, Arnold.

Doesn't it please you? After all, I'm finally singing a true song. Do you hear me? My sounds are genuine, damn genuine. I learned this song tonight. Tonight I studied bird calls. It involves visiting all the places where birds nest. It's contagious and I caught it. Now I'm a bird myself.

What are you telling me?

I am a bird. Hear me sing a true song. Admire my courtship-display.

Hush, Arnold. You're hurting me.

But he continued to act up with his body, his mouth, his eyes. He argued his insubstantiality: already an early eighteenth-century German maintains in his study *Naturgeschichte der Stubenvögel* that in choosing her mate from one hundred males, the female bird selects the one whose singing she likes best. And what does Darwin tell us? Well, all bird-watchers simply and clearly agree that the male of the species uses his singing to attract the mute females.—How quiet you are, Cinnamoncandy.

Make me real. Make me exist.

Only her words pleaded with him. Standing absolutely still, she waited with closed eyes. He turned quiet and stood still. She could not hear him. When she opened her eyes again, she saw that he had become real. They stood like this for a long time, facing each other without uttering a word. He was not drunk. Having jumped out of himself, he was turning somersaults into the impossible. Facing her, he protested in two directions. Formerly sad, he refused to be sad any longer. He had discarded his superiority and irony. His earlier cool curiosity had disappeared. The bitter intelligence in his eyes was gone. Britt-Mari discovered suddenly a boyish face, giving her the feeling that they were almost the same age. His outfit was less elegant than the clothes he had worn the times she had seen him before. Tieless, his shirt was open, and his light pants were not pressed recently.

Where are you headed? he asked at long last.

Nowhere.

He tried to smile.

It's been a long time since we last saw each other.

I've seen you downtown a few times. Three or four maybe.

Didn't you want to meet me?

Sometimes yes, sometimes no.

Did I frighten you the last time?

No.

I didn't think so.

He mumbled something, his face troubled. Britt-Mari turned away. She remembered the kiss she had given him, heaven blossoming out first and then knotting up around his mouth; his fear she had lifted like a dark mast right into his face; the apple and the bites taken from it.

She felt his grip on her arm. Without looking up at him, she sensed his torture.

There are certain thoughts one should not divulge, he said, his voice strangely tense. But what I told you is true. That is the truth. Don't try to find out why I can see the truth. Don't come with some cheap explanations about my private life.

He was quiet, but did not loosen his grip around her arm. She did not say anything.

Here is the truth, he continued. Don't ever ask me: Who are you? You must ask: Where are you?—Then I shall answer: Arnold. I am inside Arnold. That is the name of my standing. It is my longitude and latitude. Whatever is inside Arnold does not separate us. We are much alike, we human beings. We are comparable. But my standing in Arnold divides us, it separates me from the rest of the world.

He laughed without happiness. Silence fell between them, became tangible. Britt-Mari repeated her request,

Make me real. Act so that I may exist.

He moved one foot, the earth grinding under his sole.

Would you dare come up to my room?

Britt-Mari gave him a quiet look,

Why shouldn't I dare?

32

When they entered his room, he first pulled the curtains shut before he lit the lamp. Now he was turning the light off before opening the curtains again. He remained standing by the window, his forehead on the pane. The streetlight surrounded his tanned back and dark head with a faint blue-yellow glow. She watched his bare arm and the lowered hand. She was no longer interested in looking at his books in the bookcase, or his bed, or his desk standing by the wall instead of by the window because he did not want any distractions while studying or writing. From his entertainment center radiated a warm yellow sheen.

He liked music very much and played his favorite records for her. The art of music is the best of all, he said. They listened to modern music and he translated the titles for her. He tried to teach her the names of the composers, spelling their names and she had to repeat them. By now they had slipped her mind, but their works excited her without taxing her emotions. In a painful-lucky way her excitement could rise into beautiful designs and shapes. The music flowed through her, making it impossible for her to tear herself away.

Her senses, thoughts and feelings emulated the music in a constant round of creation and recreation inside her. The music shaped her experience, lifted it up from the invisible and gave it shape, broke it down and rebuilt it further, hurling into the past its rapture, its care, its indivisible thought, its sensual joy while hurrying toward the future in energetic, deliberate, humble, peaceful structures.

The emptiness and want afterwards. How could she organize her experience in the way music did? How could she lift the compact matter that often threatened to choke her under its weight? Music could touch the most difficult and make it light, dark but light, solid with clear-cut contours, deadly dark though purifyingly luminous.

Only more music could heal her grief over her inability to recreate herself. With music her languid hands could rise like white figurines, but she did not feel their caresses on her cheeks, her forehead, her hair, her breasts, her shoulders. Only when her hands returned to their heavy and powerless state did she notice them again.

She sat, listening. She did not look at the window. He was silent—it was as if he had stepped through the window and disappeared.

Britt-Mari bent down to take off her sandals. She wore no stockings. The rug was red, but that did not show in the dusk. She rubbed her feet lightly against it and a tingle came rushing up her legs. She set her feet on the floor, waiting, her arms resting on the easy chair's comfortable armrests. It suddenly occurred to her that she sat up straight, her back tense. She smiled to herself as she leaned backward.

Never before had she sat in an expensive easy chair like this. At first her back was very respectful, not wanting to become too intimate. Probably misunderstanding the reason, Arnold playfully pressed her backward when he noticed it. She finally understood what "taking it easy" meant. She caught herself sitting up straight while he was playing his records. That's when she was unable to take it easy. Not later either, when Arnold got up and paced the floor. She sat up, on the outer edge, at times even gripping the tip of the bulging armrests.

Arnold was honest with her. She believed it, no, she was totally convinced of it. The things he said would never have been said otherwise. He sharply rebuked himself, even scorned his misery. But

that was about a minor phenomenon on the surface of human misery. That's why his concentrated unrest was so bizarre, he judged, so
bare of deeper motives. She would be unable to share in his longitude and latitude. His position was irrevocably located inside Arnold. But they could touch each other, one place moving close to
the other place. Position Arnold and position Britt-Mari could an-
chor as closely as possible to each other.

She found it impossible to be honest. She had not worried about
it then and did not do it now. A confession on her part would concern the past, and the past no longer existed. Her filching from the
future from the person she would once become was a closed chapter
now. She loved him, loved him exactly the way she was. She could
not help that, as absurd as she found herself to be. At any rate it was
this absurdity in her that was in love. To tell him that she did not
share his problems in earnest just for the sake of truth, why should
she? He knew by now that she believed in God. And what is God,
but the placeless place? And what is salvation, if but the life of the
blessed in this placeless place? Where distance is neutralized and our
position is not fixed in the ego's enclosure. It is determined by one
thing only: love.

The easy chair's security was pressing firmly against her back,
and an intuitive foreknowledge of whatever lay in store for her in
the future came to her. All the difficulties were gone. She had fought
her way up. Her husband was standing there by the window. He
loved her. She was sitting in her own home, in his den. What day
was this? Their engagement anniversary. Seven, nine or twelve years
ago they got engaged. They were celebrating. That's why she sat in
his room, so like the one he had once in the home of his parents.
Their anniversary involved a secret known only to them. They pre-
sented each other with something beautiful. They repeated this every
year. That's what they were about to do now.

Britt-Mari could wait no longer. Separating from the security of
the chairback, she sat up and looked toward the window. Arnold
had turned around and was sitting on the windowsill, looking into
the room's darkness. Britt-Mari raised her arms, but dropped them
again. If he had continued staring out of the window, she would
have slipped off her dress. Now she could not. It was the very act of
undressing that did not correlate with her feelings. Nudity would

have been all right. She knew what was about to happen. They had talked about it, and they had mutually agreed.

She glanced at the door to see whether perhaps it was darker over there. She remembered a drapery in front of it and hoped for enough room for her in the space between.

He jumped off the window sill, petting her over her forehead as he walked past. His white shirt stopped where she knew his bed stood. The way his hands moved told her that he was unbuttoning his shirt. She lifted her skirt and struggled out of her dress. Then she quickly took off the remaining underwear. She walked a few steps over to the window. Not before she heard him come closer did she turn around.

They did not look at each other's naked bodies. Their hands met for a short second before their eyes flowed into each other. He led her toward the window and they stood there the way they had agreed to do. Half a step away from each other and holding hands. Her feet close together, she let her right leg carry her body weight. He pushed one foot forward and his toes touched hers. They stood at an angle and the dim light coming through the window settled slightly stronger on her.

For a second time their eyes locked into each other and now their gazes remained steady. Their tension loosened, their furtive ogling and angle-shy tightness. They were unaware of their flesh, their skin, their warmth. Leaving no room for anything else, they lived the act, let it progress in a thousand tiny motions. The full balance, the severe rest, the quiet breathing were reaching perfection—their necks outlined in solemnity, their lips turned serious and taut. In unison they experienced the exalted, formed an image they both shared. She felt as if neither one of them existed separately, but in some third dimension that included both of them and made them one. Her feelings were in every respect in this unity. She experienced its winglike contour. She felt how they were moving in its motions, and how they were resting in its rest.

When his gaze unlocked, she looked at his shoulders and breast and his mouth. He squeezed her hands and she noticed with surprise that his lips came apart. He moistened them with his tongue. His grip around her hands became harder and harder, the wings enclosing them trembled. Suddenly he came down on his knees in front of her and pressed his cheek against her body. The wing stretched wide and returned to its original form. She knew it. She felt it. She understood that she would never lose her connection with this form, no matter what would happen inside its absolute contour.

Keeping his tight grip on her hands, he pulled them behind her back and bound them in his strength. He stroked his head and cheek back and forth across her abdomen and made a faint noise that sounded as if it came from an insect.

Suddenly he stopped, and she felt him resting against her. Her vision expanded to include the fact that the form encasing them was larger by far than either of them separately. Her humble happiness, her singing gratitude placed her on the proper level of greatness.

Finally I am happy, she whispered then.

He let go of her hands. She lifted them up to her bent face and whispered into his palms, I am happy, I am happy. He asked her to be quiet, and she grew silent. She straightened out, finding that she still existed in every respect in the form they had created. His hands stroked the back of her legs, starting at her calves, then moving up to the crease under her knees. He uttered a low moan and he stroked his forehead ever faster over her skin. Suddenly he left her and got up. Turning his back toward her, he told her that she had to leave now. He repeated the few words several times,

You have to go now. You have to go now.

He walked over to his bed and got dressed. Looking for her clothes in the darkness, Britt-Mari found the easy chair. He finished dressing before her and moved over to the window. When he heard that she was done, he pulled the curtains and switched on the light of the floorlamp. Britt-Mari could see that he had pulled a mask over his face. Hiding inside his front, he would not express his thoughts.

You're going to find your way home on your own?

She nodded.

You don't regret it?

She shook her head.

He followed her to the outer door. They walked through a wide hall with parquet flooring. The only guide showing their way, besides his own familiarity, was the streak of light coming from his room. Down on the street she remembered the soft sounds of his bare feet and she was surprised that she had not expected him to kiss her in the open door before the lock slammed shut. Suddenly she understood herself and him. She smiled a quick smile and walked quickly toward Storgatan 33.

33

She must have known it while still asleep. When she opened her eyes she was prepared for what was waiting for her—a dreary Sunday morning. Lifeless, a time burdened with the past, a solidified past that did away with the scanty present she was forced to live in now. It was the same for her mother as for her, she thought. Neither one could reach for what had happened to her these last twenty-four hours. They were unable to continue. They hardly existed. Only whatever had happened to them was fixedly alive, was unyieldingly, starkly and powerfully present.

She moved under the Sunday roof. Reality faded gradually into the background. A step of empty space remained constant between her and what had happened. One step of nothingness backward and forward and to the sides. She was solidly encased in her experience.

It was the same for her mother. But she stayed in bed.

The Sunday hours were ticking away. Nothing of what Britt-Mari had hoped for happened. Slowly she stopped hoping, and eventually she concluded that there was nothing to hope for. Every attempt foundered, every start to action faded away and vanished. Even though she knew exactly what to do in certain instances to get results, she refrained from doing it. She could not understand her passivity. It was so simple. It was easy. Still, she never acted. Did nothing. All she did was to consider doing it over and over again; I'm going to do it now.—But she never did. Actually, even that did not bother her.

She went over to her mother again. Sucking at her underlip, biting and holding it between her teeth, she tried to prevent a smile which, she knew, was inappropriate, yes, forbidden, and in no way corresponded to her true feelings.

Her mother was lying in the same position she had been in hours ago. Looking at her that morning, Britt-Mari was convinced that her mother had been awake all night. Her eyes immobile and her body rigid, she looked like a lifeless doll and gave the impression of someone easy to understand. Supine on her back, she kept staring at the ceiling, her blanket barely reaching her groin. The skin around her left eye where she was hit was discolored and looked like a gaudy dark flower. Of course she did not see the ceiling. She saw nothing and not one blink indicated that she had heard Britt-Mari enter the room. Her body was drained of all feeling. She was concentrating on one thing only: her heart's pain, and the wall she needed to encase this immensely active, constant onslaught. Her pain had come like a peep-show's distinct spectacle. But her war did not reach through to her limbs and voice organ.

Was there possibly something else happening behind her mother's easily comprehensible exterior? There were times when Britt-Mari suspected it, but the thought never lasted. Just one question returned: Isn't there something else behind that which is visible?

She felt no pity. What she knew gave her no reason to shudder. She understood that her mother's heart would break open and over-flow sooner or later. Her mother's difficulties were never hopeless. Eventually they disappeared and then she wished to be somewhere else. Out of reach. At that point it did not bother her any longer.

It was terrible realizing how much she loved her mother and that she needed to do something for her. It was terrible too knowing that the wonder created last night when Arnold took her hands was still alive in her. Worse was her desire to cry before the living, beautiful form that enclosed her, and her urge to laugh in front of her mother. But she did not feel bad about all this. The difficulty was knowing these things. It was like falling without feeling dizzy, or losing a hand without feeling pain. The sights are terrible and grim, the eyes can see them, but the pain does not burn.

You have to eat, she told her mother. Can't I heat up something for you?

Her mother did not answer. Again Britt-Mari chewed on her underlip to prevent the smile from materializing. Earlier she had tried to pull up the shades, but her mother had said, "Don't," the only word she had uttered all day. Don't, don't. . . A handbreadth of daylight streaked across the floor, generating a gradually thinning glory of golden sheen.

You have to work tomorrow morning, Britt-Mari said. So you know that you have to eat.

She could see that her mother would not go to the plant tomorrow. How could she appear with this eye? Was it possible that she no longer could stand seeing Stellan at her place of work? But it was a child's task to believe that everything will repeat, or that everything will come to a catastrophic end. And now she really smiled. She turned away, thinking that it was cruel having to live so miserably and lost. She did not feel the cruelty of her position, but she knew that it was a fact.

Full of spite, she sat down. If she remained sitting in her mother's room long enough, perhaps something would happen. Her mother might get impatient or furious in some way, or something unpredictable might happen, such as for example her mother sitting up in bed, saying that everything was over: vacation is gone, love is gone, the wonderful, simple week-day has begun.

But nothing like that did happen. Not even her suspicions received any boost. What she thought she was detecting at times were illusions, like catching sight of a figure that turns out to be a tree. Or hearing a frightening sound that turns out to be the wind.

Soon she forgot her mother. She failed to remember her scheme to make her mother eat, the way she used to do. Ask no questions. No, but put a tray with food in front of her. Her mother had always eaten the food on the trays she used to put on the chair next to her bed. Half an hour later there was no breadcrumb left. And the coffee she would prepare afterward was always welcome. Perhaps not in words, but the coffeepot was soon empty. She had watched her mother once putting as much as five sugar lumps in her first cup.

But today she wanted her mother to ask for the food, or else go without it. She declined to run wordless errands. She did not understand why she did not want to.

Love's outline started taking shape as she was sitting on the chair, ever so near her and with far greater force this time. She could feel its form rising above her, before her, under her and behind her, pressing hard against her back. It made her freeze and shiver. She became aware of how ugly, how pitiable, how lost she was. Lost, and yet strapped. Lost in whatever encased her. It was like standing under a sparkling, starry sky; like escaping cramped and stifling quarters out into the enormity of a sparkling, starry sky, its eternal lights silent and mute.

Up above nothing happens. Happenings come to the onlooker. She feels her insignificance. She feels her insignificance and ugliness. But, her perception of the glorious stars and the brilliance of the boundless sky reveals to her also the distinctness of her existence. Do trees shudder? Does the earth's gravel tremble? Do things created to stand up on the surface of the earth shake? Do buildings tumble down? The very ability of beholding arouses jubilation and the beholding eye is yet another star whose illuminated centerpoint becomes part of the glorious, mute, lofty design.

What happens when the eyes return to the reality of the hand and the thing at the foot, making her shudder again?

Beauty retains its hold on the human heart and threatens to destroy it. In order to save herself, she needs to crash into the densest ugliness, her beautiful eyes looking out, terrorstricken.

Suddenly her mother is talking. Her voice is totally sober.

I could get up now. Of course I could. I could also stop thinking of him, starting right now. I could live on as if nothing had happened between us. Of course I could. And go to work tomorrow. What would prevent me? Nothing. Listen to what I'm saying. Nothing at all. Right at this moment I could cut a deep line and say that I don't care. Of course I can. I could easily do it. I couldn't care less about what has happened. What he has done means nothing to me. I am my own person. Always. I'm alive. I should say that I'm alive. Can't you see that I'm alive and kicking in spite of everything I went through?—But I don't want to live like that.

She raised herself up on her elbows and looked at Britt-Mari who sat, a vague expression on her face, as if she had not heard or seen anything.

That's just it. I don't want to. Of all the choices the worst would be to say: I don't want to live that way.

She sat up straight and both her arms flew up in a gesture of strength,

I don't want to.

A glow spread over her ravaged face born of an anger she relished.

Can't you understand that I don't want to? She sank back into her pillow and concentrated on something that more and more looked like pleasure.

It feels good that I don't want to, she said, her voice loud and clear. If I were any different I wouldn't be worth a straw.

It was at this point that Britt-Mari began to laugh. Neither a roar, nor a giggle, it sounded artificial and strained.

Then she left.

34

When she returned a few hours later her mother, quite unexpectedly, was up and almost dressed. But for her nothing had changed. She was still lost, locked into what she loved, encased in something that was stronger than she. In contrast, her mother was very busy and had a smile for her when she arrived. Britt-Mari was stunned.

Poor girl, her mother said, and Britt-Mari did not know where to turn. Her wretchedness was evident and she knew it. Knew also that her mother had pulled herself up by her own bootstraps, up above what had happened to her, and was now working on a solution. Britt-Mari had laughed. She realized that her mother's words by no means meant an empty rebellion. She was going to act.

Stop pretending, her mother said.

Her new thoughts and decisions showed in her face. The discoloration around her eyes was covered up with cosmetics. Britt-Mari could only wait.

Good that you showed up now, her mother said, putting away her jars. I was afraid that you'd be too late.

She gave the girl a swift glance and Britt-Mari watched a strange transition follow—her mother's wish becoming feeling, and the feeling creating a behavior pattern independent of the fact that the course of events her mother so desperately wanted had not yet come to pass. Suddenly her mother lived again the world of a lover. Her happiness existed only in her imagination, not on the outside of herself. She knew beforehand what life would be like before whatever was about to happen had happened. She already lived it. It invaded her, took hold of her. Her lips separated, though not her hands. She moved them in a distinct way, hands pressed together,

I don't demand that you understand, she mumbled, her face straying from the girl right into the beloved space.

Again Britt-Mari was impressed by something she had suspected earlier that day regarding what had happened to her mother. It was the clarity of one of anger's thousandfold manifestations that struck her. What had happened to her mother. What she had in mind. She was ready to let anger rule and she knew what she wanted destroyed. She enclosed herself into a beloved space to be able to see whatever she could not allow to exist.

No, I really don't ask for that, her mother repeated, her voice absent. A short silence followed. Then her mother came out with what she wanted to outwit, eliminate and drown in her future,

I don't want to live like a decent, dustproof robot, she said, raising her voice. I can, but that's just it, I don't want to. I know what's ahead of me. But I've never been disciplined with common discipline. I'll be my own discipline. I don't want to. Do you hear, I don't want to. But . . .

As if taking a step backward and again withdrawing from reality and a space created by others, she continued.

About him, it's going to be the way I want. Even if he hits me. Do you hear? There's something he'll never crush, however much he may hit me. But if he is not mine, I don't have anything, not even something that is frayed. When I raise my cup to my lips it's cold china I'm drinking. Do you understand? Eating spoons, eating forks. Dressing up an aluminum doll with clothes.

Her facial expression shifted and her beloved time disappeared now that it faded from her imagination. Her first practical anger entered her body, still rather undemanding and humbly shrewd. She lowered her eyelids into a crafty slant, a slight sneer drew around the corner of her mouth, and tiny grooves of anger stretched from her nose up to her eyebrows.

I want you to go to the station, she said. You have forty-five minutes until his train comes in. You are to tell him that I forgive him.—No, no, not that. You tell him that I long for him and want him to come here right away. Tell him that I no longer make any demands on him. No unreasonable demands. Tell him that I love him. Yeah, tell him with your mouth and in your voice. Tell him also that real love has no demands. I mean, doesn't stand on marriage or stuff like that.

Her mother laughed lightly; lightly spiteful.

Don't look so upset. As if I were a lush asking you to get me more liquor, screaming at you without giving you the money or without telling you where to go, screaming: don't dare to come home without booze, you snot.

But I don't even know what Stellan looks like. I've never seen his face.

That's easily taken care of. I'll give you a snapshot. I've several in my handbag. I couldn't get myself to tear them up. So there you can see.

She went to get the snapshots and spread them out on the kitchen table. Refusing to look at them, Britt-Mari turned her back and clenched her fists. She wanted to get angry, but she could not. Even though she was conscious of her anger, she did not feel it. How could she seriously get angry? How was she to act when anger got the upper hand?—Her hands automatically lost their grip.—Oh, why are we never trained to show rightful anger? this open hand wondered. She knew how necessary her anger was. There was much she ought to destroy. But where would she have to draw the line? How was she to distinguish between what should be dismissed and what should be retained?

But go ahead and look, her mother urged her. See whichever you think is best and take it along.

How can you? Britt-Mari said without daring to hope for her anger to materialize, only thinking: I ought to prevent you from doing this. You're going to be ugly doing this, Mommy. You're not up to this. It was better when you lay there, stiff like a doll. You should never have fought that which hurt you. It was the truth that bothered you. You should have submitted to the truth. Now you are angry.

She stepped forward and glanced at the pictures.

If he hits you again?

Then it's he who does it.

He might murder you next time.

Then it's he who's murdering me, her mother said, waving with scornfully expressive hands.

Well, if he doesn't come?

He will if you tell him what I told you to say.

I can't believe that.

You don't need to. I do. I'm certain. Almost fully certain. He told me that much. And I know more about him than he himself does.

What do you know?

That he's going to come back to me. He's not rid of me yet.

No, you're not letting go of him.

That's not what I mean. I mean that I'm in his blood. That's what. I've become like hunger or thirst for him. There's a fire in him that only I can put out.

Then why did he hit you?

We're not going to talk about it any more.

Well, yes, you have to. You have to tell me why he hit you.

Britt-Mari lifted her hands as if now she was ready to hit. She could not understand it, could not grasp why her arms and hands were so upset. She saw them shaking. She herself was not upset.

Her mother stroked across Britt-Mari's forehead. The caress burned in her.

Haven't I told you that it was your fault? her mother said with terrible mildness. Be glad that I'm not taking up this issue again. It was your fault that he hit me. In a way, she added, getting still milder.

I can't go. I just can't.

You are going.

Why?

So that he can hear you tell him: Mommy loves you. She longs for you. You have made her happier than she has ever been.

How can you think that I can say such things!

I know that you can.

I can't!

Suddenly she was crying. It had come over her with as much surprise as a sneeze. It passed just as quickly.

I'll go, she said.

Don't look like such a hero, her mother scoffed. What you're doing is the simplest thing on earth. Don't you see? Her mother spoke at an ever quickening pace, underlining it with fleeting, darting gestures.

He's coming directly from his wife. You've understood that much at any rate? What do you think he told her? I know. He told her how it is when he gets home. He lies his head off. Even if there's nothing to lie, he does. He's the worst liar I've ever met. In certain respects, that is. He lies to his wife. He's always done that. First he lies that he's finished with me. Then he admits that he's told a lie. She forgives him everything. First she forgives him the truth. Then she forgives him the lies. Finally she forgives him his future lies too. Her forgiveness knows no limits. There's no end. He doesn't get out of it. And even though he has tested her forgiveness for years, he doesn't believe that it's true. Basically, it's beyond him why a person would keep on forgiving in this way. He is like one possessed with this forgiveness and makes himself worse than he really is. Why does he do it? Why? I wonder. There's only one answer. He wants her finally to get fed up with him.

Her mother was talking to herself. It was a repetition of what had gone through her mind yesterday and last night and perhaps for many days.

Britt-Mari stood in the entrance, the door already slightly ajar. Casting a last glance at her mother, she thought that nothing was strange. There was no longer anything to be surprised about. Her mother was standing by the kitchen table, talking and knocking her knuckles on the tabletop while she did so.

He wants her finally to get enough. That's what he's hoping for. That this woman finally has enough. He keeps on looking for lies and throws them at her, one blacker than the other. He hates her. He wants to get free of her and her damn forgiveness.

I'm going to do what you told me, Britt-Mari said, closing the door on her mother's words—stirring, imploring, angry words.

35

But she did not. A strange, quite unnecessary confusion got underneath her actual bewilderment and it determined her behavior when she arrived at the station to wait for the train's arrival. Just waiting was not enough, she felt, only she did not know what else she could do. Catching sight of the many beautiful flowers growing in front of the ugly building of the railroad station, she walked over to look at them. The flower bed was compact, its rows rising stepwise up against the wall. She felt sorry for not knowing the name of even one of these flowers and considered this a sign of her general ignorance. She could see, but did not know what she was seeing. The flowers were beautiful. By the wall they were grouped in clumps according to kind, the rest were arranged in rows for each sort. The first row looked like potted plants with green leaves that were covered with large red spots and the flowers were salmon-colored and very tiny. She walked along this row, curious about the name of the plants.

Suddenly overcome with longing for herself, with love for her own name, she stopped abruptly and stood very still. She whispered her name quietly under her breath: Britt-Mari, Britt-Mari, Britt-Mari. But that would not do. It did not bring her closer to herself. She felt foolish and stupid.

A policeman came, as they usually do with the arrival of the more important trains. Standing with his hands on his back, he too looked at the flowers in the flower bed. Would he know their names? Did he think they were beautiful? Or was he out to make sure that no one swiped them? In a way, Britt-Mary felt sorry for policemen on patrol. They really had nothing to do, just cruise around and shine with their idleness. And when they finally had an opportunity to do something, then people said they did something awful. The police interfered, the police busted two of the troublemakers. She had hardly completed this thought when he proved her case. She heard him call out,

Hello there!

She looked around and at first did not see what it was about.

Is that your dog? she heard him ask a lady.

She saw a little terrier at the far end of the flower bed, sniffing carefully the first flower. Dogs were not allowed to go without a leash, but it was not the lady's dog. She gripped her handbag tightly while voicing her protests and definite denials. The dog on his part declined his relationship to any of the people around him and took off with a snort when the policeman shooed him off.

Britt-Mari walked in his shadow when the policeman walked to the platform. The train was rolling in from the south. Standing quite close behind the policeman, Britt-Mari pulled out Stellan's picture and looked at it. It was a snapshot of the time Stellan was Sweden's champion, dressed in his soccer garb and ready for the match. At least, the ball was not far from his feet. His smile full of the winner's certainty stood above a solid chin, as round as a knee. He had large eyes and his nose looked sensitive and romantic, like his mouth. All of him looked sensitive and romantic. Though not his chin, and his hair was thin and his hairline high and round. Now his hair was much thicker and his forehead was not so naked up high. That was because many years had gone by since he last headed balls. He had been known for his headers.

She recognized Stellan as soon as she saw him. He was not alone and kept on talking to some acquaintance all the way up the platform. They separated by the taxistand, and the other took a cab. He also took the two heavy suitcases. Stellan, who had been carrying one of them, stood there without any luggage, not even a briefcase or package.

Was it tomorrow you said your wife would arrive?

Right, Stellan answered.

Well, see you later?

Sure, Stellan said.

They waved to each other and Stellan continued in a brisk walk. It began to look as though he was in a hurry to get somewhere. Britt-Mari had to scoot in order to catch up with him and around him. Yes, she walked past him and, in doing that, she sideswiped him with her left arm. The sidewalk was not exactly crowded, but there were enough people so he wouldn't be surprised. Now I've touched him for the first time, she thought. But she didn't get very excited. Turning around, she saw that he didn't even look at her.

She stopped at the next newspaperstand and pretended reading the weekly magazine placards. He did not stop, so she walked around him again on Järnvägsbron bridge. Again she sideswiped his body with her arm, but even this time around it did not cause him to notice her. He continued at his rapid pace, although he no longer seemed to be in such a hurry.

His suit was brown with narrow dark-red stripes. She did not like the stripes in the material. For one, they ruined the look of the material, and then they hardly showed good taste. His shoes too were rather ridiculous, a sort of sandal-type shoe, with bright yellow woven leather uppers. She considered the difference between the shoes he was wearing and the heavy soccerboots. But she liked his ruby-red shirt, unbuttoned at the neck.

Stopping at a store window, she let him pass her again. Nothing would stop or distract him. All he seemed interested in was getting wherever it was he wanted to go. Britt-Mari called his name behind his back, but so softly that he could not hear her.

Listen you, Stellan, she said, walking about ten steps behind him. Where are you going, Stellan? Why did you do what you did to my Mommy? Are these your sportsman's manners to hit a woman! I'm not even going to mention that you loved this woman . . .

She continued, but quietly,

I don't believe all she told me about you. Not even most of it. But I believe one thing. What kind of ugly habit you picked up here? Always thinking in the future. Better coming up, just wait. You'll have to get rid of this habit if you want to be happy. You're unhappy, this much I understand. Perhaps it's just an ugly habit that's in the way. I'm going to be angry! Just wait! Better coming up. I'm going to get that hang-up out of you.

His lips aren't the way I imagined, she thought all of a sudden. And it struck her that he was not on his way to his rented room. Where was he going? It looked as if he were headed straight for Storgatan 33. She felt seriously uneasy, but was glad about that. Rushing ahead, she walked beside him for an entire block, by now rather certain where he was going. She fought her desire to talk to him.

She grew quiet, her apprehension gone. Sadly she lagged behind and followed him at a gradually widening distance. Only once she got frightened—when he passed Göstas Sporting Goods and for a tenth of a second their gilded boxing glove hung above his head and suddenly he looked cruel from the back. Alarmed, she cut a sign with her hands: the broken triangle. Was he going straight on to murder her mother? If what her mother had said was true, his wife must have forgiven him, and so he was desperate and disgusted and could see no end to all this, and so he might do anything. No, not anything—but kill, so he finally got something on him that his wife could not forgive. If that was true . . .

Britt-Mari ran until she almost caught up with him. Walking past him, she pushed him with her arm, obliging her to turn her head and excuse herself. He mumbled something, but nothing else happened. For a short moment his blue eyes fastened on her and he seemed to be laughing or smiling. A moment later she was convinced that he was and was no longer afraid.

She walked on at a quick pace in order to get further ahead of him. Time and again she turned to check the increasing distance. Eventually she started running, in this way reaching Storgatan 33 far ahead of him. She walked in and waited for a short while in the entrance, at a loss as to what she ought to do. She wanted to prevent him from seeing her mother, and again she did not. She wanted to tell him what her mother had told her to say, and she did not. She wanted to become angry, extremely angry. She wanted to talk sense with him, and again she did not, fearing that her anger would fail her.

She paced about in the hall and up the staircase, getting ever more nervous and excited. Very seriously so. By the time she reached the second floor she stopped suddenly, struck with the thought that if they could meet on the stairs it would look quite spontaneous. I can hear him coming! No, she did not. Her cheeks grew flushed and she tried to cool them by sliding them along the smooth wall, one cheek at a time. He did not appear. Unable to take the strain of waiting the way she did, she turned abruptly and walked down the stairs again.

He was standing outside Entrance A, his back toward the gate, his hands in his pockets. Obviously he had turned around. Did he have any doubts? Why was he standing there if not . . . She became afraid again, but her anger failed to get her concerned enough to feel it. She slid along the building, away from the entrance. He walked across the street and posted himself behind one of the trees on Allén, but seemed to have a change of heart and came forward again to stare at the roof.

Britt-Mari made a secret sign with her hands behind her back. She did not trust her anger, but walked up to him anyway. Facing him squarely, she said hello. She noticed a slight sign of fear.

I am Britt-Mari.

Oh. So it's you.

Getting no further response, Britt-Mari straightened up and said, How about telling me the truth?

She could hear how dry she sounded. He shrank somewhat in his open shirt and looked aside. But he remained silent.

You have to tell me the truth.

Are you addressing me in the familiar way?

It didn't occur to me, she lied.

Well, it doesn't bother me. Once upon a time everybody did. They called me Nicken. You, Nicken! they used to say to me.

He eyed her with a slight attempt at a wink.

Guess you're pretty sour on me?

She did not answer.

How's your Mom?

D'you want to know?

You heard my question.

Yep. Yep I heard you.

Hi, listen here, you trying to make fun of me?

I want to know the truth.

You're taking her part of course.

Why should I?

Naturally.

Is your wife coming here tomorrow?

Yeah, she is. How d'you know?

Is she going to look at houses?

You know that too.

Can't you tell me the truth?

Truth? If I knew that myself.

Tell me everything.

Haven't you pretty ears for that?

Don't be silly.

Your Mom told me that you're far ahead for your age, talented and such stuff. But she didn't say a thing about how damn cute you are.

It's my dress. She smiled as if she were about to cry.

I haven't even looked at the dress yet, he said, eyeing her up and down.

Shall we walk up to the church and talk?

Yeah. Why not?

He bent forward toward her, smiling. Not as big as he did on that snapshot. It was a searching, curious smile, showing a certain relief. Suddenly he took her hand.

I like your Mom, he said. Lucky that she doesn't know how much I like her.

She sure does.

Is that true? He gave a strained laugh and dropped her hand.

Is that true? Too bad that she never introduced us.

We'll go up to the church.

My wife is an angel, he said and his gaze became as clear as water.

Britt-Mari touched his arm and they started walking to the church. She led the way.

36

Three times they walked around the tile-red church. He was walking on her left side. In the west they could see the sun set and in the east dawn was flickering on the horizon. When they got there the first time, he put his hand on her shoulder. They stopped to look up to the sky beyond the top of the trees. Like heat and cold meeting in the skin, she felt a wail billowing up inside her and coming alive. She did not say anything, but listened to him.

It was an accident, he explained. Believe me, it was purely accidental.

She continued walking and he followed her.

She says that she doesn't ever want to meet you again.

She ought to understand that it was an accident.

Never.

But you believe what I'm telling you?

I sure do.

She kept holding me back, you see, and she was ghastly strong just then. She put both her arms around my body and squeezed so hard that my arms were locked. Of course I had to free myself, and that's when the accident happened. It went the way it goes when you lock arms with someone who's not going to give up before he's busted. The crash follows, and pang, there goes the arm like a rag. When I finally got my arms free, they sort of flew up, and that's when my right happened to hit her full speed. That's what happened.

She says that she'll never get over that.

But she will. Don't you think so?

She's not going to work tomorrow.

I'd like to meet her now.

Don't if you're smart. She needs time to get over this.

You want to help me?

Of course I'll help you. Why else would I be here?

Tell her that you've met me. Explain to her that it was just an accident. Tell her that I long for her. Tell her that I regret everything I said. Ask her to try and understand me. It's really not easy for me. My wife, she's an angel.

She is?

If someone is an angel, she sure is.

Isn't my Mommy an angel?

No. Your Mom is a real woman.

If things come all right between Mommy and you, then you mustn't always talk about the future.

But it's she who keeps talking about the future.

Not you?

When she starts, well, clearly I can't avoid saying something.

Don't you keep telling her: just wait, better coming up?

Well, that.

Yeaahh?

But that's nothing to chew over.

I think so. D'you think that you can get away with all this pen-
dulating back and forth?

That's unimportant.

You don't even believe that yourself.

You're pretty strange, hee hee? Real funny. Why am I not laughing?

You know that I'm right. You love this swinging back and forth.
You should find a better way to enjoy life. If you did, you wouldn't
need to keep on running back and forth.

As if I didn't enjoy being with your Mom. I love her.

That so?

I'm telling you.

Then why are things not right between you?

Who knows?

Perhaps they'll be someday.

They have to be right. You'll have to help me. I rely on you.

They continued this discussion as they walked three times around
the tile-red church. Sundown disappeared in the west and in the
east the sun continued rising. Thanks to its splendor Britt-Mari's
inner wails became more subdued. It is not yet completed, she
mumbled at one time, and it was for the power of these words that
splendor came surging through her. It is not completed yet, she kept
on thinking time and again after that. She could feel these words
separating and lifting her. She became a white silhouette against the
darkness she lived in, a slender wing—slim, brittle, lovely, charming, rapturous. It is not completed yet. Why couldn't she say these
words to him? Stellan, it is not completed yet.

Can't we sit down for a while? she asked.

She selected the bench she wanted to sit on. It stood on a sandy
path between rows of old graves. He settled comfortably right next
to her and took her hand. A light evening breeze rustled in the
branches of the willow birches and they listened for a while to the
cautious breeze. It is not completed yet, Britt-Mari thought, sitting
straight up, sensing how white she looked under her freckles. She
could feel her smile making her lips bloom.

I'm glad that I happened to meet you, he said, and it sounded to
her ears as if he were smacking his lips or making some other sound
of comfort.

Your wife looked rather gentle in the picture. Was it grey hair she had?

She dyes her hair nowadays.

What color?

Brown. Medium brown.

And she's coming here tomorrow? What time?

She's taking the eight-seventeen train.

Are you going to meet her?

How could I? I'm going to be at work then.

I thought that you might take off.

He laughed lightly and pressed her hand. She pulled it back. He mumbled something. She did not hear. It is not completed yet, she thought. A dream bent her down. She pulled off her sandals and showed her bare feet.

Why are you doing this?

She did not answer. He stroked her shoulders.

Are the sandals too tight?

She laughed and blew up her cheeks.

I saw a fat lady with two heavy bags . . .

She laughed again, then pressed her hand over her mouth and got frightened in a funny way, caught up in her train of thought and shaking with enthusiasm under her dress.

Finally it's going to happen, she said and showed her feet.

What is it that's going to happen?

She became restless and looked around.

I've been dreaming about this for so long. Ever since I was a little girl going to kindergarten, I think.

What do you want to do?

Can you see that red earth in front of that tombstone over there?

Yes. What about it?

Isn't it strange that the earth is red just there? Just wonderful? There, nowhere else.

That earth must have been brought here because someone wanted it that way.

A long time ago. There are only very old graves here. He was a shipbroker, he who's lying there. That's what it says on the stone. Family plot, it says too, so there are several lying under there. The family still live in the city. But why did he want red earth? And look at that little, darkgreen hedge. So well-trimmed. There was another hedge two years ago. Higher and not so pretty. If I just knew the name of these bushes. Do you?

No.

Oh, most people don't know a thing. Someone ought to know. Who does? I haven't met that person yet. All my life I've been living with people who know nothing.

She laughed and got up. He stood up too, getting rather nervous.

What are you going to do? he asked.

Stay and you'll see, she said.

He watched her walking to the grave with the red earth. She walked barefoot across the grass and then dried her feet before entering through the hedge. He could see her head and make out that she was looking for something. She took a long stride. Then she turned back to look at the place where she had stood before. She seemed disappointed at something that was not the way she wanted it to be. She took a few decisive steps across the red earth. Looking down again, she shook her head, then held her arm across her forehead. She seemed to hesitate and looked once more down at the red earth. Eventually she walked over to the tomb-stone and a green vase containing some tall white flowers that stood under the stone. She pushed her fingers down the vase. Then she lifted the vase up. He watched her pouring the water from the vase out over the red earth. Then she got busy doing something over there. A quick glance aside told him that her sandals were lying on the gravel path. Although he could not make out what exactly she was doing, he could tell that it had something to do with her feet, her bare feet. Bent over, she kept staring down. He took two steps toward her. Suddenly she straightened up and put her hands crosswise on her shoulders. He called her name softly. Finally she returned.

I'll be back early tomorrow morning to check, she whispered.

What is it you're going to check?

My footprints. My footprints are in that red earth now. It's something I've been dreaming about ever since I was small. I've never seen this kind of red earth anywhere. The prints are going to be beautiful when they're dry, especially when the sun is shining. Come here and check, you too. You must!

Without saying anything, he sat down on the bench.

When you see the prints, you too are going to see how beautiful they are. That earth comes perhaps from Italy or Siam or Peru. All the toes came out, I saw. She sat down and put on her sandals,

You do like things that are beautiful, don't you?

That goes without saying that I like beautiful things, he answered. It is not completed yet.

She could not stop herself. Her tears came quickly. She sat up stiffly, looking through her tears into his eyes and seeing him upset in that crystalline-brittle charming way. On an impulse she threw her arms around him and put her head against his breast, faintly moaning.

What makes you so unhappy? he asked, stroking her head. Tell me what it is that bothers you.

It feels like some weight, she whispered.

Are you sad that your Mommy and I. . .

It feels like some weight in my heart, she whispered.

Tell me, he pleaded. Talk about it. It'll be a long time before I forget this here.

Just hold me tight, she begged.

He did.

How about this? he asked.

I can feel it passing, she whispered.

But say something.

I can't. There is a weight in my heart. Sometimes it makes everything stick together and then my arms and legs start moving around so much and my throat gets so soft and my tongue so quick.

What is that you're saying?

The terrible thing is gone now. Can't you feel how heavy I am?

I don't feel that.

Laughing, she jumped up and went to check her footprints in the red earth once more. They were hardly visible now. Darkness had settled between the trees. She came back to him and told him how to go. He followed her and they came to Allén. Britt-Mari repeated her promise to talk to her mother and they agreed to meet the following day as soon as he finished his work at the plant. Then she would tell him what her mother had said.

37

On her way to the river Britt-Mari checked several times with her left hand, but her breast would not change. It remained as hard as treated wood. She felt dismayed in the same unreal sense as before, without responsiveness, without trembling in her fingertips, without vibrations in the roots of her heart. Still, she obeyed the command. She had started her walk of penance and was determined to complete her sacrifice. It will come, she thought. It must come. At the end of Åbacken hill she stopped and this time she checked with her right hand and in the area of her heartbeat. Her breast remained as hard as an elegant, wooden door.

To her right Åbrinken bluff rose high, like a ski slope, and the pale green staircase leaped skyward step by step. The city lay asleep in the black, warm darkness. She walked on along the sidewalk in the direction of the embankment. Pausing outside the coffee-roasting plant, she took a deep breath to test herself. Many a time she had stood here, savoring the exhilarating aroma of roasted coffee beans. For tonight the enjoyment of the place was prohibited. The air was warm and humid. A faint odor of decay wafted up from the river waters. She walked over to the dark doorway planks to see whether the wood had absorbed some of the smell. Suddenly it struck her that she was facing herself. Indeed, it had been that way all through the evening and night, even though she was not conscious of it.

She had seen herself, faced herself all along; whatever had happened, she had seen herself. That's why her breast was so hard and everything about her so unreal, she thought, everything except the naked command she obeyed. It is horrible to see yourself, she reflected and closed her eyes right in front of the planks of the doorway. But that did not help now. It was not enough to cover her eyes with her hands. She had seen herself even in front of her mother, and that was when her mother was lying in her bed, burning in a black fire, groaning about the fire that was slowly consuming her, the ashgrey future in store for her.

Didn't you see him? her mother had asked right away.

Yeah.

Did you tell him what I said you . . .

His wife was there.

Was she! Didn't you get to see him alone?

Yeah.

What did you say, what did he say?

He said: no one can live with your mother.

Did he say, live? Are you sure he didn't say, love?

Then he said, my regards to your Mom, I've never loved her.

You're lying, he's lying.

That's what he said.

And then, and then?

Our encounter was a disaster, he said.

That's not true.

That's what he said. He said: never again.

Never again! Oh, that's what he thinks. I'm going to him right away!

His wife is there.

I don't care. I'm going there and . . .

Talk? He said: your Mom thinks that life sits in her kisser; she lies so she gets what she wants; I'm not going to be taken in anymore; lies have short legs.

He's going to see.

Are you going there and just tell lies, Mommy?

Her mother did not answer. She got dressed and put on her makeup. But she never left. The consuming fire seized her with a flashing blaze.

That's my punishment, she complained, baring her teeth.

Punishment?

My punishment caught up with me.

Her mother did not know what to do with her body. She searched and searched, but no one welcomed her except her bed. She hid under the blanket and threw it off.

Punishment, Mommy?

Don't you see!

What is it you're seeing, Mommy?

Your Daddy.

What are you seeing?

The way he was.

How was he?

Not like me.

Weren't you like him?

I ought to have been. Now I'm being punished.

Wasn't it an accident?

No.

How would you know?

I know.

Did he write?

No.

What did he say?

He blamed himself. I'm not enough for you, he said. I'm not right for you, he said. And he hated himself and thought that he was worthless and unfit to live. I am getting so much from you, he said. And still, I'm not enough, he said.

And you?

I wanted to be enough for many.

And now?

I'm not enough for anyone.

Is there someone enough for you?

You heard what he said. He doesn't want to.

No, Stellan doesn't want to.

Britt-Mari turned her back to the plank doorway. Looking straight ahead, she remembered a sewerpipe draining into the river just outside this coffee-roasting plant. She recalled the boys who used to sit on the embankment with their fishing rods because whitefish and perch like to congregate around these drains.

She went there and acted according to her commands. All through she kept on seeing herself, but without rebellion, without aching pain. She fastened the white envelope, containing the ashes from the furnace in her mother's room, on her head. It was pasted together and had a striped paper string tied around it. She could see what she looked like and thought that it looked like a nurse's cap at best. Then she wound the sackcloth matting like a shawl around herself. She could see herself, but it did not burn in her eyes. Her eyelids were as cold as fish skin in the sea. On the embankment at her feet was the box containing the things she had stolen from the grown-ups, adults she loved and admired. These pawns reminded her of their perfection and assured her of reaching it some day.

She stood erect, dressed in sackcloth, ashes on her head. Folding her hands, she pressed her palms tightly together and lifted them up to her face. There she separated her fingers and then prayed for her heart's true contrition. She prayed for a long time and for only one thing, but there was no answer to her prayer. Her heart remained quiet and calm in her breast and she could still see herself. Eventually she pressed her wrists to her forehead and opened her fingers like a flower. Not even that helped. No, she needed to tear her hands apart and let them wilt.

She did so and fell down on her knees. Her hands lay uselessly and ineffectually at her feet. She lay quiet, listening, inhaling the musty smell from the river waters and hearing the sighs of bursting gasbubbles. She could see herself. She watched herself pushing the box with her forehead ahead of her, centimeter by centimeter. Getting the box to the outer rim, she collected herself and waited. Even though she felt no answer to her prayers, she butted the box out into the water. The waters splashed up around it. Then she sat down on her heels, surmising that perhaps true atonement for her heart's contrition did not reach her because she had spared her hair. She should have strewn the ashes directly on her hair instead of putting the ashes first in the white envelope. It was the wrong idea.

She got up, at a loss as to what she should do. But then she decided that it was too late now to put the ashes on her hair. She untied the string under her chin, tore up the envelope and tossed it over the water below her. She proceeded to take off her sackcloth mat and rolled it up. After that she did not know what else to do. Hard and stiff, she felt unable even to turn around. Her own vision surrounded her, scrutinizing her physical abandonment. She lived only in the sphere around her body and she lived there as a mere observer. Why did life not want to enter her body again? Was there anything else she needed to do for it to happen?

At that point her body reacted mechanically, finding in all seriousness that it ought to act as if her feelings of despair should still be in control. She watched herself putting her arms around her breast, swaying to and fro, then bending and doubling up as if cramps were pulling her together.

My God, my God, show me the way.

Even that course of action effected no change. She simply became weak, nothing else but weak in her body. Standing still again, she tried to reflect. But all her thoughts returned time and again to her mother lying on her bed, her feelings and body fused and consumed in a black fire of fear and remorse. Her anger had taken the upper hand, but it was not the right, pure anger. Britt-Mari did not feel angry, though she had acted in anger. She knew that she needed to destroy something in her mother, destroy that which stood in the way of her intentions. But anger's white flame had not touched her. She had acted like a moral guide and told one cold lie after another. That was why she stood here. Something was bound to happen to her.

She sat down on the wooden hood covering the motor of a cross-cutting saw nearby, thinking that what was happening to her now was the highest degree of despair. She had never felt real despair before, but now she did. Every fiber in her body suffered in her white-cold moon-despair. Muteness calling: touch me so that I may know I exist.

Moon-despair, she whispered and gave in to an urge to touch her lips with her finger. They felt strange and the strangeness reverberated through her finger, felt how they shivered, froze, lived in despair, and its tip shared in both the cold and the despair. Through her finger, this cold stream flowed down into hand and arm, finally hitting her heart with its steely cold sting.

The moment after she smiled. Her finger was wrong. Her lips were warm. Her heart was not cut open. A tight, solid form had taken shape in her breast. She could feel it. An urn around her heart, blessed and graceful. If the urn were a solid object and if it had been possible, she would have guided her finger around the urn's soft outline. She was not cold. A quiet ecstasy burned in her. What was it that took shape inside her? Something that not even she could comprehend—an unfathomable secret lived hidden inside her, protected and safeguarded by that blessed, condensed, rounded form. What is the name of this urn? Peace is its name. What was it the urn contained? Your life, they say. What is the name of what is bound to happen? Your death, they say. Then I know also the name of what has happened. More than enough is its name. The urn's peace embraces my entire life. I am old, I am very old. I have had enough and more than that. There is no more room inside of me. I have received all that I can take. The urn keeps it safe. Now the urn will be broken while I am sleeping, because peace . . . What is the name of the sleep of the blessed? Peace, they say.

She felt a warm ease in her body. She got up from the motor hood and started walking. She no longer faced herself. She saw the city. She was happy about the holy sleep that every night frees the human race from their cross. No trees are visible during the night because the truth is forest enough. During the night the cross lies supine and people may sleep. "If someone will follow me, so let him forsake himself and shoulder his cross every day . . ." It was night now and the human race was asleep. The cross lay still. Neither guileful nor truthful people lived in the city. Throughout the world sleep encloses and safeguards none but a holy man. During the night the earth is truly God's earth.

She did not see herself and she did not notice where she was going, did not know the design that led her onward. Filled with this warm ease, this solid tranquility, this shining peace, she looked at the city and its holy sleepers. She was on her way up to the Stadsberg, now hidden in the darkness, but she felt its slumbering presence like a scent in the air and a heavensent form in her eyes and on her skin and against her body's balance.

It happened on her way up Stadsbacken hill that she saw his back as he walked through the light-ring of the street lamp. Someone was awake. Was he carrying a cross? Was he walking in blessed sleep? He was tall and big and had a mighty back. His coat shimmered in sea-green before he disappeared in the darkness.

She hurried up to catch up with him. Three times she saw his sea-green form gleam under the light-circles from street lamps. She was pretty close to him now and could hear the determined strides of the boots he wore on his feet. She could see them flash up when he turned left off the main road. She knew that path and she was glad that he took just this one to walk up the hill because it was the most beautiful. She too took a turn and hastened into the darkness. Forest was forest on both sides of the path.

38

I am a sanitary worker, the man told Britt-Mari in answer to her question. My job starts in three hours, for me and the horse. His name is simply Boy, although he's getting pretty old now. We empty garbage cans. We work on contract and have our fixed customers. It's a good job. Both Boy and I like it. He's not too weak for the service, and neither am I. During the night and early morning hours we have the streets for ourselves.

I wish I could see you properly, kinsman. We may sit very close to each other, but I can't see you the way I want to. Do you have a match?

What's the use of getting a light? I can tell you that I look ugly.

Light up anyway.

Oh no. Besides, I have no matches. And I find it unpleasant now. What do you look like?

I have freckles. And I have red hair.

Copper-red?

No, my red hair isn't so beautiful, it's lighter.

He was up to something, she could hear metal clanking on him.

Feel here, and you can feel it, he said.

His raincoat, its sea-green color indistinguishable in the dark, rustled and the metal clanked. He led her hands to his stomach. She could feel a steel ring as large as a child's head and lots of keys. His fingers toyed with the keys.

Do you like keys, he asked?

Do you?

I like keys very much.

I like perhaps two.

I haven't always liked keys that much.

Is there something special about them?

Keys open doors, and then you can walk into the dwellings.

She reflected on that, sensing the uncommon, and fumbled further like a palp in the dark.

Why do you say dwellings? she asked.

Because that word sounds nicer and is better than house, villa, farm or whatever else they use. Human dwellings, doesn't that sound great and correct?

Is it true that you carry no match?

There was a time when I didn't dare walk into a human dwelling. My own truth forbade me.

Would it hurt your feelings if I ask to feel your face with my hands? I would so very much like to know what you look like, kinsman.

You have red hair?

I'm reddish-blond.

And bareheaded, I noticed. May I touch your hair?

By all means.

You have long hair.

A ponytail.

Well, that's not much. Will it frighten you if I wind your hair around my hand?

Why should I be afraid?

We don't know each other, you and I. But why should you be afraid?

I can hear you. That says a lot.

And I hear you.

You have pouchy cheeks, kinsman. I can wiggle your cheeks.

I may have had too much beer these past fifteen years.

Is it from beer you got these cheeks?

How would I know? I got them.

But you feel so thin over your forehead. There you're skinny and narrow and seem famished.

There's actual warmth in your thin hair.

Why were you afraid of dwellings once upon a time?

That's a long story. Can you hear the brook?

Yes, I sure do.

Water is unlike anything here on earth. But I wonder whether people recognize how special water is if they don't have a horse. Have you ever seen a thirsty horse drink?

Not that I can remember.

I feel sorry for you for that. You have no idea how special a thing on earth water is. To water a horse is really . . .

I usually come up here to the brook and drink.

But a horse.

Are you thirsty now?

Not now. I drink always when I water Boy. First I watch him drink. It's so special the way he reveres water. When Boy has had his fill, then I drink too. He's such a happy one. He looks on when I drink. I can't be careless about it. So sometimes we have fun with each other. I pretend that I don't want to drink. Then he's real stern. He snaps at me, pulls my shoulder, you see, and finally pushes me. Then I fill the whole scoop and drink in front of him. Not before he sees that I do it right—and I have to snort with pleasure— he goes and drinks the second time. When he sees that I'm not watching him, he gets cross and starts scraping with his right hind-hoof. Horses are marvelous animals. They revere water like no one else on earth.

You revere beer too.

There's a lot of water in beer, girl.

You're probably rather red-faced?

I sure am.

But your narrow forehead is white?

That's correct. And I'm bald. My pate is badly whitewashed too, and wrinkled. Little girl, your hair is warm, thin as it is.

Do you always wear a raincoat?

Nope.

I thought that you always go around and wait for rainwater too.

There's thunder in the air tonight. Can't you smell it? We'll have a few thunderstorms around here before morning. I'd say that they're already blowing out on the sea. The clouds are hanging heavily across the roofs in the city. It makes me sad.

Why? Because of your job?

No, it's something else.

Don't you want to tell me?

Of course I do. I can tell by your voice that you'll understand me.

Nevertheless, he hesitated. They had not reached very high up in the mountain and were sitting on a rock by the side of the path. The forest stood dense around them and branches came low over their heads. They could not see them, but their outlines were present in the darkness and their scent permeated the air. He kept her hair wound around his left hand. She felt the weight of his arm on her back. Sometimes a hair pulled too tight and pinched and then he moved his arm slightly.

This night I usually stay awake, he said eventually. She could hear his breathing.

I usually come up here on this mountain the nights I stay awake. Why? That's hard to explain. But it's easy to tell. I want to watch the lighthouse out there in the sea. You can see it from up here. The lonely cliff and the tiny lighthouse. Have you been there?

No.

I have. It was there I became human and dared to walk into a dwelling again.

In a dwelling.

I became a human there and a dwelling goes with a human. I could no longer forbid myself to enter a dwelling.

Enter a dwelling.

Before that my anger had broken me. My face was blackened and I shied away from facing anyone. I dared not enter into any person's eye dwelling, so to speak.

Were you young at the time?

I considered myself an old man, though I was just twenty-three.

And your parents?

Mom died when I was twelve. Dad was beaten to death. I was twenty-one then. A guy dressed out as a woman killed him. He was really a baker, and ever since I've always thought that bakers have something of a woman in them. He was the son of an old woman, a widow, who lived in a cottage my father owned. Her boy did day labor for the rent. You see, we homesteaded up there on Södra Berget. We owned a lot of ground up there. Dad assaulted her. He was a hard man. My four brothers too. Only I turned out soft and wet. Youngest child, they said, sort of explaining. I would have liked so much to be as hard as my brothers, yeah, at least as my brothers. The widow died a week after Dad's assault, but it didn't get into the courts. Dad palmed off some hard cash, a few hundred or whatever it was, to the frightened boy. Then he disappeared from our view and years went by. There was so much that happened. I've hardly the time to tell you everything.

We have all night.

Well, we have. But what is it to you how I lived so long ago?

I'd like to learn how you became human and dared to go into a dwelling.

In that case I have to tell you about the anxiety and fear the hard ones had to suffer. It concerned our property. One day our city revised the laws on land grants and started legal proceedings. We had to show papers on how the ground had come into our hands. Dad got frightened because the forests and hills belong to the city, and our property was part of old grants and in the course of time the borderlines had been moved pretty arbitrarily, without authorization. That's the way it was, but the city left us alone up there. They were primarily concerned with choice land down in the city, like that by the harbor and along the shores—lumber yards, and large warehouses, and depositories. They sued them first, and that dragged on in the courts. It took several years. Dad no longer trusted the land. He cut it up and sold it in lots. That went well because times were good and many people moved here from all over town. He became wealthy. Yes, Dad became wealthy. He put up shacks and rented out apartments. Finally that dressed-up baker came to him, told him that he was a seamstress and wanted to see a few rooms that were for rent—and killed him. My brothers sold most and went to the United States. All four in one day. I was too soft and wet, I didn't dare go. They didn't want me to tag along either. You can take care of what is left of the farm, they said and took off. So I went there to the farm and didn't want to live on. Everything was against me, I thought. Distrust blackened my face. My anger tore me up.

Tore you up.

I felt worse than an animal. After all I was a human without dwelling. Many animals manage without a dwelling. It's nice to think of an elk lying down on the ground. It doesn't hurt him. He is created for the naked earth. Other animals have caves or nests where they sleep and feed. And man builds dwellings for the other animals that serve him. The horse has his stable and the cow her barn. The pig its sty and the dog his doghouse. One morning I decided to leave for good the place where I was born. I made a contract with my farmhand and he became leaseholder. It was in the middle of the harvest. It was today many years ago. I went to the stone city never to return. I didn't know quite how to go about my disappearance. I was soft and wet. For the time being I sat in a pub.

A pub.

I drank a lot. Still, I didn't get really drunk. There's a certain sadness you can't drink under the table. If I could describe for you how I felt, but I can't. Wait—perhaps I can anyway.

Perhaps anyway.

I walked down to the harbor and by that time it was dark. I roamed around and then went out to Rosenborg and then on toward Mon. I found a rowboat there, I got in and rowed out of the bay. The city lights sparkled. Never before had I understood our Savior's sufferings; that went beyond my understanding. The cross never shook my heart. The *only* sinner had no reality for me. But now I rested on the oars, looking toward the city, and suddenly I remembered His word: The foxes have their lair and the birds their nests; but the Son of Man has no place to rest his head.— I rowed on in my despair. A Western wind blew up over the city that night. I threw away the oars and threw myself down on the skiff's bottom planks. My anger came to me like an assault and knocked me unconscious.

He was quiet.

Can you hear the soughing in the trees? he asked.

Has the rain come?

Not yet.

Not yet.

The lighthouse-tender's daughter saved me. She saw the boat and someone lying in it. She rowed out and piloted me and the skiff to the cliff and the lighthouse. I was still unconscious from my anger's assault, but she poured vodka down my mouth and I woke up. I'll always remember what I saw when my eyes cleared, as long as I live. Her face, her melancholy face. It was the face of the November seas I saw. Not the sea of the November storms. No. The despondent, dreadfully depressing November sea that is not able to raise itself, much less glitter even a little. Her face is more melancholy than mine, that was my first thought.

Was it the first?

And it was this woman I came to love, and she came to love just me. And I realized my love while I was lying there on my back, and before I saw her hair.

The copper-red hair?

The copper-red hair, her thick, wonderful, warm hair.

What color was your hair?

I was darkhaired.

Then you were happy together.

Yes, we were happy. We became happy and remained happy—always in our hearts throughout our life.

Is she dead?

Yes, she died twenty years now. She gave me a dwelling, a re-markable dwelling. I carried one half, she the other. And when we met these two halves were united. An invisible dwelling. The rent can't be paid in money. You can't pay for this. You just take and owe more and more.

Owe more and more.

But I was still afraid of the visible dwellings. Can you imagine? I lied about who I was. I didn't want to admit my past; its dwelling was closed. I told my beloved that I was a bad farmhand. Quite correct. I went to town and hired out as a farmhand. She followed me and worked as a maid for a family in Sotkroken. We drudged and saved our money for a home so we could get married. I still did not tell her anything about my circumstances, and no one else told her either because no one knew me. That shows you how lonely I lived. I was a farmhand and she a maid for three years. We couldn't scrape together very much. But we met every week and put our pennies together if we had some left. And all the time I warmed my hands in her heavy, copper-red hair. There was nothing like it. She would sit on the floor in front of me in my hole or in the hay by the stall in the barn and put her head on my knees. Not even then did we talk much to each other. No, we were mostly silent. My hands were no longer cold. They had a dwelling. They lived deep in her copper-red hair. And so three years went by.

Well, a new winter came and something terrible happened. She came to me in my stable one cold winter evening. I had not ex-pected her and was very happy. My hands would get what they wanted most. But that night she had no hair under her shawl. She had sold her gorgeous braids to a wigmaker. The money she showed me in her hand was for our still invisible home. I rushed to her, knowing that all was my fault. I finally told her the truth. Lying at her feet and holding the hem of her skirt, I asked for her forgiveness. She cried too. She understood me and why I had doomed myself to live without a human dwelling. Our life turned beautiful there on the stable floor. Yes, it became beautiful, my girl. My beloved finally dared to respect her extraordinary hair that had given my hands a dwelling. And what happened in these short minutes was such a formidable cure that I became an entity, a whole human being on earth. Hand in hand we walked up the hills to look at the home of my childhood. We got married that winter and moved there.

And you had children?

Yes. A girl. We had been married for five years by then.

What's her name?

Her name was Lisa.

Is she dead?

Yes, fourteen years.

Then you're alone now?

Yes, if you want to call it that. Perhaps you've misunderstood me. Not everything became humanly perfect all at once. There are many kinds of dwellings here on earth. And our faces were blackened; my beloved's face was even darker than mine. There was a dwelling I had not dared to touch yet—the dwelling inside a woman's body, created for a man to enter. I was full of anger and had no trust in my future, fearing that something wrong might come out of my body and inhabit the earth. But the time came when I dared knocking on that door too. Finally Lisa was born. Then a lot happened. Then it happened that the mower cut off both of Lisa's feet.

The mower!

And I was its driver. I didn't see how it happened. She wanted to surprise me and had sneaked up through the grass. So she lay there, with an irreplaceable loss. And I stood there, crushed with hostility and anger. I can still feel it. The worst had come true. All man's dwellings are vain. They burn. They collapse. They stand bloodred and gall-yellow in a fiery plague. My wife could not console me. Her warm hair could no longer warm my hands. I sat, my hands buried in her copper-red hair. I sat for hours, days and nights with dead hands. Don't forget, my wife begged.—I did not forget, but no life remained besides the accident. It lived. My anger lived, because I could have prevented the accident. If I had not been so wet and soft. Nobody could convince me that there is no reason for anger in a man's life.

She did.

In my case the little one cast my anger overboard. She came home from the hospital with her mangled legs. She was too little to fathom her misfortune. She rippled with happiness, she was made that way. It was strange, but there was nothing like bending down over her bed, watching her. You can say that she was maimed, and she was, but not in her mind. She loved to live, and I lifted her on my shoulders and carried her around in our rooms and then out on our property. We made this tour every day. And now I'm going to tell you, my girl, the most special thing that ever happened to me.

You began to love still another dwelling.

Yes, you said it correctly.

Was it she who showed you?

Yes, it was. It was her face above my head. She bent it down to mine. Her wonderful face above my head when I carried her on my shoulders. It happened that she bent down and threw her arms around my head, and from up there she came down with her mouth against my forehead, my nose, my mouth. That may sound childish, but I'm a childish kind of fellow. These kisses made me dare to love myself in God. And do you know what these words mean in my book?

Tell me.

They mean that I permit the Creator's hand to shape me. I don't find it humiliating. It hurts in a mundane context, but it is not humiliating. Anger not only wants to kill, anger also implies its readiness to withhold creation. I loved her as soon as I saw her blackened face. My love was ripe in me. That's not humiliating. The stranger makes himself known in the process of creation. He becomes us. The lighthouse-tender's daughter became my wife. She was a stranger, but I got to know her and thus we created something: a dwelling for us. That's nothing humiliating. The strange thing remains strange and I get angry, because the strange thing makes me into a stranger and I want to be known. To talk about an idiot and find that his idiot talk has a meaning.

Many think that it's humiliating when they hear it said. Living totally outside of life, they forget how they came into being.

There are men who are afraid of the female, of the maternal, of that in life which gives birth. They dare approach it only to destroy it.

And women.

I can feel the hand above me. I feel it now. The hand is strange. It hesitates to create. I feel it and it hurts. The hand is creating. It enters me so that creation may take place inside. It becomes my thoughts, my feelings, my wishes, my belief, my life. I come to know some of all that is converging. The face that was like the November sea's face, the warm, copper-red hair, my daughter's face bending down to me from above, my horse drinking water. I love all this. I burn with longing to see the places again where I was created for others and others for me. I am filled with love when I think of these dwellings. I know that the hand is still above my head. I can feel this hand. It is stretching forth quite near me, in a new manner and with a different intent.

But your anger, kinsman!

Are you angry?

Not tonight. The cross is resting quietly. I am sleeping in peace. Death has no pointed tip. But tomorrow. My anger is bound to come then. And I need to act.

Can you do that?

I don't know. I'm afraid that my anger may turn ugly. I want to feel a clean anger. The anger should make me happy. Anger is beautiful because it does not submit to humiliation. Anger's children ought to be lauded because their contribution might bring about the betterment of the world. I don't know how I will fare. Anger often turns inside, and rightly so. Perhaps I can't do anything. Perhaps all I can do is press my forehead to the ground and cry.

She pressed it now against his knees. Then she left him.

She did not take the path up the steep mountain. She walked down to the road. From there she turned eastward and fifteen minutes later she passed the quiet sanatorium. Continuing in an eastward direction, she reached a vast construction site another fifteen minutes later. At the outskirts she found several one- and two-family homes under construction. She selected one whose lot was not graded yet. She saw the shadows of earthen mounds and stepped across lumber planks put in readiness. The yellow lumber glowed faintly in the darkness. The windows and doors were not in yet. She walked up a cement staircase, its wooden moldings still sticking up. Entering the villa, she hesitated near one wall. She thought of her father as she was leaning against an unknown wall in the darkness.

39

She woke up, hearing the woman's penetrating, peculiar singing and thought that the noise had awakened her. Though greatly affected by the singing, she took the time to sink back into her body. She did not need to trouble it for a while yet and it felt wonderful to have the time to enjoy its drowsiness. She closed her eyes in order to hear and feel better.

The woman could not be more than a few steps away from the window. She sang home-made lyrics and the melody came haphazardly, if it was a melody at all. Her improvisations seemed to arise out of the moment's necessity. It did not take long before Britt-Mari understood that the woman was working non-stop in an alternating, rising and falling pattern on something demanding strength. The rattling sounds came in thrusts as if she were flinging water against a hard object that splintered it. The woman's song came in uneven doses. Sometimes it sounded cuttingly monotonous, sometimes rugged and husky, sometimes like a horse's neigh. All through, a kind of shadowy figure seemed to keep on creating this song, tossing it forth and somehow altering herself in the course of it.

"These are good times," she sang. "No one's unemployed. All those with kids have prams. No kid has nipples. God did I freeze when I was little." Not long after that she sang, "I remember the high heels I wore to a ball one time. A ninny jumping downstairs had a miscarriage. Lousy heels, yelled the baby, 'cause he couldn't see the sun." Then, "Why should people swear when there's so many beautiful words?—Stupid are those who read books. And I agree. Grandmother knew the Bible cover to cover, and still got the corpse-hiccups before she died. Then I ran up to the loft. Uff, uff, said Karlsson's cat. A big spider was crawling on her sheet. That ain't any good."

Though Britt-Mari felt like seeing the woman, her body found her wish difficult to satisfy. She started rolling her body across the floor to the open window. But about halfway she caught sight of something played out on the unpainted walls and stopped. She heard a strong wind blowing outside and suddenly caught a whiff of early fall. The woman went on again, "It's great to work on your own plot. It's great that baby sleeps. My fellow works piecework every day. Lovely money. Praise and joy be advised. Blessed be strong arms. Soon the building stands done an' ready. But the rent, the rent."

Music, music, Britt-Mari sang in a low voice and stared, fascinated and frightened, at the wall. She made her body do an act on the floor. Looking at her image she could see how she looked—charming, and funny, her head resting on her hand, her sackcloth mat carelessly wound around her bare legs. She changed her act and looked even more charming. She could feel that her purse had dropped out of her dress pocket. She found it lying on the floor and put it back again. The woman was still singing,

"In past times all mamas mended stockings for hours and hours until darkness came. Now no one mends stockings. But the runs are still there. I go with bare legs in summer."

She looked at the wall and sang in a whisper,

Music's trick, music's trick.

She thought of Arnold, remembering how they had stood hand in hand and foot against foot. Again she experienced the delicate dialogue of her nerves' antennae and felt the form love had created for her. She felt no longer lost. She stood skyhigh in her feelings.

Was this peace? Peace, the carefree and deep sleep of the holy ones when they wander through this world, intervening with angry or giving hands, or when they gently die away from here.

Or was it music? Was everything about her now fulfilled? She looked at the wall. No longer touched, she had at her disposal a kind of wheel that would turn her world according to her wishes. Play or sincerity, suffering or happiness, enjoyment or indifference no longer touched her. She could look at herself and she could look away. She could play and she could leave it alone. She could feel pain, but it never reached her center. Her new ability was neither artificial nor abnormal. It was as natural as one of her organs, as natural as her moving eye.

She looked at the wall. An intense, lively play of lights was surging back and forth across it. The sunspots, in the form of slender daggers, came all at once rushing forward and then disappeared in unison, leaving wounds of various sizes as brown knots in the wood. Here and there a droplet of resin, oozed out and hardened, glittered up. Watching the wounding and stabbing was deeply upsetting, but deeply pleasurable at the same time. Nothing died. No one screamed. Nothing was touched in a hopeless manner. The performance was playfully elegant, so without sound and suffering, so untiring and all carried on with smiling enthusiasm.

She tore herself away from watching this in order to get herself interested in some of the other things happening in her life. She listened again to the singing woman.

"My father boozed. Aye so I cried. My fellow boozes just a little. An' I too take five swigs. Five words to send on third-class mail. But the rent, the rent."

Britt-Mari rolled over to the open window and got up on her knees, careful not to reveal her presence.

Britt-Mari was shocked. It felt as if all spokes of a wheel had come loose from their band. It was no longer possible to drive. She saved herself with a sudden application of brakes. The broken front-wheel rose up high. Most life exists beyond all music, lives outside the borders of peace. It cannot be formed into beauty and strength. In vain the lover bends over the splintered material. In vain his hands toil against broken keyboards. His fingers stiffen while they work, his hands swell with gout. His work looks ugly. The musician must be a master warrior, pursuing the martial arts. He must be strong and shrewd, persistent and ruthless. The weak remain weak, but they become organized in the master warrior's powerful pattern and the attack can go forth.

The master warrior must love the powerful pattern and with his anger put the weakling into his place when he comes and fills the entire viewing range with poor performance, his grotesque and ugly gestures signaling that he, the weakling, expects to be loved and appreciated as an individual, and to receive beauty and strength as an individual.

The woman sang. The singing did not affect her, it was a by-product. She was busy with her work and it made her pull faces. It was the unspoken that howled,

"Why do we never win in the lottery? Axel Persson won and had fun as long as it lasted. He bought a car. It went bad for him in the end. Now his old woman sits alone with her furcoat."

She was busy sifting out suitable gravel from a till heap. There was nothing young or innocent or carefree about her. She was little and wiry and unevenly tied together with her wild energy. She looked like a strangely compiled package of small meatballs, flat muscles and crooked angles, which some power kept busily trying to dissolve, rearrange and tie together again. She rolled her drablooking eyes and looked with exasperation at her work with till and gravel.

What had Britt-Mari expected?

She expected something of herself. She curled up on the floor, her elbows against the boards and in a rather uncomfortable position, in order to meditate. The hour was getting closer and could not be stopped. There was a woman in that hour. Stellan's wife. What would she have to do when the woman stepped into that hour? Everything there was unborn, uncertain. Only her will knew something, but that was knowledge which saw nothing. It was uninhabitable. There was a blind thought without form: do it cleanly, do it well.

Her anger had to be in charge. But in what way?

The woman outside her window continued her singing, her words undulating like crows' wings.

Britt-Mari was amazed, amazed at the human ability to utter words. Small, ugly people hustle together and tittle-tattle. Two people meet and babble garrulously, their muddled words signifying muddleheaded man as clearly as maggot flies the carrion. His ability to talk stirs an anthill like a stick. Even the dirty and vulgar spit out their words, their hands take hold, their feet move on and their lips search other lips. People signal their desires and entice each other with squeaky noises—like rats gathering on the moonlit meadow, seized by desire to increase their kind on garbage heaps.

The little, movable tongue serves, far removed from music, beyond all peace, and speech follows. That thought pleased her. She got up, satisfied that this was so. There is a good sign in the halls of the mouth: obedience and command. We are not abandoned, we are not sold on hypocrisy or isolation, human life is born with moans and cries of joy and constant changes. Only the lovers are silent. Love's unification happens in silence. And the sufferers, silenced by fear? Silence protects them from humiliation, and self-love rises proudly and talks clearly with sealed lips.

We talk the most when far away from music, Britt-Mari mused. Fearful and desirous, the weak build their rookeries in the sand. The ugly buzz with activity until sleep does them justice. The powerless have their sphere of dialogue. The angels searching for the needy sweep forth, their giant ears extended, and a newspaper is dropped on the ground every morning. The confused speakers can neither avoid expressing their humaneness, nor escape the hand that constantly shapes in anger and love.

Britt-Mari peeked through the opening, but shied back. Did the waiting hour necessarily wait for her? She thought to hear words running in false scales. Was that necessary? There had been so many false scales of words in her hearing before. Her own tongue tended to shape them. A few talked to her because she lived somewhere and not wherever, and she talked only to some for the same reason.

But she had something to say, no matter how it was judged.

She looked out again. No, fall had not arrived yet. After the heavy rainstorm last night and the strong wind afterward, the greenery stood renewed in the sunshine. The woman stood no longer by the oblique gravel sieve. A babycarriage stood in the sunlight, its hood down, the baby screaming with a shrill voice. Its mother cooed, bending down to it with adjusting hands, her boundless energy no longer constrained.

Gra, ga, ga, she coaxed, pressing her finger into the child's abdomen. I'm going to feed you, gra, ga, because you've been a good boy, gra, ga, ga. She pulled the babycarriage out of the wind into the shade.

Britt-Mari left without thanking anyone for her lodging. The woman did not see her go. She went toward the hour waiting for her, hoping to make it inhabitable.

40

Grönängen, she said. Single to Grönängen. The name of the first stop pushed out through the slot. The frosty agitation in her hair roots told her that something of importance was in the making. Her fingers were numb with cold and she found it difficult to get the money out for the ticket. The man behind the window started drumming with his finger on the sliding counter.

Her ticket in her hand, she returned to the point where she first got her inspiration. Grönängen . . . all at once its appeal was too obvious and her means too simple. She cradled the ticket in her hand. It did not bend and its sharp edges cut into her skin.

It was quiet in the large waiting hall with its green tile walls. The restaurant was not open yet, but she could see two waitresses inside, talking. The girl in the newsstand was counting leftover newspapers to be returned. The doors to the luggage service were closed, but above its white button it said PUSH. It was necessary to knock on the window over at the ticket office to get a counterperson's attention. The personnel was in a sideroom whose door stood halfway open. There were two old men sitting on the wooden bench. They were the only people besides Britt-Mari, who had given herself a reason to be here.

On seeing the old fellows a short while ago, she felt a sudden urge to call across the hall, "Do you think too that I am beautiful?" She thought that she was and went closer to see herself in the green tiles. She looked especially good against this color and she imagined seeing herself from the vantage point of the old fellows. Her reddish-blond hair, the very shape of her head, hardly disguised by the hairstyle she wore, the violet-blue shading of her eyes against her milky-white skin, the contrast of her cinnamon-brown freckles on her skin, the shape of her neck and the goodwill of her shoulders . . .

It hurt her to be able to see herself in that way. Her gaze turned unclean, though the picture was clean. The beholder felt pained, the pain of the admirer's first stage of adoration. The onlooker is dangerously humble, the adored rich, rich with exposure. A condensed danger stands between eye and picture. The eye calls silently for help not to obliterate the picture, not to sink it, not to let it corrode under any devastating, downgrading looks.

It was then that the idea of Grönängen took shape in her, and she walked over to the ticket counter. She could turn her world any old way she wished.

It began to frighten her. She watched the old men as they sat talking to each other. They talked very softly and she could not hear them, only see the movements of their lips. For sure, they were not deaf. But it looked very strange to see them talking without facing each other. One was tall and skinny and unusually pale, and his nose stood out sharply from under the peak of his cap. His eyelids were strained and the incision between his lips expanded, like a chink, toward his cheeks. He held his hands flat on the bench at the lower end of his back, his arms straight and his shoulders turned upward. It looked as though he was hanging between his hands as if to keep his body above some nuisance.

Britt-Mari walked slowly closer to them.

The other one looked more pleasant and his skin healthier. Holding a walking stick between his legs, he let his hands rest on its handle. He had a white mustache, cropped close to his skin. His small, beautiful eyes looked amused. His hat was black, wide and dented. Every once in a while he sucked on his upperlip and it looked as though his mustache stubs stung him then. A worn, flat briefcase lay beside him. He talked the least.

The skinny one started gesturing with his hand and raised it slightly. Britt-Mari was touched by the beauty of this movement, outlining hesitation before it carefully erased its significance as it stood in the air. Having held his body somewhat above his pain with his hand, he now sank slightly down the back of the bench. But when he put his hand down again, his body came up as before.

Britt-Mari sat down next to them. She discerned a similarity between them and herself, a sharing of the same terms. If they disliked her presence, she neither saw, nor believed it. They did not let her presence disrupt their ongoing conversation.

Remember that cat and tiger are related, and so are dog and wolf, the skinny one said.

They're called felines, the other said.

Once when I was a child, I saw a strange dog's performance. He wore a horrible leather coat, closed on the neck, back and rump and fastened with leather straps. The gruesome thing about it was the rusty, inch-long nails sticking out from everywhere.

The very idea!

It sure was in this case. Some friends wanted to frighten me when they found this leather coat among old trash. Originally, this coat was supposed to protect the watchdog on the farm against wolves who might attack during winter nights.

They had their inventions in those old days. But getting off the subject, I got myself a good laugh last night. What would you say if, in talking about a hunting dog, I would say, During Tuesday's hunt, the well-known harrier created a furor?

Furor? How can a harrier go up in furor?

That's what I thought, the other said and his hands laughed on his stick-handle. Yesterday morning I read in the newspaper about a singer. He created a furor, it said, and I couldn't understand it. I asked all the people I met during the day and wouldn't give up, but not before last night my neighbor's boy explained that creating a furor is like a storming success. Of course, I didn't want to believe him, but the fellow got out a dictionary and showed me in black and white.

They had fun for a little while, each one in his particular way.

Anyway, the skinny one resumed, Thinking about a dog, or seeing one, doesn't really make me think of brutalities. I think of cheesecake.

Cheesecake. I've never tasted it. Though, I've heard them talk about it.

Well, that was in Småland province a long time ago. Nineteenhundred and two, I think it was. I was on the road looking for work. That entire summer I earned good money as a construction worker—considering the times' niggardly wages—but it was about the end. So that fall I was more like a hobo, because I used to ride Shank's mare to get from here to there. Not that I begged, I worked for my food. Chopped wood. Really. And now I'm getting to the cheesecake. Almost. First I had to chop a good amount of wood. That was on a rather big farm not far from Kalmar. Yeah, it was surely all right to get a decent meal for woodcutting, said the girl in the kitchen. A beautiful girl, I tell you. Grand and . . .

If you go off on that subject I . . .

No, I'm going to talk about that there cheesecake. Because I did get cheesecake, you see, and sweet-preserves with it.

So that was like a delicacy?

You can say that again and add an even finer word. I have eaten cheesecake before, and after that too. So I can assure you that it was an unusually good cheesecake that time. Yeah, it was luscious. My mouth waters just thinking of it, sitting here.

Did you get as much as you wanted?

I sure did. They weren't stingy in that kitchen. The girl offered me that cake three times.

She offered? That was nice and polite.

But I never took it three times. Just twice.

How do you explain that?

I wanted to be refined at the time because the whole place was so refined and so was the girl toward me. And that even though I was literally a hobo and almost a beggar.

So you ate with the other people?

No, I didn't. The others had gotten theirs already. There were only I and that grandlooking girl in the kitchen, yeah, there was a dog lying under the table and I was rather afraid of him at first. But that was unnecessary, he was peaceful and well-trained, refined just like everything else on that homestead. Well, the first time I took it, it was a healthy piece. Second time it was pretty substantial. Perhaps I gave the rest a longing look, who knows? At any rate, the girl offered me a third helping. She did it in such a well-mannered and respectful way, it made me feel like a real human being, a real gentleman. Thank you, but I had enough, I said and bowed, perhaps even eased something out of my butt. Then, you see—

Well?

Then that girl sets the pan on the floor. There was a real big piece of cheesecake left.

The dog.

Yeah, can you imagine. I stared at the dog and watched what he'd do and couldn't help seeing it. He swallowed that tremendous piece of cheesecake with one yap. It simply slid down that throat of his. Then he lay down again, licking his chops.

You damn better believe it. If it was cheesecake.

Yeah, and what a big piece! Perhaps even bigger than the one I took the first time. And it disappeared in one single yap. I didn't look at anything else, but I still didn't see how it happened. He nosed at it and then that huge piece was gone, and I heard it slosh in that throat of his. It hurt, you know. It hurt many times and for a long while, and it's not without hurt yet, come to think of it. Cheesecake is special, a party dish.

You said it. People have told me. Perhaps you can say that cheesecake has created a furor with you.

His hands laughed on the stick-handle.

It shows that girl in a different light, the skinny fellow said hesitatingly. Suddenly she looked different, and I had trouble remembering the way she looked when I first came in to see how grand and polite she was.

She probably wanted to get her dishes done.

Yeah, that's it, you see. But to feed a dog cheesecake. It still makes me mad today.

It seems unnatural.

On my soul, if that isn't so! It's unnatural to feed a dog cheesecake. Because cheesecake is one of the most distinguished foods man has invented. And it costs a pretty penny too.

And I've never even tasted cheesecake!

You'd have gotten it, and this very week if my old lady were still alive. She could make cheesecake, she too, though it wasn't exactly her big thing. To be honest, I must say that hers were never quite as good as what I got in Småland. No, not as distinguished as that huge piece that mutt swallowed in one yap.

It's expensive, didn't you say?

It is, if you take the proper ingredients. They know what price to set on the good things. So you wouldn't have gotten it even if my old lady had lived. Social security won't allow for delicacies.

Delicacies, did you say? How should social security be enough for delicacies? We can't even afford a nip.

He patted his hand,

You're a decent fellow and thanks once again, he said.

Don't mention it, the skinny one said.

As you say. Still, I'm asking you once more. Are you serious that I can take out both liters on your monthly alcohol allowance?

I've told you that.

Then I'll buy something real good for my old lady.

Do that. She needs all the encouragement she can get. Just don't mention me.

Why not?

She doesn't know me. We've never met. And you and I? We've only seen each other here downtown and been sitting and talking on parkbenches.

Well, you must excuse me, but I'm telling you what I think. You're perhaps a little too refined for me. Yeah, I had that suspicion.

Unnecessary.

You did it out of your own free will, right?

I did.

I didn't even ask for it.

No you didn't, the skinny one said. You mentioned your troubles, and then I offered it to you voluntarily.

Guess what occurred to me?

How would I know?

Imagine us fixing a cheesecake at my place. You could tell me how to do it. Besides, we should have an old cookbook at home, to be sure.

That won't work.

Of course it would! I'm not too stupid to cook and fry. Even an old dog is bound to learn something in seven years. And still my old lady tells me what to do from her bed. She can lie there and read the cookbook, if cheesecake's in there, and then I mix the ingredients and buy them and all that stuff.

You know nothing about cheesecake, I can tell. It's difficult to make a decent cheesecake.

But it could at least taste like a weak memory.of one if I try.

D'you think you can sell those liters?

Why don't you want to talk about what I'm talking about?

You've misunderstood me. I'm not walking around trying to be refined. You know very well that I don't feel pity for you. It's better to have a wife alive, even if she's bedridden, than to have none at all.

Now it's perhaps you who's suspecting me of feeling pity for you? I'm not suspecting anything at all.

All I wanted was for us to have a good time. Actually now I've really gotten to feel like tasting that there cheesecake.

Forget it. To make that cheesecake takes time, and it's difficult.

You keep on saying that.

I do hope that you meet someone off this train who wants to buy those liters. That must be difficult, that too.

Not nowadays. I've been standing here every month for almost seven years. It went well, always. It seems that you develop a special eye to pick them out. Nowadays I can see immediately on the outside who can pay best.

Every month? the skinny one asked. Do you come here in December too?

Yeah. Though not the first year. It seemed too difficult not to keep some booze for Christmas. But after that.

Is that right!

Well, I'm not going to lie. To tell the truth, I do keep one liter of the December ration.

What does she say about it, where she's lying down?

It's she who gets me to do it, every year. "If you don't permit yourself a Christmas nip, I'm not going to permit myself that Christmas ham." These are her words, and so it goes.

I understand that. Yeah, sure, I understand that. A swig gets better when the wife . . . It's the guzzlers on the sly that I'm thinking of. To guzzle all by yourself . . . I couldn't get a nip down, even one. I don't understand them, on the sly. That's against nature.

Well, I'm going to ask you again about that cheesecake. Couldn't we try?

We won't mention that subject any more.

I do respect that. Well, in that case it'll be to buy some marrowbones. Do you like marrowbones?

Reindeerbones are best, if you ask me.

Of course. But around this time of year . . .

It's almost time, the skinny one said.

41

Britt-Mari stood at the outermost edge of the sidewalk, waiting. She could see the church tower and two sides of its dials. The time was a quarter past eleven. One lonesome sound had just died away. By now she had been keeping close to Stellan's wife for almost three hours, shown her interest countless times, given small, unabashed signs, at one point even walked straight toward her and said some words straight out into the air with an indifferent face. Now it was Stellan's wife who stayed close to her. Britt-Mari could stand still and wait for the instant when their encounter would become un-avoidable.

That you are Hildur, she thought.

Stellan's wife was as slender as a girl, and that worried her immediately. A frail and impractical body had overworked its will and shied forward on the platform. She knew her face well by now, having recognized it right from the start: her neck, expression, hat. She wore a cream colored straw hat with padded brim and a green riband streaming down the brim's edge in the back. Her oval face had smooth contours and seemed as stuck-up as a balloon. Her skin, thin and translucent, had a healthy hue. Her reactions were quick and light.

Come, Hildur. Hildur, come, she whispered, playing with her foot over the gutter.

Behind her was the park where the bloodred maple tree grew. The telephone booth on the park's western side stood empty and unoccupied, its doors immobile. On the other side of the street was a house of stone she knew well. A brown drainpipe marked a well-defined borderline on the outside plaster. Whenever she looked at that house, her eyes would always turn back at that brown dividing line.

Hildur, come.

She had talked into the air around Hildur's head: The likes of you and me shouldn't continue—continue doing what?—To live, of course, she thought.

Hildur, come. Come, Hildur.

Now it was burning again. Stellan's wife stopped over there, riddled with doubts, cast frightened glances, then turned with a pleat in her doubtfulness and came toward her with her puzzled, frightened body, no longer denying that she was anxious. To her Britt-Mari was like an organ exposed to hysterical pains. She had been walking for at least three hours now with something that felt like pain whenever she stroked her hand across her slim neck. She was sure not to have a goiter that could frighten her hand. Leave your neck alone, she commanded herself. But her strictness was without success. Her hand was permitted to stroke many a time without being interrupted.

That you are Hildur, Britt-Mari thought. You ought not to look like a young girl. That's unforgivably wrong. I'm going to look like you—if I get old.

Hildur walked past her three times. The third time Stellan's wife stopped as if to say something, but then Britt-Mari suddenly looked the other way and stood markedly unapproachable.

Hildur, come.

She was merely a few steps away from her when Britt-Mari took off. She rounded the park and walked down Åbacken. Hildur, come, she whispered and hurried toward the quay without turning even once. Their parts reversed, Britt-Mari was now the pursued, she who received obvious signals. Walking across Ågatan, a mere stone's throw away from the coffee-roasting factory, she heard,

Wait, wait . . .

She did not, but walked over to the quay and stopped there. The crosscutting saw was toiling about twenty meters off, its labor an acoustic sensation of spitting red streaks.

Do you want anything from me?

Britt-Mari looked away. By now she knew that face only too well. She was sitting behind a table in the drugstore. Suddenly her way of eating was like that of a dove among a flock of other doves with plenty of food around them. An unnecessary greed, an ugly fear of not getting enough, her behavior displayed characteristics of mental aberration.

But say something.

She let Stellan's wife come close to her.

How do you know me?

What does that matter? Britt-Mari said, her gaze far off down the river. It doesn't occur to me to ask you why you've come to me.

Is that surprising? You've been following me for several hours now. Wherever I went, you've been right on my heels.

And it ended with your coming to me.

I have an important appointment at twelve. What do you want from me?

Don't you understand what it is I want?

Don't talk in riddles.

I'm sure you know it's about Stellan.

Stellan. I had a hunch. Do you know him?

I'm sure you know.

Tell me, straight out.

I intend to tell the truth.

What truth?

It's perhaps unpleasant to hear, but you're his wife, after all, and so you're the first to . . .

She turned silent, not knowing what to say. Stellan's wife became impatient. She moved her head like a feeding dove, surrounded by too many of the likes of her.

It's about a girl, Britt-Mari said.

A girl. What kind of girl?

She's just a child still.

What about it?

Does Stellan tell you everything?

We've been married for twelve years.

Has he told you about Sylvia Månsson too?

Do you know her?

I do. And you forgive Stellan everything?

What do you know about that?

I heard it.

What kind of girl are you?

One who wants to tell you something. Do you forgive Stellan everything, whatever he does?

So far I have.

Why?

How could I answer that? He hasn't committed any crimes, at any rate.

He has.

What's that you're saying?

He has committed a crime. I know a girl . . .

Is she a minor?

Britt-Mari looked at the straightened oval. It was so sensitive because it encompassed something that would never break. Still, its entirety rested uselessly inside her, forever unable to regenerate. Something of importance had happened to her, and she should have withdrawn. Whatever had happened should never have made her demand the visible. She was forced to make it work. She became ugly because of her demands.

It concerns a minor, Britt-Mari said, thinking, that includes you, Hildur. And she thought, that's just the difficulty, the great experience hits a minor who never amounts to anything more than a minor.

I don't believe what you're saying, Stellan's wife said.

But it's so, anyway.

How would you know? Do you know the girl?

I do.

Has this been going on for a long time?

Sure has.

I don't believe you. He's been busy with that Sylvia.

I know. I know the other too.

Is there anyone besides you who knows?

Not yet.

Do you think that he . . .

It's me, that girl.

You're lying.

I am that girl.

Are you thinking of going to the police?

To the police?

Do you want to charge him?

Britt-Mari put her hand in front of her eyes. She smiled a bitter smile.

Yes, I intend to, she said. He has destroyed my life. Do you hear, he has destroyed my life.

Your life! You little bitch. I've a good mind to claw you.

Hit me? Why is it me you want to hit?

You have a dirty fantasy. I don't believe a word of what you're saying.

It's true too. We used to meet up there on the mountain. Look up there. Over there, right under the lookout tower. Not directly underneath. It's more to this side. Above the precipice. That's where we used to meet. On a cliff ledge. Don't you believe me? You really don't?

What do you have in mind?

I love him. I hate myself for loving him. Love came too early to me. I'm not grown up yet. He doesn't want to love me properly because I'm not grown up.

Then nothing has really happened?

Oh yes it has. But he doesn't want to love me the way one loves a grown woman.

What do you mean?

He doesn't dare. I'm in the way of myself.

Has something happened between you or has it not?

We're going to meet tonight. At eight o'clock we'll meet up there.

You mustn't. I forbid you.

How could you? I love him and he wants to meet me. Something wonderful happens every time we're together. Even though I am the way I am.

You're disgusting!

I'm going to meet him there at eight o'clock. And I'm standing here, telling you.

Yes, why are you doing this? I don't believe a thing you're saying.

I want you to help me. I love him. By myself, I can't stop myself from going up there tonight at eight. Besides him and me it's only you who knows. Save me!

What do you mean?

I don't know myself what I mean. All I know is that love is a terrible torment. You can't tear yourself away all on your own. Someone has to help. Help me, please. Oh, please do. I need help. Someone has to tear me away from this love. I should not be in love. Look at me. I'm the wrong person. Just look at me. Look and save me. Tear me away. Keep me away. Find a place where I can stay. Look at me. Where is the right . . .

Hush! Be silent, girl.—What shall I do? Tell me what I can do? I can't tell you. I don't know what needs to be done to save me. No. How could one seeking help know how she ought to be saved? If I could see help somewhere, I would stretch out my hand. Help me. Do something. Stretch out your hand.

Hush, girl—No, you mustn't go. Stay here, girl.

His name is Arnold.

Do you call Stellan Arnold?

Do something, save me. At eight tonight we're going to meet up there. We have the most wonderful time. He never knows quite where I am. I always walk ahead. Because we have to be careful. No one must see us. I've made up a game. The precautiongame. It's a wonderful game. I decide the places where we're going to meet. I put marks along the road I take, and I always start from the lookout tower.

Stellan! It's him!

I have flower paper that I've cut into ribbons. Tonight I'll have white. White shines through the dusk so we'll find our way back without danger. I'll tie a ribbon at even intervals on branches of trees and bushes. And if there is no branch, I shall put a little pebble on a bigger stone and the ribbon in between. So he can look for me. Just like ski tournaments where no one really knows where the tracks run. He climbs in the mountains. The track goes east and west. It runs up and down. So that he can find me. Or it's me who first sees him from my place deep in a cleft. He is standing right over me, but doesn't see me. Arnold, I call out. Softly and cautiously, Arnold, here I am.

Wait! Stop!

But Britt-Mari continued to run in the direction of Åbacken.

42

They found the first ribbon of crêpe paper on the backside of the lookout tower where it was tied around a rusty nail. On the wall behind it hung a piece of thick, weatherbeaten rope. Having gone around north first, they were on their way back in a southward direction when they saw the white strip shining between two pine trees. They looked at each other. Without saying anything he walked up the road and raised his hand. But then he changed his mind and waited until she caught up with him.

What do you say now?

Nothing, Sylvia answered.

You don't mean that you think . . .

Gosh, darling. I know my girl so well. I knew right away what was true and what was a lie.

I don't like this at all.

That's not the question now. We'll have to get the girl.

Of course she's cute, but she went too far. She sure was absolutely adorable with me last night. But now, afterward . . .

It's just that you're not used to her. She's always been somewhat high-strung.

They stood still next to each other and discovered two new strips. At a distance they looked like gauze hanging from the branches.

What a damned mess! he said.

Sylvia gave a muffled laugh and looked down at the city in the valley.

We're going to follow the track, he said. No use taking short-cuts.

It's not that we're in a hurry, now that we know what she's up to. She gave him a tender look. Don't you think it's beautiful up here?

Beautiful? That's what she said too. "You like beautiful things, don't you?"—Of course, I like things that are beautiful.

We are very much alike, the girl and I.

Sylvia slid toward him and put her hand on his arm. They looked into each other's eyes and the world around them came together, existing for one purpose only. Their lips began to smile. The distance between their faces ripened and their mutual desire delighted in its ripeness, slowly consuming it. Afterward she was reluctant to leave his skin and brushed her cheek, her nose, her chin against his face. Hundreds of tiny sensations died and regenerated, thousands and thousands more stood in wait. Gradually her ardor increased. Tightly gripping his head, she stroked her eyelids against his forehead. Then she took his hair, gripped his forehead tightly and let her eyelids ever so lightly and softly flip against this forehead, the left first, then the right. Then, stepping back, she put her hand across his chin and mouth, all admiration.

There's something about tonight I don't like, she said suddenly, and her tone of voice made him look up.

Exactly what I said.

That's not what I'm thinking of. She hesitated.

Did you see the flying ants? she asked.

Weren't those mosquitoes?

No, those were ants. I didn't want to mention that it was ants. I've always thought it awful when ants swarm about. Once as a child I got terribly frightened. I thought it was impossible and didn't know that an ant can fly. And it looked to me like an eclipse when I saw them. There were small, glittering streaks of dead and dying ants and their long wings twitched, and some labored to get ahead, dragging their fishscale-like wings, small drifts of terror, and real ants crawling around too and they looked now real naked and they were carrying the winged ants and biting them. It was terrible. It looked impossible.—And it was the same tonight, only on a smaller scale.

She was silent. Then she said,

Ants should walk on their legs.

He delighted in the cloud of fear she created around herself, her face hardening in its center.

Ants ought to walk on their legs, he said, taking her hand to follow in the track of the white signs.

They took it easy. The track led eastward first, then west. Up and down it went. The white streamers dangled from slim pine trees and maple branches. On occasion Sylvia made him sit down and enjoy the view. A deep silence in her heart overwhelmed her and silenced her tongue's light chatter. At times she called down the mountain,

Cinnamoncandy, Cinnamoncandy.

But there was no answer.

Sylvia called,

Now we're behind you, my little, sweet witch.

The tracks led on. When there were no longer any trees, the girl had solved the problem by putting one little stone on a larger one, or simply the little one on the mountain directly—and the white strip lay there, glimmering.

It was when they sat down again to admire the view that he thought he heard someone singing. At first she did not hear, but then she did.

It's Cinnamoncandy, she said with certainty.

They continued and the singing became more distinct, though they could not make out what she was singing. The song was like nothing they knew. There were lyrics to the song, but the words were indiscernible.

It can't be anyone else but Cinnamoncandy, Sylvia said. Hush, we're going to sneak up on her.

But the singing grew silent after a while and they had to find the paper strips again to lead them on. The terrain grew more difficult for them, and they had to jump from one mountain path to another. Actually, these were not even paths, but something like mountain shelves with a thin grass rind, smooth and meadowlike at times and overgrown with bearberry brushwood, shelves that went up and down, twisting and turning and suddenly ending. Out of breath, they stood still every once in a while and listened.

Then they heard her singing again.

What a youngster! Sylvia said.

You can say that again, Stellan said.

Suddenly they saw her, diagonally below them. They stopped and stood very still. The girl was lying stretched out on a cliff shelf with dry grass. She was singing, but somehow the melody did not fit together. They watched her busily doing some tricks with her hands, lifting them and trying to put them together in various configurations, but somehow it wouldn't work. Her hands insisted on remaining independent of each other.

How miserable she sounds! he said.

Well, you can see she's having fun there carrying on by herself.

Maybe. But it sounds sinister.

You can say what you want, but she is cute, said Sylvia. Let's sit down here and watch her for a while.

They tried, but they could not see her too well from this position. They stood up again and leaned against the mountain.

You can get dizzy just looking straight down, he said.

They watched the girl now moving her legs. First she pulled her knees toward her abdomen and kicked her feet, then she stretched her arms out, trying to catch hold of the tips of her sandals. When she could not bring this off, she kicked her feet more impetuously, trying over and over again. She lifted her head and stretched herself forward. But somehow, she could not get things the way she wanted them. They understood that she was playing at not being able to get things the way she wanted them, and they thought that this looked funny and cute.

She is squirming like a little toad that has landed on its back. Stellan said this, making the comparison.

But she is certainly not coldblooded, Sylvia countered, adding adoringly,

She is so much like me! It's as if I was watching myself as a youngster.

They kept on looking down at her.

Now this should be enough, Stellan thought. Sylvia agreed after a little while. She bent forward and called as loudly as she could,

Cinnamoncandy.

They saw the girl's arms and legs sink back on the dry, yellow grass. For about a minute she lay absolutely still. It looked as though she had closed her eyes, but they were not certain.

Cinnamoncandy, Sylvia called.

The girl stood up. She did this in stages, sitting up, turning around, carefully getting down on her knees, setting down one foot, at long last slowly raising herself. Then she stood straight, looking up. The woman started beckoning and the man joined her in waving eagerly and kindly down to her. They watched the girl raising her arms. It looked as if she were trying to wind them in a wreath around her head, but she did not succeed. Her arms dropped down. They saw it. Her arms dropped down. The girl turned and took two short steps. Then she took a longer step straight out into the air.

Acknowledgments

I wish to thank the Fulbright Commission for their generous grant which enabled me to travel to Stockholm to interview Lars Ahlin and to research his work at the Royal Library as well as the archives of his first publisher *Tidens Förlag*. My most sincere thanks go to the Commission's Excutive Director Jeannette Lindström for her invaluable help and support in every way, to Ms. Eva Roxeheim, her secretary, for making my stay run smoothly, and to Nina Forssblad for helpful advice.

My warmest thanks go to Lars Ahlin and his wife Gunnel for inviting me to their home in Äppleviken and graciously taking the time to talk to me at length about the life and work of Lars Ahlin, despite the precarious health of the author. Thanks also to Ragnar Jones for talking to me on various occasions about Lars Ahlin.

I want to express my appreciation to the people of the "*låneexpedition*" of the Royal Library for their generous help by providing space for my research and tracking books and manuscripts. Thanks also to Ms. Mia Bjursén Karlsson at the Library of Stockholm University for facilitating my research.

Lastly, I want to thank Dr. James Wilhelm for patiently reading my manuscript and suggesting stylistic revisions. The remaining flaws are my own.

Lars Ahlin, the Writer and his Work

An Afterword

Lars Ahlin ranks high in contemporary Swedish literature. Ever since the publication of his first novel *Tåbb med manifestet* in 1943, his books have been discussed widely and many Swedish writers have been influenced by his work.

A member of the Communist party, he quite naturally became one of the revolutionary writers of the thirties and forties. His first novels reflect his concern with the wretched social conditions of the lower classes to which Ahlin belonged. But even though his settings remained largely within this framework, his focus slowly changed from socio-economical to ethical-religious concerns.

Ahlin's intellectual interest was apparent from the very start, both in his choice of friends and his affiliations. Ragnar Jones, younger brother of Ahlin's best friend Arne, recalls the often night-long discussions of literature and social topics, which always contained religious elements, during the time when the penniless Lars Ahlin stayed at their home in Stockholm.[1] Lacking the means to a formal education, Ahlin sought financial help from a variety of sources that enabled him to take various courses in literature, philosophy and theology. He read voraciously and indiscriminately in his almost compulsory effort to educate himself. Despite all the odds against it, and much well-meaning advice to give up his impossible dream, he wanted to become a writer. He has stubbornly stuck to what he felt was his calling.

It was only natural that his intellectual bent and his preoccupation with philosphical-religious questions soon showed in his writing. His major works became expressions of his desire to "teach" the world his special brand of mystical-religious orientation. Not until much later in his life did Ahlin begin talking about a mystical "experience" while lying alone, ill and hungry, in his tent in 1933. A teen-age hobo looking for work in the aftermath of the Depression, he tried to survive on peddling 2000 revolutionary poems, left over from an unclaimed order at the *Norrlands-Kuriren* newspaper, where he had been working.

One may argue with Ahlin about the role of a writer as an "educator" and "intercessor,"[2] of wanting to "preach" instead of "present." However, Ahlin has always had the good sense to couch his theological point of view in human terms, showing the frailties of man rather than what he ought to be. Indeed, like the Greek dramatists, he shows the individual in all his nakedness pitched against a seemingly uncaring fate—a loser, except for the grace of a God whom he needs to find by his own strength.

Basing his "Christian morals" on Schleiermacher's theories, he comes dangerously close to reflecting the limited opinions of early nineteenth-century German scholarship.[3] More recent research has shown that other religions not only existed and developed, but thrived alongside Christianity even in Europe during the Middle Ages. Schleiermacher's idea that Christianity is the "highest monotheistic stage of religion" can no longer hold in a world of increasingly pluralistic views and orientations. And it does not correlate with Ahlin's own professed desire for equality. Rather, Ahlin's position must be seen against the background of his largely homogeneous Lutheran-evangelical society before the Second World War, with its dismal "statare"-system where the tenant farmhand received payment in kind, and the wretched conditions of the industrial worker during the Depression—a society vulnerable to replacing Christian ethics with Communism and related social ideas. The time cried out for change and its writers became its spokesmen, each one with his own voice. Lars Ahlin became one of them, adding his brand of convictions.

Difficult to read because of his elusive style and way of expression, his novels portray mostly immature characters in crises, combating an unrelenting, impersonal fate that leaves them stunted. Helpless in their fight against insurmountable odds, his protagonists become almost willing victims to fate, sacrificing themselves in a strange, Christ-emulating way. Ahlin's rather heavily belabored prose serves well in describing his many-faceted social outsiders and misfits, underlining the ambiguity of their concepts and sentiments as well as their destinies. The object of many different interpretations, Ahlin's work is representative of our problem-ridden century. His readiness to show the dark side of human nature makes Lars Ahlin a most interesting writer.

Even though his work stands uniquely on its own, Ahlin admits to a variety of influences. He names Swedish writers Hjalmar Bergman and Eyvind Johnson, as well as Thomas Mann and, above all, Fyodor Dostoyevsky as influential early in his career. His extensive reading exposed him also to writers like Ibsen, Gide, Proust, Cervantes, Sterne, Kierkegaard, even Faulkner, all writers haunted with the problems of a "double vision" in human existence. Their works must have struck a familiar chord. Like every great writer, Ahlin has his own brand of motivating agony. Indeed, Ahlin's problems are reflected in his troubled characters and their tragic fates. Although none of his tortured creatures answers to a description of their creator, they all represent facets of himself, his environment and the people in it, and his personal concerns as he describes their struggles of trying to live with themselves in a world not of their making. He himself admits to a close, definite relationship between his own experiences and his work. It is therefore only prudent to take a short look at his life.

The youngest of seven children, Lars Ahlin was born April 4, 1915, in Sundsvall, at that time a minor agrarian-industrial seaport in Sweden. He spent most of his formative years in that city and it provides the setting for many of his stories. Ahlin's father was a traveling salesman who had moved to Sundsvall from Stockholm in search of work, but he returned to the capital in 1918. Two years later, in 1920, the mother also abandoned her family to live with another man, and the children were left to care for each other. Lars was five years old at the time. He saw his mother only once more when, "23 years later she reappeared on the scene after my first success. I was supposed to embrace her as my mother, but by that time I had no feeling for the woman."[4] Eventually, his parents divorced. When his father remarried in 1922, he moved back to Sundsvall, and Lars as well as an older brother returned to live with him. Their new relatives were mostly blue-collar workers. The family lived in a two-room apartment on Storgatan 33 (the so called "Hellbergska huset") in the Södermalm part of Sundsvall—also called "Stenhammaren" ("Stenstan")—whose wooden shacks climbed up the southern side of the "Stadsberg" mountain. The next few years on Storgatan seem to have been Ahlin's calmest and probably happiest time during his vacillating childhood.[5]

But times were bad. In 1928, barely 13 years old, Lars had to leave school to help support the family. That fall he joined the youth group of the Communist party and remained a member for five years. Lars and his brother followed their father to various other apartments in the city during his father's rocky second marriage, until that foundered too. In 1930 the suicide of a brother five-years older and closest to him of all his siblings left him with deep scars. After that his family disintegrated and Lars broke all ties with it. That was after the Depression. Through his friend Ivar Öhman, whose father was the editor, Ahlin eventually found work at the Communist-oriented newspaper *Norrlands-kuriren* as a general man to perform various kinds of jobs. When a lack of funds and friction among the Communist factions turned the daily paper into a weekly, Ahlin lost his job. Unable to find work, Ahlin decided in May 1933 to leave Sundsvall. With that Ahlin's affiliation with the party ended. His friend Ivar Öhman considered it a "desertion." [6]

Lars Ahlin became a hobo. This period in his life is important because it shows Ahlin's stubborn pursuit of his dream. Living in Ivar Öhman's tent, he tried to survive on selling the 2000 offprints of the poem "Den arbetslöses sång" (The Unemployed's Song) and various other poems he had with him. It was during this time also that he had his mystical-religious vision, which had an immense impact on his outlook and priorities in life. Never mentioned before the publication of Linder's essay in 1966, Ahlin himself describes it much later in his essay "In på benet" (*Bonniers Litterära Magasin*, 39 [Jan. 1970], 1:7–10) as a vision of "Kairo's time": a mystical, all-embracing, ever-evolving "double movement" forward, intertwining the world with man. Even though he grew up without religion, the author thinks that he came by his mystical-religious orientation quite naturally through his grandparents. In 1936 he became a novice in the *Societas Sanctae Birgittae*, and a full member of the sect in 1941. Leaving it in 1945, he has since come out in favor of a separation between church and state.

Coming to Stockholm in 1933 in search of work, he rented a typewriter and wrote articles for various papers. At this time he met the sculptor-to-be Arne Jones, with whom he developed a lifelong friendship until Jones' death in 1976. Eventually he scraped together enough money to attend a course in Swedish literature in a "folk high school" in Ålsta, where he met David Palm and his wife, who helped him in every possible way to continue his self-directed studies in world literature, philosophy, theology, and related subjects. Arne Jones went with him to Ålsta.

In the summer of 1934 Arne Jones and Lars Ahlin were once again on the road selling poems. Moving back into the Jones' household in Fränsta in 1935, they set up a small book bindery, which soon failed. Together they became involved in various church activities while Ahlin was writing his first novel *Lille Prometheus* (Little Prometheus). Finished in 1937, it was summarily rejected by Georg Svensson at Bonniers, though with the encouraging remark that Ahlin should continue his writing. Ahlin doggedly kept on. Hardly making a living at various odd jobs, he took more courses at "folk high schools" in Stockholm and Ålsta while working on his second manuscript *Underklassare av blodet* (Of Lower Class Blood). Again, there was no publisher when he finished it in 1939.

A time of utter misery followed. Well-meaning friends advised him to find a more profitable occupation, and for a short term he enrolled in a school in Uppsala to prepare for the ministry. But his inner agony could not be silenced. Compulsively, he continued to write even while he was drafted for military service in 1942. But wiser by previous experience, he mailed his next manuscript *Tåbb med manifestet* (Tåbb with the Manifest) to the literary critic Holger Ahlenius, who recognized Ahlin's talent and sympathized with his predicament. With his help, Tidens Förlag in Stockholm agreed to publish it.[7] The year was 1943 and Lars Ahlin's career as a writer was on its way.

It is only natural that Ahlin's first published novel concerns itself with the Marxist idea of equality combined with the poor man's democratic rights, which Tåbb represents with his "manifesto." Ahlin's native Sundsvall with its Stadsberg provides the setting and the blue-collar society the models for his characters. He varied this in later novels, but his strength remained with that environment. Other novels followed in almost yearly succession until the early sixties. It is not that he remained silent exactly after that, but there was no new novel until the publication of *Hannibal segraren* (Hannibal the Conqueror), a co-operative effort with his wife Gunnel, in 1982. A few others have come out since then and he is currently working on his next one.

It may seem strange to learn that Ahlin's ambition was to become a dramatist. He even had one play, *Lekpaus* (Break in the Game), performed at the Royal Dramatic Theater in 1948. Perhaps his efforts to describe his characters in minute details and from all possible angles, and his sliding into extraneous storytelling unrelated to the main plot, prevented him from writing for the stage with greater success.

It does not take an expert in psychology to recognize Ahlin's difficult, rather loveless and poverty-stricken childhood and his own moral-religious preoccupation in his work. It stands to reason that they provided the impulse for his stubborn wish to voice his feelings and concerns and they propelled him into his profession in spite of all the hardships. More often than not, his major characters are outsiders, emotionally stunted, often grotesque, dejected and dismal, lost to themselves and others, abandoned by fate and fortune. Biologically and emotionally programmed, they are searching for love in a highly unresponsive, unconcerned universe. Miserable in their anguish, they cannot help but put their trust in a compassionate God whom they cannot fully comprehend, but to whom they become willing sacrifices—Greek tragedy in modern dress. But their salvation is not a heavenly Dantesque-Miltonesque vision of divine grace. Rather, his protagonists are willing blood-sacrifices in a process akin to archetypal ancient fertility rites that later reappear in the Christian doctrine of a Messianic martyr, a sacrificial lamb for the sin of mankind. This idea eventually becomes the focal point in his novel *Fromma mord* (Pious Murders, 1952). Ahlin considers this novel to be his major work because with it he began "breaking new ground."[8]

Never insisting on developing his own style, but experimenting with the novel's form throughout his career, [9]Ahlin began with this novel a number of so-called starkly "religious" novels. The novel's protagonist is Aron, who returns home after a long absence to visit the grave of his father. But even though he wants to leave immediately afterward, Aron never gets to the grave. Instead, he is confronted with a series of old sins—sins against three different women, who symbolize three different types of love. Too weak to defend himself, he becomes an almost willing accomplice to his own, rather Christ-like sacrificial death. It is not clear whether Aron lacks the necessary physical, mental, or moral strength, or perhaps a mixture of all. The question is whether Aron wants to atone for his sins, or stands as a Christ symbol, or both? And what about his victims turned executioners? Indeed, life for him is complicated, and the human soul seems a bottomless pit, unfathomable.[10]

Ahlin developed this motif of a Christ-like sacrifice further in his next novel *Kanelbiten* (1953, *Cinnamoncandy*, 1990), published a year later. His angle shifted. The protagonist is no longer a guilt-ridden male, but an innocent, precocious girl-child on the verge of maturity who is pushed into her sacrificial martyrdom through circumstances beyond her control. Strangely enough, like her predecessor—and this seems inherent in Ahlin's novels—Britt-Mari, nicknamed Cinnamoncandy, never develops any combative spirit to fight back, but accepts her fate with a Christ-like, passive resignation.

An argument can be made that Cinnamoncandy's experience is based on the author's own. The setting is the very identifiable topography of his native Sundsvall, its streets and Stadsberg. Even the protagonist's address corresponds to Ahlin's own with the slight difference that he lived in the cheaper rear part of the building while Britt-Mari resides in the attic, the poorest part still, of the posh Entrance A. Above all, there is the close connection between the author's early life and young Britt-Mari's experience of watching helplessly and without recourse the gradual loss of her mother's love and attention to a man. Her sacrificial, Christ-like identification is mentioned already early in the story. Without having realized it, she has been walking to the place where her father, a "carpenter," died years earlier. In her mind she sees him fall from the scaffold "with outstretched arms." But she believes that at the lowest point there is an invisible curve by which his fall continues upward. And "often a longing overcomes her to fly through this invisible curve herself" to join her father in heaven (27).[11]

Likewise, her love for her mother is boundless and self-sacrificing. "There were no demands she was not willing to carry out. She would offer herself. Her entire life . . . give everything" and "tear herself apart to allow the mouth that called to feel the sweetness of life" (18).

Precocious and too wise for her age, Britt-Mari goes through life pining for her self-centered mother's ever-diminishing love and attention. Abandoned and lonely, she escapes into a consoling mystical experience where "pure happiness does not count in seconds. Bliss does not run through an hourglass" (140). Her mind tries to keep its sanity and survive with the help of its fertile imagination. She longs back to her "pure, unadulterated childhood" where the terrible truth was still hidden from her and therefore reality was still bearable.

But she cannot stop the clock and life ticks silently onward. Time and again, Britt-Mari escapes into her own world of mystical revelation. At one low point of rejection she escapes into dancing an archetypal mandala, whose center Jung establishes as representing the "self in the individual's search for 'individuation'" (Weiss, *Archetypal Images*, 14).[12] She "dances into the setting sun in the western sky" (60) with her sister and her brother—she is all three rolled into one. At another time when she has to leave because her mother wants to entertain her lover, she tries to find solace in a type of supernatural earthly love with Arnold to "become real" in her own esteem (202/6). She fights the temptation to encrust her heart with ice, praying "Love me, God, in this black night . . . Make love come alive! Awaken my heart from death! Feed your lamb!" (194). On the verge of despair, she takes "thirteen steps" to test her hearing and sanity (195). In another vision, she thinks of her "carpenter father" as she is "leaning against a wall" in the "darkness" (251). The scene is set at night, which only underlines the emotional darkness surrounding her. In another allusion to the Bible, she drinks "twelve times" from the clear water in the brook. Putting her trust in the number twelve, she tries hard to "make Grepp understand how important the number twelve was" (147). Ashes on her head, she walks down the river in a baptismal ceremony of her own to atone for her "sins" and find peace (237).

As can be expected in an Ahlin novel, biblical and other symbols abound. Ahlin himself draws attention to the fact that "there are many metaphors and the body language is subtle"; and often the girl "moves choreographically" (letter, Nov. 14, 1988). The dove, the fishes, the lamb, the triangle-bird-chalice figures Britt-Mari repeatedly tries to create with her fingers hardly need an explanation. Even the Stadsberg mountain takes on a symbolical significance with its "sun-drenched top" and trails leading "eastward" and "westward." Britt-Mari sits under the city's tallest bird-cherry tree with its "snowy-white flowers," and greets "her own" solitary maple-tree with its "darkly burning red leaves," which is "not like the others" (22). In the same category belongs Stellan's observation that Britt-Mari "squirms like a toad." Ahlin uses the word "*groda*" which not only means "frog" or "toad," but "blunder" or "howler" as well (274). She may be her mother's, or her society's, or even Nature's "blunder," neither one providing a living space for the little girl here on earth. Additionally, even in translation the symbol of the toad makes an allusion to a transformational life-cycle abundantly clear.

Significant are the scenes that symbolically build up to the final end—the sacrifice. Britt-Mari is Eva, in her budding maturity the temptation of Arnold (Adam), who resists at first, but secrectly gives in and follows her example; he takes the second bite out of the apple (94). The baptismal hairwash Britt-Mari gives her mother to "save" her reads like an ancient libation ceremony with oil and water to "accomplish a cleansing" until she can "pull a strand of hair through her fingers" and hear it "whistle like a grassblade, as glossy and darkgreen as a laurel leaf"(134). In a fleeting recognition of her impending death she cries out in the arms of Stellan (231/2). Ashes on her head, Britt-Mari stages a penitential pilgrimage to atone for her "sins." She "started her walk of penance and was determined to complete her sacrifice" (232). In the same vein is her wish to eternalize her footprints in the red clay of the graveyard while repeating the words "it is not completed" (228/31) throughout the graveyard scene, as if she had a premonition that soon her life was to complete its course (237). Finally there is the last scene on the mountain ledge when Britt-Mari tries "to wind them [her arms] in a wreath around her head" (275) before taking her final step, again an allusion to Christ's death.

Along with the Christian offering, the sacrifice itself contains the elements of ancient pagan fertility rites. Britt-Mari is going to wear white on her way east and west in the mountain where she, "lying deep in a cleft," wants to meet Arnold, her bridegroom-lover (271). But, seeing her "playing at not being able to get things the way she wanted them," (275) her mother calls down to her. As she had promised throughout the book, Britt-Mari answers the call to sacrifice herself for her mother's happiness. Stepping out from the mountain ledge she lets herself fall into that curve upward to meet her father in heaven.

Much has been written about the love aspects in Ahlin's work. According to Torborg Lundell, Ahlin's message concerns the three equalizers: love, work, and death, "and the greatest of them is love."[13] That may be. But his work is just as much about the absence of love, even a hatred of love. Talking about Britt-Mari, Ahlin explains, "she would have been stunted if she had continued to live."[14] His major characters are perpetual loners, emotionally incomplete, doomed to search for love without ever being able to give or receive it in a normal way. Aron is unable to love except in the abstract. Sylvia Månsson lacks both love and compassion for her child. Like Aron, Arnold hates the physical act of love. To both, desire is shameful and neither one can complete the physical act in a normal, loving way. Britt-Mari's normally developing maturity becomes a despicable curse and she must die before reaching fulfillment. There may even be a hint of homosexuality implied in the behavior of the three characters—Aron, Arnold, Britt-Mari—with an additional suggestion of incest and narcissism in the dance scene, where Britt-Mari imagines herself as both her brother and her sister.

The fact remains that Lars Ahlin manages to show the entire range of human emotions with an almost unequalled subtlety. It is the universal aspects of life he presents in his stories that make him a writer of international importance.

Notes

1. Talks with Ragnar Jones in his antiquariat on Norrtullsgatan in Stockholm, May-July 1989.
2. Lars Ahlin, "Om ordkonstens kris," *Kritiskt 40-tal*, Vennberg and Aspenström, eds., Stockholm: 1948.
3. Interviews with Lars Ahlin (taped) in Äppleviken on May 6 and May 18, 1989.
4. Interview with Lars Ahlin.
5. Lars Åke Augustsson, *Lars Ahlin och Sundsvall*, Sundsvall: 1978.
6. Lars Furuland, *Synpunkter på Lars Ahlin*, Stockholm: 1971, 19.
7. Torborg Lundell, *Lars Ahlin*, Boston: 1977, 20.
8. Interview with Lars Ahlin.
9. Interview with Lars Ahlin.
10. For an extensive analysis of *Fromma mord* see Gunnar D. Hansson, *Nådens oordning: Studier i Lars Ahlins roman Fromma mord*, Stockholm, 1988.
11. All page numbers are taken from *Kanelbiten*, Stockholm: Stiftelsen Litteraturfrämjandet, 1977.
12. Hanna Kalter Weiss, *Archetypal Images in Surrealist Prose: A Study in Modern Fiction*, New York and London: Garland, 1988; see also Karl Gustaf Jung, *Aion: Beiträge zur Symbolik des*

Selbst, Vol. 9, pt. 2(of 2) and I, Vol. 12 of *Gesammelte Werke*, Olten and Freiburg, Breisgau: 1976 and 1972, resp.

13. Lundell, *Lars Ahlin*, 146.

14. "Samtal med Lars Ahlin,"(Conversation with Lars Ahlin), cover of *Kanelbiten*, 1953; and interviews with Lars Ahlin.

Books by Lars Ahlin

Tåbb med manifestet, Stockholm: 1943

Inga ögon väntar mig, (short stories), Stockholm: 1944

Min död är min, Stockholm: 1945

Om, Stockholm: 1946

Fångnas glädje, Stockholm: 1947

Jungfrun i det gröna, Stockholm: 1947

Egen spis, Stockholm: 1948

Lekpaus, play performed at the Royal Dramatic Theater

Huset har ingen filial, Stockholm: 1949

Fromma mord, Stockholm: 1952

Kanelbiten, Stockholm: 1953

Stora glömskan, Stockholm: 1954

Kvinna, kvinna, Stockholm: 1955

Natt i marknadstältet, Stockholm: 1957

Nattens ögonsten, Stockholm: 1958

Gilla gång, Stockholm and Helsingfors: 1958

Bark och löv, Stockholm and Helsingfors: 1961

Händelser i felbyggt hus, Sundsvall: 1965

Sjätte munnen, Stockholm: 1985

Vaktpojkens eld, (short stories), Stockholm: 1986

Din livsfrukt, Stockholm: 1987

In cooperation with Gunnel Ahlin

Hannibal segraren, Stockholm: 1982

Some Titles in the Series

JAMES J. WILHELM

General Editor

1. Lars Ahlin, *Cinnamoncandy*.
   Translated from Swedish by Hanna Kalter Weiss.

2. *Anthology of Belgian Symbolist Poets*.
   Translated from French by Donald F. Friedman.

3. Ariosto, *Five Cantos*.
   Translated from Italian by Leslie Z. Morgan.

4. *Kassia: The Legend, the Woman, and Her Work*.
   Translated from Greek by Antonia Tripolitis.

5. Antonio de Castro Alves, *The Major Abolitionist Poems of
   Castro Alves*. Translated from Portuguese by Amy A. Peterson.

6. Li Cunbao, *The Wreath at the Foot of the Mountain*.
   Translated from Chinese by Chen Hanming and
   James O. Belcher.

7. Meïr Goldschmidt, *A Jew*.
   Translated from Danish by Kenneth Ober.

8. Árpád Göncz, *Plays and Other Writings of Árpád Göncz*.
   Translated from Hungarian by Katharina and
   Christopher Wilson.